3rd edition

SCIENCE IN EARLY CHILDHOOD

Science education is crucial to young children's discovery and understanding of the world around them. This third edition of *Science in Early Childhood* has been substantially updated to include the most current research, bringing together an author team of respected science education researchers from across Australia.

New chapters address changing priorities in early childhood science education, introducing coverage of STEM, inclusivity, Indigenous understandings of science, science in outdoor settings, intentional teaching and reflective practice.

This text complements the Australian Early Years Learning Framework and the Australian Curriculum: Science. Concepts are brought to life through detailed case studies, practical tasks and activity plans. Instructors can further supplement learning with the extensive materials located on the new companion website.

Renowned for its accessible and comprehensive content, *Science in Early Childhood* is an essential tool for all pre-service early childhood educators.

- **Coral Campbell** is Associate Professor in the School of Education at Deakin University.

- **Wendy Jobling** is Lecturer in the School of Education at Deakin University.

- **Christine Howitt** is Associate Professor in the Graduate School of Education at the University of Western Australia.

3rd edition

Science

IN EARLY CHILDHOOD

edited by

Coral Campbell
Wendy Jobling
Christine Howitt

CAMBRIDGE
UNIVERSITY PRESS

CAMBRIDGE
UNIVERSITY PRESS

University Printing House, Cambridge CB2 8BS, United Kingdom

One Liberty Plaza, 20th Floor, New York, NY 10006, USA

477 Williamstown Road, Port Melbourne, VIC 3207, Australia

314–321, 3rd Floor, Plot 3, Splendor Forum, Jasola District Centre, New Delhi – 110025, India

79 Anson Road, #06–04/06, Singapore 079906

Cambridge University Press is part of the University of Cambridge.

It furthers the University's mission by disseminating knowledge in the pursuit of education, learning and research at the highest international levels of excellence.

www.cambridge.org
Information on this title: www.cambridge.org/9781108436755

© Cambridge University Press 2012, 2015, 2018

First published 2012
Second edition 2015
Third edition 2018

Cover and text designed by Leigh Ashforth, watershed art + design
Typeset by Integra Software Services Pvt. Ltd
Printed in China by C & C Offset Printing Co. Ltd, January 2018

A catalogue record for this publication is available from the British Library

A Cataloguing-in-Publication entry is available from the catalogue of the National Library of Australia at www.nla.gov.au

ISBN 978-1-108-43675-5 Paperback

Additional resources for this publication at www.cambridge.edu.au/academic/scienceearlychildhood

Foreword

When I was five years old, an engineer named Jack Kilby demonstrated the first example of an integrated circuit: a computer chip. It was 1958, and I suspect that very few of the grown-ups noticed.

And who could blame them? Computers were in their infancy. Physically, they were enormous, filling entire rooms with heavy, hot and flammable equipment. In every other sense they were practically invisible, locked away in defence agencies or closely guarded university labs.

No-one looked at a young Alan Finkel and imagined that he would one day dictate this message to a device that he stores in his pocket, by the miracle of chips.

How different the world looks to the loving parents of a five-year-old today.

In just five years of life, she has been photographed on five generations of iPhones.

She has lived through the first ever detection of gravitational waves, a feat so stupendous that Albert Einstein himself thought that humans could never achieve it.

She was there for the arrival of technologies that make it possible to edit our basic coding, our DNA, cheaply and precisely.

Perhaps she's already travelled in an electric car. Perhaps her first car will be capable of driving itself. Perhaps she'll be able to travel into space as a tourist.

She can expect to live a full ten years longer than a baby girl of my generation. And however long she lives, we can say for certain that her world will be rich with opportunity, filled with humankind's great unfinished projects, and ripe for her contribution.

It would be easy to conclude that after thousands of years of raising humans, we know everything there is to know about education. It would also be easy to take the opposite position, and give up teaching science completely, thinking that nothing we know today could possibly be relevant to the adults our children will become.

Between the two extremes is the position that the thoughtful society adopts: to learn from the past, adapt to the present and strive to be even better in the future.

For that, we need great teachers, and inspired teaching. And the learning should begin from Day One.

From nought to eight in the lifespan of a human is a time of astonishing growth. As our hundred billion brain cells branch out into perhaps a quadrillion neural connections, we launch into our lifetime of learning.

We have done right by our children in those precious early years if we fire them with passion for that journey: if we help them grapple with questions and bring the role of science and mathematics to the fore.

To our present and future educators, I wish you every success on the path you have chosen. May this book help you to guide our children – and may science guide our nation into the future.

Dr Alan Finkel AO
13 December 2017

Contents

PART 4 HOW DO I PLAN AND ASSESS IN SCIENCE? 207

Contributors

ELAINE BLAKE works with postgraduate students in early childhood studies at Edith Cowan University in Western Australia. Her doctorate, from Curtin University, investigated the sociocultural aspects of learning and teaching science in early learning centres. Elaine's career includes contributing to early childhood science as a consultant with the Association of Independent Schools Western Australia, teaching children in early childhood classrooms for 25 years, and being principal of an independent junior school. Her current research investigates how science can assist the development of literacy for young children. Elaine is a Fellow of the Australian College of Educators and her published work includes the teacher resource *Planting the Seeds of Science*.

CORAL CAMPBELL is Associate Professor in the School of Education at Deakin University. She has contributed significantly to the fields of science, education and educational research over three careers which span forty-six years. She is on the editorial board of the *Journal of Emergent Science*, and is the European Science Education Research Association's Early Childhood Science Special Interest Group Coordinator. In 2017, she received a Fellowship from the Association of Graduates of Early Childhood Studies to undertake a research project studying Science/STEM in early childhood. With a sustained interest in early childhood science education, Coral's research focus is on young children's learning in science and teacher professional learning which is reflected in her current projects.

KATE CHEALUCK is a Lecturer in the Faculty of Arts and Education and the Institute of Koorie Education at Deakin University, Geelong. Her teaching focuses on science education and design technology for early childhood and primary pre-service teachers. Kate is a registered practising science teacher with experience teaching science in early childhood, primary and secondary classrooms.

CHRISTINE HOWITT is an Associate Professor in Early Childhood and Primary Science Education at the Graduate School of Education at the University of Western Australia, Perth. Her research has focused on young children's science learning in informal contexts, and methodological and ethical approaches to including young children in research. Christine is co-editor of the science resource *Planting the Seeds of Science*, the product of a two-year nationally funded project to develop science resources for early childhood educators. She has been awarded various teaching excellence awards at the state and national level.

WENDY JOBLING is a Lecturer at Deakin University's Burwood Campus in Victoria. Prior to joining Deakin, she taught for more than twenty years in Victorian primary schools. Her doctorate focused on the factors affecting the implementation of science and technology curricula in Victorian primary schools. Wendy has a long-held interest in teaching and learning in science and technologies education and has published extensively in these fields. Since joining Deakin, Wendy has taught undergraduate and postgraduate primary and early childhood teacher education students in science and technologies (design and digital) units. She has also been involved in research into early childhood science and technologies teaching and learning.

JANE JOHNSTON is a retired Reader in Education (Associate Professor) at Bishop Grosseteste University, Lincoln, United Kingdom. She has taught and researched extensively, both nationally and internationally, in three distinct areas: early childhood studies, primary science education and practitioner research. She has worked as a primary classroom practitioner, undertaking projects in early childhood and primary science education. She is the author of many books, chapters and journal articles on early childhood, primary and science education. In 2006, Jane was one of the first of five teachers to be awarded Chartered Science Teacher status in the United Kingdom.

ANDREA NOLAN is currently Professor of Early Childhood Education, in the School of Education, Deakin University, Melbourne, Australia. She holds Bachelor, Master and PhD degrees in early years education and before entering the university sector taught extensively in early childhood education settings as well as in primary schools. Andrea has conducted research in both schools and pre-schools and has worked on a number of state, national and international projects concerning transition to school, literacy development, mentoring and professional learning for teachers. She has researched the impact of the current Australian reform agenda on professional identities and educator practice, mentoring, inter-professional work, and reflective practice as a means to better understand practice.

KATHRYN PAIGE is a Senior Lecturer in science and mathematics education at the University of South Australia. She taught for seventeen years in primary classrooms in a range of schools, rural, inner city and in the United Kingdom. Kathryn's research interests include pre-service science and mathematics education, eco justice and place-based education. Current projects include citizen science, water literacies, connecting children to the natural world, and STEM and girls. Past projects include Redesigning Pedagogies in the North, and the Distance Education Project in the Eastern Cape, South Africa.

CHRISTINE PRESTON is a Lecturer at the University of Sydney, New South Wales. She teaches early childhood and primary science education to undergraduate and Master of Teaching students. Christine is also kindergarten science specialist teacher at Abbotsleigh. Her research interests include using toys and representations to enhance teaching and learning in science and STEM. Christine writes an early childhood series in *Teaching Science*, journal of the Australian Science Teachers Association.

JILL ROBBINS is an Adjunct Lecturer at Monash University, and Associate Lecturer at Deakin University. Working in early childhood and primary science education for many years, her research interests have included young children's thinking, young children's understanding of natural phenomena, early childhood science and mathematics, grandparents' support of children's informal learning, technology in early childhood and the application of sociocultural theory in teaching and learning.

Acknowledgements

Each chapter of the original edition of this book was submitted to a blind review by two members of an independent review panel. For this third edition of the book, Cambridge University Press instigated independent academic review processes. The editors would sincerely like to thank all contributors whose input was invaluable in refining the content of this book. We are confident that the scholarly content of each chapter reflects contemporary research in the area and will assist educators in understanding science education for children aged from birth to 8 years of age.

The authors and Cambridge University Press would like to thank the following for permission to reproduce material in this book.

Text permission: All ACARA material © Australian Curriculum, Assessment and Reporting Authority (ACARA) 2010 to present, unless otherwise indicated. This material was downloaded from the Australian Curriculum website (www.australiancurriculum.edu.au) (accessed as noted in the references) and was not modified. The material is licensed under CC BY 4.0 (https://creativecommons.org/licenses/by/4.0). Version updates are tracked on the 'Curriculum version history' page (www.australiancurriculum.edu.au/Home/CurriculumHistory) of the Australian Curriculum website.

Design images: Part opener © Getty Images/Robert Hanson; Chapter opener © Getty Images/harpazo_hope.

Figure 15.2: (from top to bottom, left to right) © Getty Images/joecicak; © Getty Images/@Hans Surfer; © Getty Images/Quirex; © Getty Images/Elke Van de Velde; © Getty Images/Martin Harvey; © Getty Images/Catherine Ledner.

Every effort has been made to trace and acknowledge copyright. The publisher apologies for any accidental infringement and welcomes information that would redress this situation.

Introduction

Coral Campbell, Christine Howitt and Wendy Jobling

Science in early childhood

As we present the third edition of this book, we are aware that science education in early childhood has moved significantly since the first edition. While retaining the essential elements of science learning and teaching that inform and guide students and educators of pre-school and early years settings, we wanted to include some new thoughts and material into this current edition – Science, Technology, Engineering and Mathematics (STEM), inclusive strategies, Indigenous approaches, outdoor learning, intentional teaching and professional learning as reflective practice. Research in early childhood science is developing internationally as well as in Australia and we have drawn on work done by the authors and reviews of the broader research literature, such that *Science in Early Childhood* provides information that is relevant and responsive to its intended audience. Each chapter helps to develop content knowledge of areas of science and instructs on how to guide children's learning in that area. Many different approaches to science learning are taken, with an understanding that science is inter-related with most other curriculum areas and, in particular, with an understanding that young children tend to learn through play, in a holistic way. There is a growing recognition of the importance of science explorations in children's lives as they try to make sense of the world around them. Cognitively, it is important for educators to have input into children's developing science understandings and to be able to guide their concept development. *Science in Early Childhood* is designed to complement Australia's Early Years Learning Framework (EYLF) and the Australian Curriculum: Science, with references in each chapter to the alignment of content with the philosophy and anticipated outcomes of the national guidelines. Internationally, the 'early years' comprise a period recognised as that time between birth and 8 years of age, and this book provides resources for practitioners working in this age range. In recognition of the general acceptance in the early years' community of 'learning through play', *Science in Early Childhood* highlights varied types of learning and learning environments: naturalistic, informal and formal. Information in chapters is illustrated through the use of detailed case studies and practical examples that relate to both pre-school and the early years of school.

The third edition maintains its four parts, constructed around the required elements of effective science teaching and learning. Our approach has been to label these sections based on questions that students and practitioners of early childhood science would ask:

Part 1   'What initial information should I know to teach science?' includes information on policy documents and learning theories. Chapters 1–4 fall within this part.

Part 2   'How can I enhance children's learning of science?' presents different approaches to science learning and the importance of play as a pedagogy. This part covers Chapters 5–9.

Part 3   'How can I use the learning environment to enhance children's science understandings?' covers learning environments, learning in informal contexts, and outside learning environments. Chapters 10–12 are within this part.

Part 4   'How do I plan and assess in science?' covers essentials of planning, intentional teaching and assessment and reflective practice. It includes Chapters 13–16.

Chapter summaries

Chapter 1 starts with a short case study of 'typical' child-instigated exploration in science, highlighting the importance of early childhood education as a whole and of developmental and cognitive psychology. This chapter describes children's wonder and curiosity towards the world as it outlines what science looks like in the early years. As part of the definition of science, the chapter introduces conceptual, procedural and attitudinal science knowledge, and outlines important aspects of each for young children's learning of science. Chapter 2 provides the reader with an overview of Australia's first national curriculum framework for early childhood educators, the EYLF, which is set out in the document *Belonging, Being and Becoming: The Early Years Learning Framework* (DEEWR, 2009). The relevance of the EYLF in relation to teaching science in the early years is explained, concluding with the identification of science outcomes for children within the framework. The voices of early childhood educators and early childhood teacher educators are highlighted to illustrate how those working in the field are engaging with the framework.

Chapter 3 introduces the reader to the Australian Curriculum: Science, starting with a brief outline of the history of the Australian Curriculum. The three curriculum strands of Science Understanding, Science as Human Endeavour and Science Inquiry Skills are described, along with how these could be woven together to provide a framework for developing experiential, connected and sequential science learning experiences for children in the early years. The seven general capabilities and three cross-curriculum priorities are presented, along with examples that relate to science in the early years. Case studies provide an insight into how the Australian Curriculum: Science can be implemented.

Chapter 4 discusses the many theories of learning that have an impact on how educators work with young children. There are accepted theories about how children (and, indeed, adults) learn science and the factors that affect learning in young children. This chapter describes those theories of children's development and the range of influences that can affect science learning. Case studies are used to illustrate various aspects of the influences on children's learning.

Chapter 5 links practice to theory with a discussion of the range of formal and informal teaching approaches used with young children to enhance their learning. It outlines the importance of such strategies as scaffolding and targeted explorations. Using illustrative case studies, attention is paid to process skills; guided discovery; interactive problem and project-based learning; and intentional teaching. Whether through the processes of science, such as the development of observation, or through the skilful questioning of the educator, the approach used should enhance children's learning. The chapter includes a discussion on the importance of children's prior knowledge in terms of the teaching and learning of science.

Chapter 6 focuses on inclusive teaching principles and practices in relation to science teaching and learning. It describes Indigenous learning in science, in particular the *8 Aboriginal Ways of Learning*. The chapter outlines the relationship between Indigenous learning and inclusive teaching practises. It indicates ways in which educators can be more inclusive, particularly in early childhood.

Chapter 7 discusses the importance of play as a developmental tool, rather than just an informal aspect of childhood. Play is of great use in early childhood, and is of value to professionals. The chapter addresses theoretical aspects of play and how play supports child development. It discusses play in the pre-school and school curriculum and the role of the professional educator in play pedagogies. Practical examples and case studies support the discussion in this chapter.

Chapter 8 explores how young children's science identity can be enhanced when thoughtful pedagogy is provided by the educator. The first part of this chapter presents the definitions of science identity and pedagogy, followed by an exploration of the relationship between educator beliefs and what they teach. The second half of the chapter presents two case studies to illustrate pedagogical practices associated with the learning and teaching of science with young children, using play as a medium, in order to enhance their science identity.

Chapter 9 focuses on STEM education in early childhood. It describes what STEM looks like in early childhood settings and identifies ways in which STEM elements can be incorporated into children's learning. The chapter describes how STEM-related play can enhance young children's appreciation of the world and provides a range of examples that have potential for STEM learning.

Chapter 10 discusses the indoor learning environment and the ways in which educators can use this to support science learning in play-based contexts. Space, layout and materials are discussed in relation to the inside learning environment, with the use of materials highlighted through the potential they offer to enhance the curriculum. The place of cooking, the science discovery table, and construction are emphasised. Examples of science opportunities available in the built learning environment are included, along with a brief discussion on the value of digital technologies.

Chapter 11 provides insight into the informal learning of science through home and community involvement. Sociocultural theory is used to examine some of the multiple and complex ways in which science skills and concepts are being developed within the everyday practices of families, and how families' 'funds of knowledge' provide a rich and meaningful basis for children's future learning in science.

Chapter 12 discusses a growing interest in the value of children learning in the outside environment. It provides examples of the benefits of outdoor learning, using case studies of bush kinders and their affordances for science learning. Environmental learning is highlighted indicating how young children can be provided with explorations of an environmental nature. The chapter embraces the notion that young children can develop empathy for living things, knowledge of ecosystems and an understanding of the inter-relationships between elements of their environment.

Chapter 13 deals with the pragmatics of planning. Planning is fundamental to all science teaching and learning. This chapter discusses how effective planning ensures that students are engaged in appropriate science learning experiences that follow a logical and coherent sequence. Planning considers not only what to teach but how to teach. Thus, an educator's science content knowledge, science pedagogical knowledge, beliefs about science teaching and learning, and beliefs about young children's capability and competence in relation to learning science all play a part in effective science planning.

Chapter 14 highlights the role of an intentional, purposeful educator. It provides ideas and examples of how an intentional educator can plan for and teach children with regard for their individual and collective learning experiences. The chapter highlights the important place of verbal scaffolding and lesson planning. The components of a lesson plan are described and illustrated.

Chapter 15 presents information on how educators monitor, assess and document science learning. Early childhood educators use evidence to determine what children know and understand. Evidence may be based on how children explore and interact within their environment or on specific competency tests. Data relating to science is usually obtained through a process of observation, anecdotal note-taking, journal entries, checklists and folios of children's work. Consequently, this chapter outlines steps associated with the assessment of learning in science as outlined in the EYLF and in the Australian Curriculum: Science, with an indication of some associated strategies that are appropriate for each developmental level. The information in this chapter is similarly supported by reference to examples of authentic practice.

The final chapter in this book, Chapter 16, refers to an important aspect of any professional educator's role – that of ongoing professional learning. This chapter discusses reflective practice as a means of ensuring that educators review and monitor their own practice and how this practice affects children's learning outcomes. Tools such as reflective journals and professional portfolios are discussed. The theoretical aspects of educators' pedagogical content knowledge, content knowledge and pedagogical knowledge are presented.

There are many people who have contributed directly or indirectly to *Science in Early Childhood*. Professional discussions with practising educators, colleagues and students have provided ideas and inspirations in the writing of this book. All new chapters have been blind peer reviewed by two academics, while the other revised chapters have been academically reviewed. Our thanks are extended to all reviewers for their insightful comments, as we recognise the value these add to the strength of the book. Our photographs came from a range of sources, including family, friends and a professional photographer. We thank these people for their trust in us and for the use of their treasured photographs.

We hope that you will find this third edition a useful addition to your science education library.

Reference

Department of Education, Employment and Workplace Relations (DEEWR). (2009). *Belonging, Being and Becoming: The Early Years Learning Framework for Australia*, Canberra: Commonwealth of Australia.

PART 1

What initial information should I know to teach science?

The place of science in the early years

1

Coral Campbell and Christine Howitt

'Where there is a child there is curiosity and where there is curiosity there is science' (Howitt & Blake, 2010, p. 3). Young children continually engage in science practices. But they do not call it science – they call it curiosity. This chapter describes children's wonder and curiosity towards the world as it outlines what science looks like in the early years. As part of the definition of science, the chapter introduces conceptual, procedural and attitudinal science knowledge, and outlines important aspects of each for young children's learning of science. The ability of science to engage and stimulate children makes it an ideal vehicle to assist in all aspects of child development.

OBJECTIVES

At the end of this chapter you will be able to:

- recognise the natural disposition young children have towards science
- describe the conceptual, procedural and attitudinal knowledge associated with science
- describe the relationship between science and creativity
- list a range of reasons why young children should engage with science
- describe young children's capacity for science at different ages.

What does science look like in the early years?

FIGURE 1.1 Young children demonstrate a sense of wonder about all things around them – such as blowing seeds from a dandelion

Fourteen-month-old Zara has her gumboots on. Holding Dad's hand tightly, she walks into the edge of the mud. Zara stands still and smiles, looking down at her feet as they slowly sink. She pulls her gumboots out of the mud, feeling the resistance. On dry land Zara stands still and looks down at her feet. She then walks back into the mud with another smile on her face.

Best friends Lily and Sam (both 3 years old) have noticed a caterpillar crawling along the branch of a bush. For 10 minutes they watch the caterpillar move, engaged in their own private conversation about what the caterpillar is doing, where it could be going, what it might eat and how it might stay dry in the rain.

Every morning 6-year-old Fatima plays with the magnets at the science learning centre. She explores the different sized and shaped magnets, watching how they 'attract' and 'repel' each other and a range of materials. When asked how she thought the magnets worked, Fatima confidently replied: 'They stick together because they have honey on the ends. I know this because honey is sticky.'

These three stories illustrate how young children are constantly exploring their world. They demonstrate a sense of wonder about all things around them and delight in the natural aspects of the world. This is demonstrated by Zara and her fascination with the feel (and possibly sounds) of the mud, and by the intensity of Lily and Sam's engagement while observing the caterpillar.

D'Arcangelo (2000) referred to the term 'scientist in a crib' to describe how young children constantly explore their world through play. She noted that if we look into a crib 'we find a little scientist peering back at us – a child who is desperately interested in making sense of the people, the objects, and the languages around him or her, a child doing mini-experiments to try to sort everything out' (pp. 8–9).

Curiosity – children's wondering, observing, exploring, questioning and discovering as they try to make sense of the world.

Everyday science – refers to the way children interpret their science experiences based on their everyday experiences.

Children learn as they grow. Through **curiosity**, play, observation, questioning, trial and error and conversations with others children develop their own explanations and understandings of the world. This is often termed **everyday science**, referring to the way children interpret their science experiences based on their everyday experiences. This is clearly illustrated by Fatima and her explanation of how magnets work.

Science learning can occur in planned situations or incidentally as children are involved or engaged in other activities. While the educator provides set activities for planned learning, incidental learning can occur in the home environment or early childhood centres as children undertake their normal play activities. Incidental science understandings can arise through observation of others or specific things (such as Zara exploring the mud and Lily and Sam watching the caterpillar), through problem-solving (working out how to balance on a tree stump) and through social interactions in which discussions with others may present new information. Incidental learning can also occur through the mistakes that children make when they adapt or accept an alternative way of doing or understanding something.

Practical task

OBSERVING A CHILD

Watch a child for an extended period of time to see how they are exploring their world.

1. How do their actions reflect curiosity and wonder?
2. How is their whole body engaged in their exploration?
3. What do you think they are learning?

Have a conversation with the child afterwards. Do your observations match up with their experiences? If not, what does this tell you about learning to see the world from a child's perspective?

What is science?

The word **science** comes from the Latin word *scientia*, meaning knowledge. However, science is much more than just a body of knowledge. Davis and Howe (2003) described science as consisting of **conceptual knowledge** (understanding of, and about, science), **procedural knowledge** (the skills and procedures associated with doing science) and **attitudinal knowledge** (attitudes and dispositions to enhance scientific thinking).

Early childhood educators require a basic understanding of key scientific concepts in order to support young children's learning. Young children also have a range of understandings of scientific concepts, developed as a consequence of their everyday interactions with the world. While their initial ideas may be far from the scientifically correct concepts,

Science – a body of knowledge and skills which help to explain our world and the interactions of living and non-living elements within it.

Conceptual knowledge – understanding of, and about, science at a detailed level.

Procedural knowledge – the skills and procedures associated with doing science.

Attitudinal knowledge – attitudes and dispositions to enhance scientific thinking.

these ideas make perfect sense to them. This was illustrated by Fatima's explanation of how magnets work.

It can take 12 years, or more, of schooling to reach the correct scientific concept. In the early childhood years educators should distinguish between the 'right' answer and the 'correct' answer (Harlen, 2001). A **right answer** allows children to answer based on their everyday experiences. While the right answer may be a long way from the scientifically correct truth, it is important to allow young children to make observations and gain confidence in their ability to describe what they think is happening and why it might be happening.

Right answer – a right answer allows children to answer based on their everyday experiences, and is not necessarily the scientifically correct answer.

Educators play a significant role in helping young children learn science. This role includes preparing the learning environment; co-constructing knowledge; being a source of expertise, skills and knowledge; encouraging children to ask questions; asking productive questions; initiating and stimulating talk; and modelling how to think things through (Blake & Howitt, 2012; Brunton & Thornton, 2010). Materials on their own do not teach scientific concepts. Rather, the best science learning opportunities occur through conversations between children and adults while interacting with materials (Fleer, 2009).

Young children's scientific understanding is also developed through the educator modelling effective scientific communication. Using appropriate scientific terminology acknowledges children as capable and competent learners and helps them develop explanations and understandings of scientific concepts (Peterson & French, 2008). Brunton and Thornton (2010) noted that scientific language provides the tools young children require to describe natural phenomena, express their ideas and communicate their discoveries. Further, questioning to challenge ideas, encourage discussion or promote further exploration or investigation assists young children to develop scientific thinking and investigation.

Young children require many opportunities in a variety of contexts to practise the practical, intellectual, communication and social skills associated with doing science. These include:

- practical skills of observation, using all the senses, manual dexterity, fine motor control, hand–eye coordination and construction
- reasoning and thinking skills, such as questioning, speculating and inferring, problem-solving, noticing similarities and differences, and reflecting
- communication skills, including speaking, listening, discussing, representing, recording and reporting
- social skills of cooperation, negotiation, leadership, following instructions and behaving in a safe manner (Brunton & Thornton, 2010, p. 15).

The provision of time to explore resources, discover ideas, construct meaning and learn skills, along with opportunities to re-visit and re-engage with materials and activities to build on their observations and ideas, permits the development of science skills and knowledge.

Enthusiasm is contagious. Thus, early childhood educators should model and display positive attitudes towards science. Important scientific attitudes to develop in young children include curiosity, enthusiasm, motivation, cooperation, responsibility, originality, independence of thought and perseverance. They also include a respect for evidence, open-mindedness, critical reflection and an ability to accept the provisional nature of knowledge (Brunton & Thornton, 2010). It is important for young children to see that unusual observations can form the basis for further investigation and that if something does not work the first time then they should try again.

REFLECTION

1. Within the Australian Curriculum, science is defined as 'a dynamic, collaborative and creative human endeavour arising from our desire to make sense of our world through exploring the unknown, investigating universal mysteries, making predictions and solving problems' (ACARA, 2014). What is your definition of science, and how does it compare to the above definition?

2. How is science dynamic, collaborative and creative? Were these words part of your definition? If not, why didn't you consider them as part of your definition?

3. How could these three words be applied to Zara, Lily and Sam, and Fatima as they experienced science?

Science and creativity

Not only are children naturally curious, they are also inherently creative. Science provides an ideal platform for young children to demonstrate and enhance their **creativity**. Creativity involves using the imagination to create a process or product that is original and has value to the user (Niland, 2016). Creativity helps children to better understand the world around them by supporting questioning, experimentation, problem solving, risk taking and shared thinking. Creativity also encourages divergent thinking and acceptance of differences.

> **Creativity** – a higher-order thinking skill which involves using the imagination to create a process or product that is original and has value to the user.

Creativity has been defined to contain a number of aspects which are both observable and, in some case, actually measureable (Cropley, 2014) based on seminal research undertaken by Torrance (1966). These factors include:

- flexibility: the ability to produce a large variety of ideas
- elaboration: the ability to develop, embellish, or fill out an idea
- originality: the ability to produce ideas that are unusual, statistically infrequent, not banal or obvious.

An early childhood educator can use her or his understanding of these factors to consider how children are displaying creativity in their science explorations, construction activities and problem-solving tasks. (See also Chapter 12, p. 188.)

CREATIVITY WITH CARDBOARD TUBES AND BALLS

Four-year-old Ethan was fascinated by balls. A range of cardboard tubes (different lengths and sizes) and balls were placed outside near the sandpit. Ethan quickly started rolling the balls down the tubes, observing how he could direct the balls by moving the tubes. His friends Coby and Sarah joined in this play. Ethan then suggested, 'Let's roll the balls into the sandpit', a distance of 3 m away. The three children spent the next 30 minutes devising and trialling many different arrangements of the cardboard tubes to get the balls to roll into the sandpit. During their play, two main problems were encountered: making sure the tubes maintained a downwards slope, and working out how to join the tubes. The former was solved through the use of buckets from the sandpit and boxes from inside the centre to provide height to the tubes. The latter was harder, with suggestions of using hands or string to join the tubes, until they realised that some tubes fitted inside others.

The science presented in this case study is based on forces (gravity) and the exploration and use of different materials. The creative thinking shown here, based on Robson's (2012) indicators of creative thinking, involved defining a challenge (how to roll the ball into the sandpit), analysing ideas (suggestions and discussion on how to do this), overcoming barriers and problems (solving their own problems through divergent thinking), having confidence to explore (offering different ideas), embracing uncertainty (persistence and taking risks), spending time (concentrating on the problem), and making mistakes (trial and error). The children posed their own science problem during play and solved it through their creativity and imagination.

REFLECTION

1. How can you set up an environment where children feel free to take risks and make mistakes?
2. Another example of creativity can be found in Case study 10.4 'Constructing a roller-coaster'. From this case study, identify the link between science and creativity, and describe the indicators of creative thinking.

The importance of science in the early years

The early childhood years are an important time for learning. These years represent a period of significant social, emotional, cognitive, linguistic and physical development in children. Research into developmental and cognitive psychology has highlighted the importance of environmental effects during the early years of development and that a lack of stimuli may result in children's development not reaching its full potential (Hadzigeorgiou, 2002). Due to its ability to engage and stimulate children, science education in the early childhood years offers the capacity to improve many aspects of child development.

Eshach and Fried (2005) presented a range of reasons for engaging young children in science. As mentioned earlier, children have a natural tendency to enjoy observing nature and to think about it. Science content and skills are a natural fit with the way young children explore and try to explain their environment. Young children are motivated to explore the world around them, and appropriate science experiences can capitalise on this motivation. Quality and developmentally appropriate science learning experiences can assist children to better understand their world, collect and organise information, and apply and test ideas. These experiences provide a solid foundation for the subsequent development of scientific concepts that children will encounter throughout their academic lives. Engaging in science experiences also allows for the development of scientifically informed language and scientific thinking. Through active engagement with science, young children can develop increased self-belief as science learners and participants in the process of science, construct understandings of science as a discipline, and come to view science as interesting and worth pursuing (Mantzicopoulos, Patrick & Samarapungavan, 2008).

Children's capacity for science

In terms of science, the developmental domains can characterise what children are capable of achieving (Gopnik, 2012; Johnston & Nahmad-Williams, 2009; Marotz & Allen, 2013). From birth to about 3 years of age, children are able to focus their attention on particular features of their world. In their explanations and play, they seek meaning for their experiences. They demonstrate an interest in why things occur and start to use others as a source of information and learning. This often emerges as children repeat activities over and over again, becoming immersed in their discoveries of new knowledge. Children's language begins to reflect their enquiries with questions starting with 'why, how, who, when, where or what?'

In the 3–5-year-old category, children show a great deal of curiosity and interest in objects and living things. They start to demonstrate an understanding of cause and effect, and realise that things can change. Children of this age are able to articulate their own understandings and ask questions of others. They investigate materials by using their senses appropriately and begin to identify features of living things and objects they observe. Further, they begin to notice similarities and patterns in objects and events around them.

Children aged 5–8 develop dispositions for learning. They become adventurous in their thinking and begin to reflect on their thinking processes. They develop further skills in problem-solving, inquiry, experimentation, researching and investigating. Increasingly, they are able to transfer information from one context to another, adapt what they have learnt, and start to develop their own explanations for observations they make based on evidence they have collected. Finally, they are able to connect people, places, technologies and materials to provide independent resources for their own learning.

Educators can build children's science learning by recognising and scaffolding these capacities in young children.

Conclusion

This chapter described what science looks like in the early years. It acknowledged the curiosity and wonder that young children show towards the natural world, and how that curiosity provides a logical connection to science learning. Descriptions of the conceptual, procedural and attitudinal science knowledge that young children can acquire through science were presented. The relationship between science and creativity was discussed. A range of reasons why young children should engage with science were also presented. The chapter highlighted that through active engagement with appropriate and meaningful science experiences and their educators young children can see themselves as science learners and value science as interesting and worth pursuing.

1 References

Australian Curriculum, Assessment and Reporting Authority (ACARA). (2014). Australian Curriculum, 'Science – Rationale', www.australiancurriculum.edu.au/science/rationale, accessed 1 October 2014.

Blake, E. & Howitt, C. (2012). Science in early learning centres: Satisfying curiosity, guided play or lost opportunities, in K.C.D. Tan & M. Kim (eds), *Issues and Challenges in Science Education Research: Moving Forwards*, Dordrecht: Springer, 281–99.

Brunton, P. & Thornton, L. (2010). *Science in the Early Years: Building Firm Foundations from Birth to Five*, London: Sage.

Cropley, D. (2014). Fighting the slump: a multi-faceted exercise for fostering creativity in children, *The International Journal of Creativity and Problem solving*, 24(2), 7–22.

D'Arcangelo, M. (2000). The scientist in the crib: A conversation with Andrew Meltzoff, *Educational Leadership*, 58(3), 8–13.

Davis, D. & Howe, A. (2003). *Teaching Science and Design Technology in the Early Years*, London: David Fulton.

Eshach, H. & Fried, M. N. (2005). Should science be taught in early childhood? *Journal of Science Education and Technology*, 14(3), 315–36.

Fleer, M. (2009). Supporting scientific conceptual consciousness of learning in 'a roundabout way' in play-based contexts, *International Journal of Science Education*, 31(8), 1069–89.

Gopnik, A. (2012). Scientific thinking in young children: Theoretical advances, empirical research, and policy implications, *Science*, 337(6102), 1623–7.

Hadzigeorgiou, Y. (2002). A study of the development of the concept of mechanical stability in pre-school children, *Research in Science Education*, 32(2), 373–91.

Harlen, W. (2001). *Primary Science: Taking the Plunge* (2nd edn), London: Heinemann.

Howitt, C. & Blake, E. (2010). *Planting the Seeds of Science: A Flexible, Integrated and Engaging Resource for Teachers of 3 to 8 Year Olds* (2nd edn), Perth: Curtin University and Australian Learning and Teaching Council.

Johnston, J. & Nahmad-Williams, L. (2009). *Early Childhood Studies*, Essex, UK: Pearson Education.

Mantzicopoulos, P., Patrick, H. & Samarapungavan, A. (2008). Young children's motivational beliefs about learning science, *Early Childhood Research Quarterly*, 23, 378–94.

Marotz, L. R. & Allen, K. E. (2013). *Developmental Profiles: Pre-birth through Adolescence*, Belmont, CA: Wadsworth Cengage Learning.

Niland, A. (2016). *Creativity and Young Children: Wondering, Exploring, Discovering, Learning*. Canberra: Early Childhood Australia.

Peterson, S. H. & French, L. (2008). Supporting young children's explanations through inquiry science in preschool, *Early Childhood Research Quarterly*, 23(3), 395–408.

Robson, S. (2012). Creative thinking in early childhood, in H. Fumoto, S. Robson, S. Greenfield & D. Hargreaves (ed.), *Young Children's Creative Thinking*, London, UK: Sage, 27–40.

Torrance, E. P. (1966). *Torrance Tests of Creative Thinking: Technical Norms Manual*. Lexington, MA: Personnel Press.

2 Science and the national Early Years Learning Framework

Andrea Nolan

This chapter provides an overview of Australia's first national curriculum framework for early childhood educators, published as *Belonging, Being and Becoming: The Early Years Learning Framework for Australia* (DEEWR, 2009). It traces the development of the EYLF, situating it alongside existing national and international frameworks and curriculum documents. It discusses the rationale for the new structure, the underpinning philosophies and the implications these have for educators' practices and children's learning. The 'belonging', 'being' and 'becoming' motifs are explained in light of teaching and learning in the early years, along with the eight practice elements, five principle elements and five learning outcomes stated within the EYLF. The relevance of these in relation to teaching science in the early years is made clear, concluding with the identification of the science outcomes for children within the framework. This chapter firmly establishes the purpose of the national framework and its ramifications for the teaching of science in the early years. Throughout the chapter, the voices of early childhood educators and early childhood teacher educators are highlighted to illustrate how those working in the sector are engaging with the framework.

OBJECTIVES

At the end of this chapter you will be able to:

- recognise how the Early Years Learning Framework (EYLF) sits historically with international research and understandings
- recognise how the EYLF provides for teaching and learning in science in early childhood settings
- describe the principles and outcomes within the EYLF, with reference to pedagogy, play and embedded values
- identify ways that educators can enhance science learning through attending to the EYLF.

Evolution of the framework

In 2009, Australia saw the development of its first national framework to guide the early childhood curriculum and practice for those working with children aged from birth to 5 years in a range of early childhood settings. This was a direct result of the **Council of Australian Governments**' (COAG, 2008) reform agenda in the areas of early childhood education and care. With the election of the Rudd Labor government in 2007, the 'productivity agenda' surfaced, underpinned by a firm commitment to increasing investment in social and human capital as a way to strengthen the Australian economy. Education was seen as a key component of this agenda, with early childhood education and care receiving attention through the commitment to improvement of program quality. The COAG vision for 2010, that 'all children have the best start in life to create a better future for themselves and for the nation', saw state and territory governments collaborate on a National Quality Agenda for Early Childhood Education and Care. The new framework, the **EYLF**, was a key element of this quality agenda as it 'form[ed] the foundation for ensuring that children in all early childhood education and care settings experience quality teaching and learning' (DEEWR, 2009, p. 5). It was aligned with the **National Quality Standard (NQS)** (Quality Area 1), with the expectation that staff working in programs for young children would engage with the framework in designing and implementing their programs, thereby ensuring that children's learning from birth to 5 years of age and through the transition to school was extended and enriched (DEEWR, 2009).

The international context

A search of the international literature (VCAA, 2008) found a proliferation of curriculum frameworks and learning documents employed in the early childhood years. While these frameworks vary in the age range catered for and differ in the definition of the term 'curriculum' and its intentions, there are common themes that have implications for practice. These include:

- recognition of the early years, especially the first three years of life, as important for laying the foundation for later learning
- the link between quality programs and later economic benefits
- acknowledgement that changes in family lifestyles require changes in the care provisions offered
- working in partnerships, leading to 'a shared sense of responsibility and shared commitment to children and their education' (VCAA, 2008, p. 24).

Within these frameworks children are positioned as competent and capable citizens. The social nature of learning is acknowledged, children are valued for who they are and what they bring to the learning situation, and play is recognised as the context through which a young child learns. Overarching elements that underpin quality programs take a

Council of Australian Governments (COAG) – the peak intergovernmental forum in Australia established in 1992. Members of COAG include the Prime Minister (chair), state and territory First Ministers and the President of the Australian Local Government Association (ALGA). Its role is to manage matters of national significance or matters that need coordinated action by all Australian governments.

Early Years Learning Framework (EYLF) – *Belonging, Being and Becoming: The Early Years Learning Framework for Australia* is Australia's first national framework for early childhood educators.

National Quality Standard (NQS) – a key aspect of the National Quality Framework (NQF) setting a national benchmark for early childhood education and care and outside school hours care services in Australia. It consists of seven key quality areas that are important to outcomes for children: educational program and practice; children's health and safety; physical environment; staffing arrangements; relationships with children; collaborative partnerships with families and communities; and leadership and service management.

strength-based approach towards documenting, assessing and planning for children, providing continuity of service provision in well-resourced programs, and ensuring practice is informed by research evidence, and that literacy and numeracy are embedded into learning documents.

Principles that can be drawn from an analysis of the frameworks (VCAA, 2008) that determine what is provided for children and how this is provided include:

■ acknowledging that children have rights (United Nations Declaration of the Rights of the Child, 1959)

■ valuing the richness and uniqueness that each child brings to learning situations (cultural diversity, different understandings of literacy)

■ understanding the impact that environments and relationships have on shaping the learning that takes place within them.

These principles have been carried into Australia's framework.

The Australian context

Most Australian states already had in place their own frameworks and curriculum documents prior to the development of the national framework. However, these differed as to the age range described and the language used within the documents. For example, in Tasmania and New South Wales, the provision was for children from birth to 5 years of age, whereas in Western Australia, Queensland, the Australian Capital Territory and the Northern Territory children aged 3–5 years were the focus, and Tasmania used a common language and common organisers across all children aged from birth to 16 years (VCAA, 2008). Therefore, with the introduction of the new framework, decisions regarding how each state or territory would engage with the new document were left up to the jurisdiction of that state or territory. For example, it was acceptable that the EYLF be used to supplement or complement existing frameworks, or that it completely replaced current documents. In Victoria, the only Australian state with no framework already in place, the EYLF was used as a foundation upon which the Victorian government developed the **Victorian Early Years Learning and Development Framework (VEYLDF)** (DEECD, 2009). While this document echoed the features of the EYLF, it broadened the scope to encompass the age range of birth to 8 years, thereby incorporating the transition to school process.

Victorian Early Years Learning and Development Framework (VEYLDF) – sets out outcomes and practices to guide early childhood educators in their work with young children and their families from birth to 8 years of age.

The EYLF structure and implications for teaching and learning in early years settings

There are different layers in the EYLF, ranging from the main concepts of 'belonging', 'being' and 'becoming' to the 'principles', 'practices' and 'learning outcomes' set out within the framework. Belonging, being and becoming are interwoven concepts or motifs that are strongly represented throughout the framework and act as a reflection of a child's life. 'Belonging' relates to feeling part of the group, family or community. 'Being' is about living in the 'now' and understanding how you are positioned, accepted and valued. 'Becoming' refers to change and how children grow, develop and adapt to new situations.

The principles, practices and learning outcomes are considered as 'inter-related elements' and valued as 'fundamental to early childhood pedagogy and curriculum decision-making' (DEEWR, 2009, p. 9). Put simply, the 'principles' relate to educators' beliefs about young children's learning and how best this learning can be supported. These, in turn, will inform educators' 'practices' – 'the doing'. The 'learning outcomes' connect with the skills, knowledge or dispositions that can be encouraged and supported in early childhood settings in collaboration with others.

The five principles, informed by research and contemporary theories of teaching and learning, are designed to strengthen and support **early childhood educators**' practices, ensuring that their work with young children demonstrates:

Early childhood educators – early childhood practitioners who work directly with children in early childhood settings.

- secure, respectful and reciprocal relationships
- partnerships with families
- high expectations and equity
- respect for diversity
- ongoing learning and reflective practice.

These principles, grounded in children's learning and early childhood pedagogy, inform educators' practice with children.

The 'practice' element of the framework recognises that early childhood educators' practices are informed by a wide range of strategies to support children's learning. The focus is on the teaching and learning context, the interactions and the assessment for learning, planning and reflection on practice. Recognising that there is interconnectedness in children's learning between their health, physical and mental wellbeing, children's individual capabilities are acknowledged and built upon, and relevant learning opportunities are offered in fitting and responsive ways. Purposeful teaching is incorporated and attention paid to the learning environment to ensure it has a welcoming atmosphere with which children can identify and in which they feel secure and supported. Indeed, practice is considered effective when the cultural and social contexts of children and their families' lives are valued, when transitions are planned for and continuity of learning is provided that has individual children's learning monitored, reflected upon and evaluated.

The 'learning outcomes' are broad in scope to cater for the complexity of each child's learning journey. These are designed to assist early childhood educators with respect to planning for children's learning outcomes and represent the inter-relatedness and complexity of children's learning. These learning outcomes are that children:

- have a strong sense of identity
- are connected with and contribute to their world
- have a strong sense of wellbeing
- are confident and involved learners
- are effective communicators.

Descriptors accompanying each learning outcome provide more guidance as to the knowledge, skills, dispositions or learning processes that will demonstrate attainment of the outcome. However, the learning outcomes, while providing the content and processes, do not clearly articulate how these can be identified and achieved (Krieg, 2011). Chapter 8 provides two detailed examples of how these five outcomes can be applied to children's science learning experiences.

Valuing different views

The EYLF was developed with the intention of not only supporting good practice, which was already happening within the sector, but also to create a space in which dialogue could take place in relation to early childhood pedagogy, curriculum and discourses (Sumsion et al., 2009). It was designed to be flexible so it could be interpreted in ways that were relevant to the culture or context of the setting and broad enough in scope to be respectful of the many theories and discourses held by those working in the early childhood education and care sector (Raban et al., 2005). This means that the language used in the framework was deliberately chosen to ensure that it could 'cross borders and divides, resonate with diverse audiences, and be taken up differently within different discourses and narratives' (Sumsion et al., 2009, p. 8).

If we believe that what a society values and strives for is reflected in a curriculum (Reid, 2008), then this leaves curriculum frameworks vulnerable to the changing beliefs of society regarding what is valuable and what should be privileged. This is true within the early childhood sector, where differing theoretical perspectives position children and their learning differently (Raban et al., 2007). This has ramifications for the planning and interactions that take place within an early childhood setting. For example, while many of the current perspectives on early childhood education embrace a sociocultural approach to working with young children and their families, there is still a well-supported discourse that takes a more developmental view of learning and teaching. The framework therefore does not impose one overarching theoretical perspective, instead allowing each educator to engage with the document in their own way. By doing this, it acknowledges educators working from theoretical perspectives, such as developmental, sociocultural, socio-behavioural, critical and post-structural, creating an opportunity for educators to connect with the framework in ways that are responsive to their own beliefs and understandings about teaching and learning.

Learning through play

Inherent to the early childhood sector are ideas held about the nature of young children and the learning processes of early childhood. Early childhood education has traditionally devised and implemented play-based programs, which have aimed to extend each child's development in the social, emotional, linguistic, cognitive and physical areas. For many years, play has been seen by the early childhood sector as the most natural and appropriate learning medium (Wood, 2009). When questioned about play, common sentiments expressed by early childhood educators include viewing play as a motivating force in a child's intellectual development, using play as a way for children to discover themselves and their world, and the importance of play in providing a vehicle for learning. Play is therefore seen as a vital component in a child's overall learning, needing to be supported and respected. In Australia this perspective on play has been articulated in policy terms by the COAG Productivity Agenda Working Group: Education, Skills, Training and Early Childhood Development (COAG, 2008), which describes the role of play in early learning as 'integral to the delivery of early learning programs for children from birth and in all care environments' (p. 16), providing 'a platform for children and teachers to participate in meaningful learning' (p. 40). Bruce (1991) proposed that a quality early years curriculum involved three aspects, defined as:

■ the child – the process of play as part of the child's development

■ the context – people, culture and environment and access to play

■ the content – what the child knows, wants to know and is expected to learn, and the role of play in facilitating this.

The role of play in supporting children's learning in care environments is the topic of Chapter 7.

There is a deliberate emphasis on play-based learning within the EYLF in recognition of play being the context within which young children learn. How play is defined in the framework has been described as encompassing both the 'historical and contemporary arguments about the role of play in children's learning' (Edwards & Cutter-Mackenzie, 2011, p. 53). As is stated in the EYLF, 'Play can expand children's thinking and enhance their desire to know and to learn' (DEEWR, 2009, p. 15). Considering play in this way exposes the many significant characteristics that can be connected to enhance a child's learning capacity, such as motivation, sense of self and empowerment, as well as a focus on the process rather than on the product (Nolan, Kilderry & O'Grady, 2006). However, finding a unity between playing, learning and teaching is important (Wood, 2009), as 'play, unfettered by adult awareness or response, is insufficiently educative for groups of young children' (Scales et al., 1991, p. 17). Enabling children to become 'builders of knowledge structures', actively receiving information and relating this to other aspects of their lives and to previous information, relies on the adult and child being seen as 'co-constructors in the learning relationship, working within a rich, stimulating learning environment'

FIGURE 2.1 Children exploring what they are interested in – the natural environment and the small animals that live beneath the leaf litter

(Nolan, Kilderry & O'Grady, 2006, p. 8). A defined role for early childhood educators has been outlined in the EYLF and is addressed in the principles and practice elements of the document.

Overall, the EYLF enables educators, no matter the context, to aspire to developing 'a clear focus on children's learning and wellbeing, a shared language for curriculum in the early childhood sector, a base for planning, promoting and assessing for learning, improved quality in early childhood settings, cultural security for Aboriginal and Torres Strait Islander children and their families, and including all families and communities in children's learning' (DEEWR, 2010, p. 3).

Differing pedagogies

Intentional teaching – educators being deliberate, purposeful and thoughtful in their decisions and actions.

The approach of the EYLF is that learning occurs through the interplay of **intentional teaching**, and through both adult-guided and child-directed experiences, which provide opportunities for free exploration and experimentation along with focused and deliberate teaching. This provides a rich range of pedagogical practices from which educators can draw to ensure they are providing a stimulating program. Nolan and colleagues (2006, p. 14) suggested that learning as a function of experience involves taking the initiative instead of waiting to be told; generating useful alternatives and making decisions; solving problems, posing problems and designing ways forward; and thinking, pondering and revisiting ideas. With the EYLF signalling intentional teaching as 'deliberate, purposeful and thoughtful' (DEEWR, 2009, p. 15), it is important that educators are exposed to the possibilities of opening up their teaching to incorporate scientific processes. Strategies such as open questioning, demonstrating, speculating and problem-solving are in harmony with encouraging children to incorporate scientific content, processes and methods into their own learning journeys.

Encouraging children to take an enquiring approach to their learning sits comfortably with the discipline of science. Considering teaching and learning from this perspective opens up possibilities in thinking and processing learning, enriching that learning, and enabling complexities to be exposed along with different ways of thinking. Fleer and Raban (2007) use the term 'consciousness raising' when outlining early childhood educators' work in enhancing young children's literacy and numeracy learning. They draw attention to the new thinking about children's learning, which highlights the importance of educators harnessing children's everyday experiences and connecting and building on the literacy and numeracy concepts they develop through these experiences. This way of working transforms children's thinking. It can also be applied to scientific concepts and fits well with the practices and outcomes of the EYLF. The following example, provided by an early childhood teacher educator exemplifies this way of working:

> As teacher educators we try and encourage our student teachers to look at everyday experiences related to the child and see the science in them. They need to be providing open-ended experiences that promote imagination and a sense of wonder and awe, where children can actually ask further questions. I suppose the big thing that I would say is that the experiences provide meaning to a child, that's very important, and that as early childhood educators we actually promote conversations that are rich with

questions. It's about building the children's language, vocabulary, scientific terms, so there is a sense of integration in all areas of the curriculum. So I think science, what does it look like, that it's really just the everyday experiences, but when you have someone who really recognises that, there will be rich things happening in the language used, and the extension of the learning taking place. It's about creating that wonder. (Interview BS, 2011)

This example outlines how an educator can work with children in a way that connects their everyday experiences to a more heightened awareness of scientific concepts, prompting further thought. However, as one early childhood educator warns:

It depends on the educator's awareness, to bring science to the surface, to make it visible for the children, because if they're not aware then it will pass and it doesn't go anywhere. (Interview JH, 2011)

It is suggested that early childhood educators 'work with children in ways that support their interaction with new ideas found in content knowledge through a process where this new knowledge is used to test their own experience' (Krieg, 2011, pp. 52–3). No singular, particular knowledge base has dominance over others in this co-construction of meaning. Denying children this engagement with discipline-based knowledge restricts their opportunities to understand the complexities of their world (Krieg, 2011).

Science and the EYLF: learning outcomes

In their text *The Scientist in the Crib: Minds, Brains and How Children Learn*, Gopnik, Melzoff and Kuhl (1999) discuss the theory and science of how young children learn and what is needed for them to thrive. They illustrate how what adults take as mundane can become rich learning environments for children. It is therefore important for educators to understand, capture and relive this sense of wonder and knowledge so they can bring it into their programming. The EYLF allows for this to happen.

The Early Years Learning Framework is like the foundations, but then you bring your own knowledge and you build your own house. Each house will look different as each educator brings different elements to their teaching. So if you're inclined to provide a sense of awe and excitement in your program you would be able to do that within the framework because you would see that in the framework. (Interview BS, 2011).

When the teaching and learning of science is considered, the EYLF does provide many opportunities to engage children in science content, scientific processes and the use of scientific language. Science is one of the discipline areas named in the framework; however, the content does not sit solely within one of the learning outcomes but is dispersed throughout the outcomes. For example, there are references to the natural and built environments, and living and non-living things, but also throughout the framework is the use of learning processes drawn from the science discipline, such as exploration, hypothesising, enquiring, researching and investigating. As one educator suggests (interview JH, 2011): 'I think science is really everything we do. It's part of everything and it's not a separate thing. It's embedded in everything and connected.'

While not always specifically nominated as science, many of the descriptors of the outcomes and the associated processes and practices do involve children engaging in science content or processes drawn from the discipline. For example, Outcome 1 focuses on children learning about themselves and their own identity within the context of families, communities and the environment. It relates to children showing increasing initiative and curiosity about their world. When safe, secure and supported, children grow in confidence to explore, discover and learn.

Outcome 2 relates to children being connected with and contributing to their world. This outcome speaks of a broadening of a child's understanding in relation to their world through the investigation and exploration of ideas. It is also concerned with children participating in problem-solving; demonstrating knowledge, respect and care for natural and constructed environments; inferring, predicting and hypothesising to increase understanding of the interdependence between land, people, plants and animals; exploring relationships with living and non-living things; observing change; and developing environmental awareness in order to become socially responsible and to show respect for the environment.

Outcome 3 focuses on wellbeing, with children encouraged to seek out new challenges, to make new discoveries, and to celebrate their own efforts and achievements and those of others. Taking increasing responsibility for their own health and physical wellbeing, children use their sensory capabilities and dispositions to explore and respond to their world.

Children are positioned as confident and involved learners in Outcome 4. This outcome

also has strong links to science through the development of dispositions for learning such as curiosity. In applying a range of skills and processes taken from the discipline of science, such as problem-solving, inquiring, experimenting, hypothesising, researching and investigating, children are able to deepen their understandings of their world, making connections between experiences, concepts and processes.

Expressing ideas, making meaning using a range of media and texts, and interacting verbally and non-verbally all relate to Outcome 5: that children are effective communicators. Science can provide the context through which children can enjoy interactions with others, applying their senses, clarifying and challenging their thinking, negotiating with others and sharing new understandings. This outcome, with its focus on communication skills, can be incorporated into many science experiences in which ideas are exchanged, the perspectives of others are

FIGURE 2.2 Science involves observing closely – sometimes aided by tools

listened to, understood and respected, and meaning is gained through experimentation with ways of expressing ideas using a range of texts.

What becomes apparent is that the EYLF provides many opportunities to engage children with science and these are dispersed throughout the five learning outcomes.

SCIENCE IN THE EYLF

Fiona, an experienced early childhood educator, offers the following interpretation of the framework in relation to science:

> The framework opens it up for science. For example in Outcome 4: children are confident and involved learners – the wording such as curiosity, problem-solving, experimenting, hypothesising, investigating and researching make you think about science. There is a nice link to taking a scientific approach to teaching and learning. The framework also enables me to provide science experiences as a way to achieve Outcome 2: children are connected with and contribute to their world. Science provides an opportunity for boys to become part of the group dynamics – whereas girls can use role-playing as a way to do that, scientific things seem a positive way to engage all children. (Interview FG, 2011)

1. Where do you see science within the EYLF?
2. Consider a science activity in which you have seen children engage. Which of the learning outcomes were addressed in this activity?

REFLECTION

The learning outcomes enable specific processes drawn from other disciplines to be harnessed in order to enhance the learning taking place, so that it presents as holistic. Engagement with discipline content and methods opens up 'another way of knowing' (Krieg, 2011, p. 53), which further acts to support children's learning. This broadens the possibility for educators to take a multidisciplinary approach to inquiry-based learning and teaching, driven by the children's desire to understand their world (Krieg, 2011). Working in this way allows the educator to view disciplinary knowledge, in this case knowledge relating to science, not as compartmentalised and reduced to a number of facts that need to be learnt but as dynamic and embedded within the context in which it was created and produced (Fleer, 2010). The following description of science teaching by an early childhood educator illustrates this:

> Well, what does science teaching really look like? It's about all the experiences children have. It's not about 'I'm going to particularly set up a science experiment'. It's about recognising the science within an everyday experience. An example I give often is the baby who tips their toy or their cup over the side of their high chair and watches it fall and somebody picks it up and gives it back to them, and so the baby tips it over again. That's about science and exploring properties of objects, and gravity … (Interview JH, 2011)

Elliott (2010b), when looking for connections with play in nature, reminds us that we need to look beyond the obvious in the framework to discover some of the different layers that can add complexity and depth to our work. For example, she challenges the extension of 'belonging', 'being' and 'becoming' to encompass children's connection to natural environments and the impact these have on children's sense of agency, relationships and empowerment (Elliott, 2010a). This notion of looking beyond the framework and using the document as a springboard to new possibilities for teaching and learning could, however, be more difficult for some educators, as suggested by an experienced early childhood educator:

> Whilst the framework is so open and offers many possibilities, it does depend on how early childhood educators engage with it. They need to be open to the possibilities it offers, not just keep doing what they have always done without questioning their practice. (Interview JH, 2011)

Practical task

LINKING SCIENCE TO THE EYLF OUTCOMES AND DESCRIPTORS

Read through Table 2.1, which provides examples of how science can be linked to the outcomes and descriptors of the EYLF. This table only presents three examples for each descriptor, and should not be considered an exhaustive list. Many of the descriptors presented in the EYLF can make strong connections to science. See if you can add two more examples for each descriptor.

TABLE 2.1	EXAMPLES OF HOW SCIENCE CAN BE LINKED TO THE OUTCOMES AND DESCRIPTORS OF THE EYLF
Learning Outcome 1: Children have a strong sense of identity	
Descriptor	**Evident when children**
Children feel safe, secure and supported	■ Interact with the natural environment with confidence ■ Undertake their own investigations ■ Readily express their ideas about the world
Children develop their emerging autonomy, interdependence, resilience and sense of agency	■ Are open to new discoveries ■ Develop their sense of agency in exploring science phenomena ■ Persevere with a science-related task
Children develop knowledgeable and confident self-identities	■ Share science done at home with other children and educators ■ Interact with other children for a specific purpose in the natural environment ■ Celebrate and share their science discoveries and successes
Children learn to interact in relation to others with care, empathy and respect	■ Express a range of thoughts and views on their understandings of the world ■ Respect others' thoughts and views of the world ■ Develop empathy towards the environment and the part they play in it

Learning Outcome 2: Children are connected with and contribute to their world	
Descriptor	Evident when children
Children develop a sense of belonging to groups and communities and an understanding of the reciprocal rights and responsibilities necessary for active community participation	■ Broaden their understanding of the world in which they live ■ Work with others to develop skills for communication and inquiry about themselves and their world ■ Contribute to ongoing indoor or outdoor science-related projects
Children respond to diversity with respect	■ Begin to understand how all people, places and living things are inter-related and coexist ■ Begin to notice similarities and differences in the characteristics of themselves and others ■ Listen to others' ideas and explanations of the world
Children become aware of fairness	■ Share with others ■ Become aware not to take more than allowed when making collections of natural objects ■ Begin to act with compassion and kindness to elements of the natural world
Children become socially responsible and show respect for the environment	■ Demonstrate an increasing knowledge of, and respect for, natural and constructed environments ■ Explore relationships with other living and non-living things and observe, notice and respond to change ■ Show an awareness of pollution and the need to pick up their own litter
Learning Outcome 3: Children have a strong sense of wellbeing	
Descriptor	Evident when children
Children become strong in their social and emotional wellbeing	■ Seek out new challenges, make new discoveries, and celebrate their own efforts and achievements and those of others ■ Recognise the contributions they make to shared projects and experiences ■ Make choices to behave in a safe manner in the outdoor environment
Children take increasing responsibility for their own health and physical wellbeing	■ Use their sensory capabilities and dispositions with increasing integration, skill and purpose to explore and respond to their world ■ Manipulate equipment and manage tools to explore their world with increasing competence and skill ■ Show enthusiasm for participating in the natural environment to ensure the safety of themselves and others

→

Learning Outcome 4: Children are confident and involved learners	
Descriptor	Evident when children
Children develop dispositions for learning, such as curiosity, cooperation, confidence, creativity, commitment, enthusiasm, persistence, imagination and reflexivity	■ Express wonder and interest in their environments ■ Use play to investigate, imagine and explore ideas ■ Follow and extend their own interests with enthusiasm, energy and concentration
Children develop a range of skills and processes, such as problem-solving, inquiry, experimentation, hypothesising, researching and investigating	■ Apply a wide variety of thinking strategies to engage with situations and solve problems, and adapt these strategies to new situations ■ Make predictions and generalisations about their daily activities and aspects of the natural world and environments ■ Manipulate objects and experiment with cause and effect, trial and error, and motion
Children transfer and adapt what they have learned from one context to another	■ Develop an ability to mirror, repeat and practise the actions of others, immediately or later ■ Make connections between experiences, concepts and processes ■ Use the process of play, reflection and investigation to solve problems
Children resource their own learning through connecting with people, place, technologies and natural and processed materials	■ Use their senses to explore natural and built environments ■ Manipulate resources to investigate, take apart, assemble, invent and construct ■ Explore ideas and theories using imagination, creativity and play
Learning Outcome 5: Children are effective communicators	
Descriptor	Evident when children
Children interact verbally and non-verbally with others for a range of purposes	■ Engage in enjoyable interactions using verbal and non-verbal language ■ Respond verbally and non-verbally to what they see, hear, touch, feel and taste ■ Interact with others to explore ideas and concepts, clarify and challenge thinking, negotiate and share understandings
Children engage with a range of texts and gain meaning from these texts	■ View and listen to science printed, visual and multimedia texts and respond with relevant gestures, actions, comments and/or questions ■ Explore science stories from a range of different perspectives and begin to analyse the meanings ■ Sing and chant science-related rhymes, jingles and songs
Children express ideas and make meaning using a range of media	■ Create artwork from a range of natural and processed materials ■ Use the creative arts, such as drawing, painting, sculpture, drama, dance, movement, music and storytelling, to express their science understandings ■ Experiment with ways of expressing ideas and meaning using a range of media

Children begin to understand how symbols and pattern systems work	■ Use symbols in play to represent and make meaning ■ Begin to be aware of the relationships between oral, written and visual representations ■ Begin to sort, categorise, order and compare collections and events and attributes of objects and materials, in their social and natural worlds
Children use information and communication technologies to access information, investigate ideas and represent their thinking	■ Use ICT to access images and information, explore diverse perspectives and make sense of their world ■ Use ICT as tools for designing, drawing, editing, reflecting and composing ■ Engage with technology for fun and to make meaning

Source: DEEWR, 2009.

Conclusion

There is no doubt that those commissioned with the job of developing and trialling the EYLF were bound by certain constraints and parameters, dictated by political considerations (Sumsion et al., 2009). Nevertheless, their vision to create a document that encourages educators to use the framework as a base, and to also look beyond it for further possibilities relating to practice, is realistic. The EYLF offers many possibilities for science teaching and learning to occur, but it is up to each individual educator to be open to and to search for opportunities to embed scientific skills, knowledge and processes into everyday programming. The role of the educator is critical in noting, interpreting and then extending a child's learning and, as such, the focus is on pedagogy. By viewing the learning environment as reciprocal and responsive, including the interactions, experiences and provocations offered, the opportunities for science within early childhood settings are many and varied.

> I think it's just the way we work in early childhood. We don't see things in little compartments. We don't say 'This is a maths lesson, pay attention … this is a science lesson, pay attention'. So in that way, I guess the framework is a very open document, and it's having the passion or the interest or the knowledge to look for the subject matter within it. (Interview BS, 2011).

Acknowledgement

I would like to thank Bess Sajfar (BS), Janette Hunt (JH) and Fiona Grainger (FG), who collectively represent experienced early childhood educators and early childhood teacher educators, and who gave so freely of their time to share their passion about young children and science. Their enthusiasm for supporting science within early childhood programs is noteworthy as they endeavour to promote curiosity, questioning and a sense of wonder in young children.

Bruce, T. (1991). *Time to Play in Early Childhood Education*, London: Hodder & Stoughton.

Council of Australian Governments (COAG) Productivity Agenda Working Group: Education, Skills, Training and Early Childhood Development. (2008). *A National Quality Framework for Early Childhood Education and Care: A Discussion Paper*, Canberra: Commonwealth of Australia.

Department of Education and Early Childhood Development (DEECD). (2009). *Victorian Early Years Learning and Development Framework: For All Children from Birth to Eight Years*, Melbourne: Early Childhood Strategy Division, Department of Education and Early Childhood Development and Victorian Curriculum and Assessment Authority.

Department of Education, Employment and Workplace Relations (DEEWR). (2009). *Belonging, Being and Becoming: The Early Years Learning Framework for Australia*, Canberra: Commonwealth of Australia.

—— (2010). *Educators' Guide to the Early Years Learning Framework for Australia*, Canberra: Commonwealth of Australia.

Edwards, S. & Cutter-Mackenzie, A. (2011). Environmentalising early childhood education curriculum through pedagogies of play, *Australasian Journal of Early Childhood*, 36(1), 51–9.

Elliott, S. (2010a). Children in the natural world, in J. Davis (ed.), *Young Children and the Environment: Early Education for Sustainability*, Melbourne: Cambridge University Press, 43–75.

—— (2010b). Natural playspaces, *Community Child Care Victoria Early Years, Term 1*, 11–14.

Fleer, M. (2010). *Early Learning and Development: Cultural-Historical Concepts in Play*, Melbourne: Cambridge University Press.

Fleer, M. & Raban, B. (2007). *Early Childhood Literacy and Numeracy: Building Good Practice*, Canberra: Commonwealth of Australia.

Gopnik, A., Metzoff, A. & Kuhl, P. (1999). *The Scientist in the Crib: Minds, Brains and How Children Learn*, New York: Morrow.

Krieg, S. (2011). The Australian Early Years Learning Framework: Learning what? *Contemporary Issues in Early Childhood*, 12(1), 46–55.

Nolan, A., Kilderry, A. & O'Grady, R. (2006). *Young Children as Active Learners*, Canberra: Early Childhood Australia.

Raban, B., Nolan, A., Waniganayake, M., Ure, C., Deans, J. & Brown, R. (2005). Empowering practitioners to critically examine their current practice, *Australian Research in Early Childhood Education*, 2(2), 1–16.

Raban, B., Waniganayake, M., Nolan, A., Brown, R., Deans, J. & Ure, C. (2007). *Building Capacity: Strategic Professional Development for Early Childhood Practitioners*, Sydney: Thomson Learning Australia.

Reid, A. (2008). It's time: A national curriculum for the 21st century? *Professional Educator*, 7(4), 9–11.

Scales, B., Almy, M., Nicolopoulou, A. & Ervin-Tripp, S. (1991). *Play and the Social Context of Development in Early Care and Education*, New York: Teachers College Press.

Sumsion, J., Cheeseman, S., Kennedy, A., Barnes, S., Harrison, L. & Stonehouse, A. (2009). Insider perspectives on developing Belonging, Being and Becoming: The Early Years Learning Framework for Australia, *Australasian Journal of Early Childhood*, 34(4), 4–13.

UN Declaration of the Rights of the Child (1959) adopted by UN General Assembly Resolution 1386 (XIV), 10 December.

Victorian Curriculum and Assessment Authority (VCAA). (2008). *Analysis of Curriculum/Learning Frameworks for the Early Years (Birth to Age 8)*, Melbourne: Victorian Curriculum and Assessment Authority.

Wood, E. (2009). Developing a pedagogy of play, in A. Anning, J. Cullen & M. Fleer (eds), *Early Childhood Education: Society and Culture* (2nd edn), London: Sage, 19–30.

3 Science in the Australian Curriculum

Kathryn Paige

This chapter provides an overview of the Australian Curriculum: Science. The chapter starts with a brief outline of the history of the Australian Curriculum. It then describes the three science strands of Science Understanding, Science as Human Endeavour and Science Inquiry Skills, and considers how these should be woven together to provide a framework for developing experiential, connected and sequential science learning experiences for children in the early years. The seven general capabilities (literacy, numeracy, information and communication technology [ICT] competence, critical and creative thinking, ethical behaviour, personal and social competence, and intercultural understanding) and three cross-curriculum priorities (Aboriginal and Torres Strait Islander histories and cultures, Asia and Australia's engagement with Asia, and sustainability) are presented, along with examples that relate to science in the early years. Various case studies provide an insight into how the Australian Curriculum: Science can be implemented through connection to nature, citizen science and place-based education.

OBJECTIVES

At the end of this chapter you will be able to:

- outline the development of the Australian Curriculum: Science

- describe the three strands of the Australian Curriculum: Science (Science Understanding, Science as Human Endeavour and Science Inquiry Skills) and their associated sub-strands

- relate the general capabilities and cross-curriculum priorities to science in the early years.

A short history of the Australian Curriculum

In December 2008 the Melbourne Declaration on Educational Goals for Young Australians was agreed to by all state, territory and Commonwealth Ministers of Education at a meeting of the Ministerial Council on Education, Employment, Training and Youth Affairs (MCEETYA). This set the direction for schooling for the next 10 years in Australia. The key goals were, first, that Australian schooling promote equity and excellence and, second, that all young Australians become successful learners, confident and creative individuals, who are active and informed citizens (MCEETYA, 2008). In May 2009 the Australian Curriculum, Assessment and Reporting Authority (ACARA) board was established. Its responsibility was to write Australia's first national curriculum for Foundation (the first year of school) to Year 12 (F–12) in specified learning areas along with a national assessment program to measure students' progress. The 'purpose and framework' was outlined in a paper titled *The Shape of the Australian Curriculum*, which provided background to the development and for the implementation of the Australian Curriculum. A team of experts from each of the learning areas also developed shaping papers; for example, *The Shape of the Australian Curriculum: Science* guides the writing of the Australian science curriculum for F–12 (**Australian Curriculum: Science**).

The Australian Curriculum was developed in collaboration with a wide range of stakeholders, including teachers, principals, governments, state and territory education authorities, professional education associations, community groups and the general public. The process of rolling out the curriculum began in 2010 with English, history, mathematics and science. The Australian Curriculum is the first national curriculum to be made available online, which allows for ready access and also supports the ease of responsive changes that can easily be tracked. ACARA is the overarching authority for school education. However, as education is a function of each state, boards of education implement their own state curriculum documents that must adhere to the national curriculum document.

> **Australian Curriculum: Science** – the mandated science curriculum for all Australian students from Foundation year to Year 12.

The Australian Curriculum incorporates three key components that teachers must address in their learning and teaching programs: learning areas, general capabilities and **cross-curriculum priorities**. Each of these will be addressed in relation to teaching science in the early years.

The science learning area

Science is one of eight learning areas that must be taught in the Australian Curriculum. Each learning area is structured around a rationale, aims, year or band-level descriptions, information on the organisation of the curriculum, content elaborations, annotated portfolios of student work samples and a glossary. Science is described as a way of knowing and thinking that uses reproducible evidence to develop understandings and explanations about how the world works. It is a human endeavour with an emphasis on both science as a body of knowledge and understandings and the process of obtaining and using evidence to finding answers to the 'big' questions arising from our curiosity and interest (National Curriculum Board, 2009).

> **Cross-curriculum priorities** – embedded in all learning areas, these priorities provide students with knowledge, understanding and skills in three areas deemed to be important for children to know, and they have a strong but varying presence depending on their relevance to the learning areas.

The Australian Curriculum: Science aims to provide:

> opportunities for students to develop an understanding of important science concepts and processes, the practices used to develop scientific knowledge of science's contribution to our culture and society, and its applications in our lives. The curriculum supports students to develop the scientific knowledge, understandings and skills to make informed decisions about local, national and global issues and to participate, if they so wish, in science-related careers. (ACARA, 2014c)

The aims of the Australian Curriculum: Science include developing an interest in and being curious about science, understanding the process of science, recognising the place of evidence in science, an appreciation of the historical contributions to the development of science, building science content knowledge, and communicating science effectively.

Science year groupings

The content of the Australian Curriculum: Science can be described across four year groupings that relate to the nature of learners and the relevant curriculum. Foundation to Year 2 covers children aged 5–8 years. The major curriculum focus in this age range is the awareness of self and the local world. This includes an experiential approach with children using their senses to connect to the natural world and make sense of how the world works. It also acknowledges the natural curiosity of young children and the place of exploratory play in their learning. Further, these young children should be encouraged to:

> observe and gather information, describing, making comparisons, sorting and classifying to create an order that is meaningful. They observe and explore changes that vary in their rate and magnitude and begin to describe relationships in the world around them. Students' questions and ideas about the world become increasingly purposeful. They are encouraged to develop explanatory ideas and test them through further exploration. (ACARA, 2014d)

Science Understanding – the ability to select and integrate appropriate science knowledge to explain and predict phenomena, and apply that knowledge to new situations.

Science as a Human Endeavour – relates to the nature and influence of science in our world and how humans interact with science as a unique way of understanding our world.

Science Inquiry Skills – the skills essential for working scientifically. These include: questioning and predicting; planning and conducting; processing and analysing data and information; evaluating; communicating.

Children in Years 3–6 (8–12 years of age) have a science focus on recognising questions that can be investigated scientifically and conducting those investigations. Students in junior secondary years – that is, Years 7–10 (12–15 years of age) – focus on explaining phenomena involving science and its applications. Finally, senior secondary science students focus on the specific disciplines of science.

Content structure of the Australian Curriculum: Science

The Australian Curriculum: Science consists of three inter-related strands. These are **Science Understanding**, **Science as a Human Endeavour** and **Science Inquiry Skills**. Science Understanding relates to science concepts, Science as a Human Endeavour relates to the nature and influence of science, while Science Inquiry Skills refer to the skills essential for working scientifically. Together, these three strands 'provide students with understanding, knowledge and skills through which they can develop a scientific view of the world' (ACARA, 2014a). A summary of these three strands and their associated sub-strands are presented in Table 3.1. All three strands should be woven together when planning and implementing a science unit.

TABLE 3.1	THE THREE STRANDS OF THE AUSTRALIAN CURRICULUM: SCIENCE AND ASSOCIATED SUB-STRANDS		
	Science strands		
	Science Understanding	Science as a Human Endeavour	Science Inquiry Skills
Sub-strands	Biological sciences	Nature and development of science	Questioning and predicting
	Chemical sciences	Use and influence of science	Planning and conducting
	Earth and space sciences		Processing and analysing data and information
	Physical sciences		Evaluating Communicating

Source: ACARA, 2014a.

Science Understanding (SU)

> Science Understanding is evident when a person selects and integrates appropriate science knowledge to explain and predict phenomena, and applies that knowledge to new situations. Science knowledge refers to facts, concepts, principles, laws, theories and models that have been established by scientists over time. (ACARA, 2014a)

The content of SU is described by year level. The descriptors of SU across Foundation to Year 2 are presented in Table 3.2. The SU strand comprises four sub-strands:

- biological sciences: understanding living things
- chemical sciences: understanding the composition and behaviour of substances
- Earth and space sciences: understanding Earth's dynamic structure and its place in the cosmos
- physical sciences: understanding the nature of forces and motion, along with matter and energy.

Science as a Human Endeavour (SHE)

Science as a Human Endeavour highlights:

> the development of science as a unique way of knowing and doing, and the role of science in contemporary decision making and problem solving. It acknowledges that in making decisions about science practices and applications, ethical and social implications must be taken into account. This strand also recognises that science advances through the contributions of many different people from different cultures and that there are many rewarding science-based career paths. (ACARA, 2014a)

The content in the SHE strand is described in two-year bands. The descriptors of SHE across Foundation to Year 2 are presented in Table 3.3. There are two sub-strands of SHE:

TABLE 3.2 DESCRIPTORS FOR SCIENCE UNDERSTANDING (SU) SUB-STRANDS FOR FOUNDATION TO YEAR 2

Sub-strand	Foundation	Year1	Year 2
Biological sciences	Living things have basic needs, including food and water (ACSSU002).	Living things have a variety of external features (ACSSU017). Living things live in different places where their needs are met (ACSSU211).	Living things grow, change and have offspring similar to themselves (ACSSU030).
Chemical sciences	Objects are made of materials that have observable properties (ACSSU003).	Everyday materials can be physically changed in a variety of ways (ACSSU018).	Different materials can be combined, including by mixing, for a particular purpose (ACSSU031).
Earth and space sciences	Daily and seasonal changes in our environment, including the weather, affect everyday life (ACSSU004).	Observable changes occur in the sky and landscape (ACSSU019).	Earth's resources, including water, are used in a variety of ways (ACSSU032).
Physical sciences	The way objects move depends on a variety of factors, including their size and shape (ACSSU005).	Light and sound are produced by a range of sources and can be sensed (ACSSU020).	A push or a pull affects how an object moves or changes shape (ACSSU033).

Source: ACARA, 2014d.

Note: sub-strand codes from the Australian Curriculum are included. Table 3.3 and Table 3.4 also include sub-strand codes.

TABLE 3.3 DESCRIPTORS OF SCIENCE AS HUMAN ENDEAVOUR (SHE) SUB-STRANDS FOR FOUNDATION TO YEAR 2

Sub-strand	Foundation	Year1	Year 2
Nature and development of science	Science involves exploring and observing the world using the senses (ACSHE013).	Science involves asking questions about, and describing changes in, objects and events (ACSHE021).	Science involves asking questions about, and describing changes in objects and events (ACSHE034).
Use and influence of science		People use science in their daily lives, including when caring for their environment and living things (ACSHE022).	People use science in their daily lives, including when caring for their environment and living things (ACSHE035).

Source: ACARA, 2014d.

- nature and development of science: this sub-strand develops an appreciation of the unique nature of science and scientific knowledge, including how current knowledge has developed over time through the actions of many people
- use and influence of science: this sub-strand explores how science knowledge and applications affect people's lives, including their work, and how science is influenced by society and can be used to inform decisions and actions.

Science Inquiry Skills (SIS)

Science Inquiry Skills involve:

> identifying and posing questions; planning, conducting and reflecting on investigations; processing, analysing and interpreting evidence; and communicating findings. This strand is concerned with evaluating claims, investigating ideas, solving problems, drawing valid conclusions and developing evidence-based arguments. (ACARA, 2014a)

The content in the SIS strand is described in two-year bands. A summary of SIS across Foundation to Year 2 is presented in Table 3.4. There are five sub-strands of SIS:

- questioning and predicting: identifying and constructing questions, proposing hypotheses and suggesting possible outcomes
- planning and conducting: making decisions regarding how to investigate or solve a problem and carrying out an investigation, including the collection of data
- processing and analysing data and information: representing data in meaningful and useful ways, identifying trends, patterns and relationships in data, and using this evidence to justify conclusions
- evaluating: considering the quality of available evidence and the merit or significance of a claim, proposition or conclusion with reference to that evidence
- communicating: conveying information or ideas to others through appropriate representations, text types and modes.

Practical task

MIND MAPS

Create a mind map that presents the strands and sub-strands of the Australian Curriculum: Science. Provide a definition for SU, SHE and SIS on this mind map. Indicate how these definitions fit with the descriptors in the Early Years Learning Framework which make strong connections to science.

TABLE 3.4 SCIENCE INQUIRY SKILLS (SIS) SUB-STRANDS AND CONTENT DESCRIPTORS FOR FOUNDATION TO YEAR 2

Sub-strand	Foundation	Year1	Year 2
Questioning and predicting	Respond to questions about familiar objects and events (ACSIS014).	Respond to and pose questions, and make predictions about familiar objects and events (ACSIS024).	Respond to and pose questions, and make predictions about familiar objects and events (ACSIS037).
Planning and conducting	Explore and make observations by using the senses (ACSIS011).	Participate in different types of guided investigations to explore and answer questions, such as manipulating materials, testing ideas, and accessing information sources (ACSIS025).	Participate in different types of guided investigations to explore and answer questions, such as manipulating materials, testing ideas, and accessing information sources (ACSIS038).
		Use informal measurements in the collection and recording of observations, with the assistance of digital technologies as appropriate (ACSIS026).	Use informal measurements in the collection and recording of observations, with the assistance of digital technologies as appropriate (ACSIS039).
Processing and analysing data and information	Engage in discussions about observations and use methods such as drawing to represent ideas (ACSIS233).	Use a range of methods to sort information, including drawings and provided tables (ACSIS027)	Use a range of methods to sort information, including drawings and provided tables (ACSIS040).
Evaluating		Compare observations with those of others (ACSIS213).	Compare observations with those of others (ACSIS041).
Communicating	Share observations and ideas (ACSIS012)	Represent and communicate observations and ideas in a variety of ways such as oral and written language, drawing and role play (ACSIS029).	Represent and communicate observations and ideas in a variety of ways such as oral and written language, drawing and role play (ACSIS042).

Source: ACARA, 2014d.

Citizen science as a means of teaching and learning science

Citizen science involves scientists and the community collecting scientific data together. Using the community allows scientists to collect extensive data sets that are normally beyond their reach (Bonney et al., 2009). From an educator's point of view, using the community provides opportunities for children to be involved in science with their parents and grandparents (Paige et al., 2010). Participating in citizen science projects allows teachers to interweave the three strands of SU, SHE and SIS to create a rich and engaging unit that connects children to the natural environment as well as an opportunity for children to build their sense of community contribution and belonging (Paige et al., 2012). The inquiry process underpinning citizen science is also a key to teaching science in a Foundation year class. This process has an emphasis on active learning through incorporating scientific skills and abilities, such as posing questions and planning investigations in order to develop conceptual understanding.

Case Study 3.1

'OPERATION SPIDER' FOR THE EARLY YEARS

In 2010 a Foundation class in a primary school conducted a citizen science project in South Australia entitled 'Operation Spider'. Spiders were an ideal topic for schools as they inhabit locations, such as home and school gardens, that are common places in which children spend time.

The term program engaged parents and children by asking them to tick a large graph on the classroom wall to indicate whether they thought spiders had one, two or three body parts. Beginning a topic by eliciting prior knowledge values the experiences and knowledge of the children and is an effective way of creating engagement as well as a useful method for formative assessment. Including parents reflects the importance placed on community involvement in supporting children's learning. There was a wide variety of understandings in the children, educators and parents, with many adults holding alternative conceptions of the physical characteristics of a spider. Following this, the children used a variety of material, such as egg cartons, pipe cleaners, plasticine and play dough to construct a spider and label the parts they knew. This also determined their prior knowledge about the number of body parts and the number of legs. Photographs were taken and included in the children's workbooks. These were referred to when showing how the children's ideas were developing over the course of the unit.

In order to develop the children's understanding towards a more scientifically accurate view of spiders, a series of exploratory experiences were undertaken. Children observed spiders from three different sources: those caught from home and brought to school in large glass jars, a set of spiders in Perspex, and full-sized images of spiders shown on the interactive whiteboard. Conversations about how to look after spiders and what they need to survive became a focus of early morning talks with the children. Transferring a spider into a larger terrarium that contained water, twigs and ground matter allowed for ongoing observation of spiders' behavior. Fact sheets about local spiders were helpful in assisting the children with identification of different spiders. Subsequently, the children were able to identify local species, such as huntsman, redback and garden orb spiders.

The children were asked to use their imagination and draw a crazy spider based on the artwork of an artist exaggerating the features of a spider. This helped the children to reflect on their understanding about physical characteristics and the behaviour of spiders and to use their creative thinking skills to represent this knowledge in a cartoon-type drawing. During these

→

exploratory experiences, questions that the children had about spiders were written on a large chart. These included: 'Is a daddy long legs a spider?', 'Can a spider live in snow?', 'What are fangs for?', 'Do spiders have mouths?', 'Where do spiders live in the school grounds?', 'Do all spiders spin webs?', 'What is the biggest spider?' and 'What do spiders eat?' These questions led to specific investigations, including locating and marking spider webs and spiders on a school map and observing what and how the spider in the terrarium ate as different insects were added.

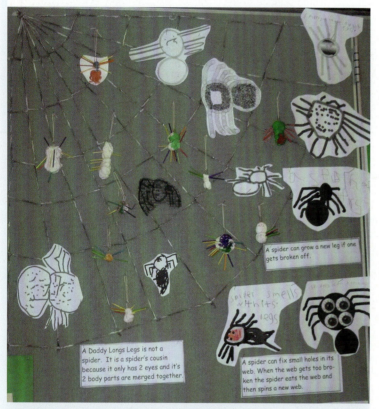

FIGURE 3.1 Children's drawings of spiders in a web

Source: © Janette Leibhardt.

The class then used this information about local spiders and contributed to a state-based citizen science online survey. The survey had two main tasks. The first involved asking questions about attitudes to spiders and what we would do if we saw a redback or a huntsman. Options ranging from 'leave it where it was' to 'kill it with fly spray' were provided. The conversation was rich as children discussed which option best reflected their view of their attitude towards spiders. The educator noted the children's attitude over the course of the unit: it changed from one of fear, to one of knowing spiders have a role in the ecosystem and we should leave them if there is no danger. The second task was completing an observational survey. This was a comprehensive survey asking for data about survey area, spider type and count and requiring the children to upload a photograph. The class uploaded information about three different spiders as a collaborative response to the series of questions on the website. This information was used by scientists to produce a more accurate picture of the urban ecology of the area. One 5-year-old boy who became totally engaged with spiders uploaded several of his observations at home with the support of his family, including his grandfather.

'Operation Spider' linked to all three strands of the Australian Curriculum: Science. The SU strand (biological sciences) at Foundation level has a focus on living things and their needs. Questions such as the following could be addressed: 'Should we keep a spider as a pet?', 'How would we care for it?', 'Where do spiders live?', 'What do they eat?' In Year 1 the focus is on the external features of living things. Thus, identifying whether you have a spider, and what key structures they have (two body parts, fangs, pedipalps, spinnerets and eight legs attached to the cephalothorax) could be addressed. In Year 2 the emphasis is on how livings things grow: how do spiders grow (exoskeletons and moult) and reproduce (egg sacs). Thus, working with the topic of spiders allows the SU sub-strand of biological sciences to be covered. Further, this case study also highlights how different focuses for different year levels could be covered if working with a composite class.

In the SIS strand children learnt about spiders by actively developing their inquiry skills of observation, drawing, counting, labelling, asking questions and communicating. Science investigations emerging from the children's questions about spiders were a key aspect of the science inquiry process, with this process replicating how scientists work. The SHE strand was covered as the children were acting as scientists themselves, asking questions and describing changes, and seeing how science is used in everyday lives and when caring for living things. It was also evident when exploring Indigenous stories about spiders (for example, 'Wankaku Ngura: A Pitjantjatjara Story'), and contributing information to a scientific database.

Overall, this case study shows how the three strands of the Australian Curriculum: Science can be woven together in teaching a unit of work. It also highlights the value of connecting with citizen science projects to assist in programming and delivering engaging units of work. The citizen science work on spiders extended learning beyond science. Students engaged in art, communication, relationship-building and connectivity to their natural world, which illustrates the interdisciplinary nature of learning when topics are connected to students' lives. This is recognised in the Australian Curriculum through the general capabilities.

1. When children 'act as scientists', many strands and sub-strands of the Australian Curriculum: Science can be covered. What does it mean to allow children to 'act as scientists'?

2. What strategies were used in Case study 3.1 to weave SU, SHE and SIS into the science program? How can you incorporate these into your practice?

REFLECTION

General capabilities

General capability – knowledge, skills, behaviours and dispositions that assist children to live and work successfully in the 21st century.

General capabilities are described as knowledge, skills, behaviours and dispositions that assist students to live and work successfully in the 21st century (ACARA, 2014b). The seven general capabilities are literacy, numeracy, information and communication technology (ICT) competence, critical and creative thinking, ethical understanding, personal and social competence, and intercultural understanding. The inclusion of the capabilities of intercultural understanding and ethical understanding innovatively set the Australian general capabilities apart from most other generated lists of required skills for 21st-century citizens. It is important to be aware that the general capabilities are inter-related and inter-connected, and several may be evident within the same activity. Further, they complement the key learning outcomes of the Early Years Learning Framework. The ACARA website has detailed descriptions of each general capability. Table 3.5 presents a summary of the general capabilities, along with a definition of each and examples of how the capabilities can be embedded in the early year's science curriculum.

BUILDING MUD BRICKS

This case study shows how the general capabilities are evident in the science learning area. A Year 2 class in a small rural school setting took many opportunities to teach and learn science (and other learning areas) in the outdoor classroom. In this particular school there was an area of natural space where children often chose to play during lunch breaks, and making cubby houses with natural materials was a popular activity.

On one occasion, during a science teaching unit on different materials and their composition, the children were asked to wear old clothes to school or overalls purchased from the local hardware store. Outside they were asked to explore the best consistency for making mud bricks. They had a range of materials to select from, including sticks, pebbles, soil, leaves and water. The children squeezed, piled, squelched and delighted as they learnt and played with the natural materials. Using their hands as moulds they set about making small structures of soil and sticks in the dirt space on the edge of the asphalt playground. The structures were left there and gradually disintegrated with play and weather.

This learning experience connects directly with chemical sciences for Year 2: different materials can be combined, including by mixing, for a particular purpose. Through trial and error the children changed the ratio of water used compared to other materials until the best combination for making mud bricks was obtained. These findings were compared and shared between different groups as a conclusion to the experience. The Australian Curriculum: Science shows how an engaging activity is strengthened as a science investigation by including questions that invoke the use of SIS, SHE and critical and creative thinking. Such questions included: 'How did the bricks change as they dried in the sun?', 'What mix of materials do you think was best?', 'Why?'

On another occasion, when working in groups exploring the properties of clay, the children came up with the idea of allocating tasks and setting themselves up along a conveyor line to build small clay houses. Each child was organised to contribute a small action to complete the task. One child was cutting the clay 'bricks' to a standard size $2 \times 3 \times 3$ cm rectangular prism. The next child smoothed the brick, the following child added water and the next joined the prisms together. This resulted in a series of small clay structures being completed. The sense of teamwork and cooperation was evidenced by a spontaneous rendition of the song 'I've Been Working on the Railroad'.

TABLE 3.5 SUMMARY OF THE GENERAL CAPABILITIES AND THEIR APPLICATION TO SCIENCE IN THE EARLY YEARS

General capability	Definition	Examples
Numeracy	Children become numerate as they use and choose mathematics confidently across other learning areas at school and in their lives more broadly.	Collect and describe data about the distance cars roll on different surfaces – e.g. create column graphs using cut streamers to compare distance rolled. Use a school map to show where spiders were found in different locations. Look for patterns, such as the symmetry on leaves. Estimate and measure the distance of a snail trail.
Literacy	Literacy involves children in listening to, reading, viewing, speaking, writing and creating oral, print, visual and digital texts, and using and modifying language for different purposes in a range of contexts.	Read fiction and non-fiction books about day and night to infer how environmental changes affect living things. Sketch and annotate a diagram of the external parts of a plant or animal. Create a sequential explanation of changes over time (e.g. using annotated photographs of a tree in different seasons). Compare a cartoon drawing to a real animal, discussing why and how it is different, and inferring why the artist has made those modifications.
ICT	ICT capability is based on the assumption that technologies are digital tools that enable children to solve problems and carry out tasks.	Use a digital camera to take photographs of a flower over time. Use slowmation to show how a toy works. Use an iPad app to identify invertebrates found in the schoolyard. Share ideas and data with students and parents on a class blog.
Critical and creative thinking	Critical and creative thinking involves children thinking broadly and deeply using skills, behaviours and dispositions such as reason, logic, resourcefulness, imagination and innovation.	Pose questions or make suggestions about how to look after the local environment. Explain the similarities and differences between spiders and Spiderman. Make decisions about what to plant in the garden for each season using information about the plant's needs for rain, sunshine, etc. Generate questions about where and when to obtain the longest shadows.

General capability	Definition	Examples
Personal and social competence	Personal and social competence involves children recognising and regulating emotions, developing empathy for others and understanding relationships, establishing and building positive relationships, making responsible decisions and working effectively in teams.	Work in a small group to role play, demonstrating skills in independent decision-making and cooperation. Organise their team with specific roles to complete tasks effectively – e.g. contributing to the care of a class pet, or taking different team roles in a science experiment. Contribute to the improvement of a small section of the schoolyard. Build community connections between children's school and home lives as they relate to both teachers and parents in their learning.
Ethical understanding	Ethical understanding involves children building a strong personal and socially oriented ethical outlook that helps them to manage context, conflict and uncertainty.	Discuss the suitability of keeping an animal as a class pet, and the responsibility for meeting its needs. Give reasons for differences in points of view about their attitudes to and actions regarding different things, e.g. animals, foods, activities, issues or environments. Think about how the decisions they make positively or negatively impact the environment. Consider fairness when sharing equipment or allocating group roles.
Intercultural understanding	Intercultural understanding involves children in learning about and engaging with diverse cultures in ways that recognise commonalities and differences, create connections with others and cultivate mutual respect.	Discuss why different materials are chosen (e.g. for housing, clothes) in different places in the world. Collect information about the temperature and weather conditions in other places. Listen to stories from other cultures about scientific phenomena, e.g. Indigenous stories of the night sky, and consider the underlying message. Explore different cultural ways of cooking.

Source: ACARA, 2014b.

As this case study shows, the children were addressing various general capabilities. They used their literacy capability when they were using familiar vocabulary to describe what it felt like when they were making mud bricks. The learning experience became an orally rich task using a context related to everyday experiences and children's interests. Critical and creative thinking was evident when the children were posing questions about the best ratio of each material to make mud bricks as well as the idea of setting up the construction as a team. The numeracy capability was evident when they were estimating and comparing the shape and size of each of the clay 'bricks' so that the similar shapes stacked together for their structures. Finally, personal and social capability was demonstrated when the children organised themselves into a cooperative team to make the bricks.

The general capabilities continuum defines different elements of each of the seven capabilities of the Australian curriculum and shows how these different elements develop in complexity using two-year banded year levels. This continuum can be particularly helpful for teachers to use as a guide when designing activities, when differentiating a task for different learner needs or when extending learner thinking.

Table 3.6 gives examples of how the continuum might be used as a differentiation tool. Additionally, the illustrations in the 'student diversity' section of the Australian Curriculum website give video examples using the continuum to differentiate for learner diversity.

TABLE 3.6 THE GENERAL CAPABILITIES CONTINUUM AS A DIFFERENTIATION TOOL

Action	General capabilities continuum	Action for differentiation/ extending thinking	General capabilities continuum
Children posed questions about spiders. These were written on a large chart. Children asked whether scats were kangaroo or emu droppings, or whether gumnuts on the eucalyptus tree were the same as those in their backyard.	Critical and creative thinking, Sub-element 'Pose questions', Level 1 students: *pose factual and exploratory questions based on personal interests and experiences.*	Teacher asks 'Why do you ask that? or 'What are you thinking when you ask that?' to support children to analyse their thinking and give reasons for asking the questions they pose.	Critical and creative thinking, Sub-element 'Pose questions', Level 2 students: *pose questions to identify and clarify issues and compare information in their world.*
Children allocated themselves tasks and set up a conveyor line … each child contributing a small action to complete the task.	Personal and social capability Sub-element 'Make decisions' Level 2 students: *practice individual and group decision making in situations such as class meetings and when working in pairs and small groups.*	After the lesson, the teacher shows a video to the class of the group working on their conveyor line, and has the class brainstorm the cooperative behaviours they can see.	Personal and social capability Sub-element 'Work collaboratively' Level 2 students: *identify cooperative behaviours in a range of group activities.*

Consider Case study 3.2 and the following questions:
1. How does the use of questioning encourage children's critical and creative thinking?
2. How could ICT be included in the mud brick making experiences? How could this use of ICT link back to literacy and numeracy?
3. Think of ways that ethical understanding and intercultural understanding could be addressed in subsequent mud brick experiences.

Cross-curriculum priorities

The three cross-curriculum priorities are Aboriginal and Torres Strait Islander histories and cultures, Asia and Australia's engagement with Asia, and sustainability. The purpose of the cross-curriculum priorities is to ensure that Australian children are able to engage effectively in a global world and to contribute to Australian society through social, intellectual and creative pursuits. The priorities provide contexts for children to participate in science. Cross-curriculum priorities are to be embedded in science when appropriate or when relevant links can be made. All three science strands can be enhanced through these contexts at appropriate times.

Aboriginal and Torres Strait Islander histories and cultures

By embedding Aboriginal and Torres Strait Islander histories and cultures where appropriate in the science learning area, young children have the opportunity to understand that Australian scientific knowledge has been developing over tens of thousands of years, originally through the knowledge of the Aboriginal and Torres Strait Islander peoples and more recently enriched and developed through the knowledge of European and Asian peoples. This cross-curriculum priority links well with the general capability of intercultural understanding. Table 3.7 provides examples of how this cross-curriculum priority can be included in the early childhood classroom.

Asia and Australia's engagement with Asia

Asian countries are Australia's closest neighbours. Early years children should start to develop an awareness of how Asian cultures have contributed to both contemporary and historical knowledge of the way the world works scientifically. Significant contributions in science have been made by people from Asia in areas such as medicine and natural disaster management. Table 3.7 provides examples of how this cross-curriculum priority can be included in the early childhood classroom.

Sustainability

Providing opportunities for children to explore and connect to the natural world around them will offer insights into the importance of caring for environments. Young children should be developing scientific knowledge and understanding about how the natural world works and the effect of human impact on the environment. Through understanding

TABLE 3.7 SUMMARY OF THE CROSS-CURRICULUM PRIORITIES AND THEIR APPLICATION TO SCIENCE IN THE EARLY YEARS

Cross-curriculum priority	Example
Aboriginal and Torres Strait Islander histories and cultures	How do our ideas about the weather compare with what we notice? E.g. have you seen snow in winter? Explain whether you think there would be many Aboriginal stories about snow? (Foundation – seasonal changes affecting everyday life, Year 1 – observable changes occur in the sky and landscape.)
	Investigate how the local Aboriginal or Torres Strait Islander communities used the land in different seasons (e.g. the Kaurna people lived in the Adelaide Hills in winter and came down to the plains and beaches in summer). (Year 1 – living things live in different places where their needs are met.)
	Investigate how particular materials were changed or used – e.g. creating paints and paintings from natural materials. (Foundation – observing properties of materials, Year 1 – changing everyday materials, Year 2 – using Earth's resources.)
	Visit a local Indigenous garden to explore plants and their uses (food, medicinal, clothing).
	Include traditional Aboriginal musical instruments when investigating how different sounds are made.
	Describe Aboriginal seasons and how they are similar and different to Western seasons.
Asia and Australia's engagement with Asia	Plant and care for a range of Asian and Australian vegetables in the school garden.
	Include traditional Asian musical instruments when investigating how different sounds are made.
	Include traditional Asian toys and tools when investigating how different objects move (Foundation and Year 2).
	Explore the different shapes and structures of houses in Asia and Australia, and why they are different.
Sustainability	Explore materials that can be re-used, reduced and recycled and set up systems in classrooms to reduce daily waste.
	Connect to the natural world through spending time in wild places.
	Use senses to experience the change of weather: see, hear, feel, taste and smell the summer rain.
	Explore the properties of natural materials, such as seeds, leaves, flowers, rocks and soils to create works of art.

sustainability, children can make informed decisions about their behaviour to ensure they contribute to socially and ecologically sustainable future. Table 3.7 provides examples of how this cross-curriculum priority can be included in the early childhood classroom. Chapter 10 provides detailed information on environmental education in the early years.

Place-based learning in science

Authentic education, as Sterling (2001) argues, has always been rooted in place and tradition. Place-based learning takes hands-on experiential learning, extends it beyond the classroom curriculum, and encourages students to be co-managers of their learning (Smith, 2002; Woodhouse & Knapp, 2000). The primary value of place-based education is the way that it serves to strengthen children's connections to others and to the regions in which they live and to the natural world (Clarke, 2013; Louv, 2008; Sobel, 2008). It serves individuals and communities, helping individuals to experience what they value and hold for others, and allowing communities to benefit from the commitment and contributions of their members (Woodhouse & Knapp, 2000). The following case study demonstrates how dispositions towards sustainability can be developed in young children by creating this emotional connection. 'We cannot protect something we do not love, we cannot love what we do not know, and we cannot know what we do not see. And touch. And hear' (Louv, 2011).

TRIP TO THE BUSH

An annual event in the Foundation year class calendar was a day trip to the bush. With much preparation the day would finally arrive, and nearly all of the parents would come with their children to spend the day in a local national park. They would start with a two-hour hike through the natural bushland, following tracks. It was often the first time that children had walked that far in the bush. It was hard work to walk the distance, but the air was full of excitement and enthusiasm. Observations and questions about new discoveries found on the track were commonplace. Comments were heard about whether the scats were kangaroo or emu droppings, whether it was going to rain during the day or whether the gumnuts on the eucalyptus tree were the same as those in their backyard.

After the hike the children would break up into small group activities, run by the educator, her husband, the assistant principal and a school services officer with parental help. Finding a space on their own and sitting down in silence (very challenging for some) helped the children to notice the sounds around them and the behaviour of small birds and insects that they might have ordinarily missed. Another session was run inside a tent (a new experience for some children). This session was focused on the organisation of what children would need to carry in a backpack on an overnight hike. The children would make suggestions and the items were neatly arranged in the backpack. To feel the weight and the experience of overnight hikers, each child would then have an opportunity to walk around with the backpack on their back. Other activities included observational drawing – sketching a tree using charcoal. Children sat a distance from their tree with a clipboard trying to sketch the branches, trunk and leaves. Questions from adults, such as 'How high up do the leaves begin?' and 'How many major branches does it have?', would help them look more closely. Yoga in the bush involved the children on mats following instructions about breathing and exhaling fresh air and simple body movements. Another activity involved an alphabet chart where children would find words that started with each letter. Yet another invited children to select a random piece of commercial paint chart chip from a magic bag to locate a natural object of the same colour. An art activity involved collecting a range of natural objects, such as gum nuts, stones or feathers, and making a collage to hang in nature's art gallery, with a tour of this being the final activity of the day. While developing scientific observation skills was part of the learning focus, the real key to the day was allowing the children to experience learning outside the classroom, working with their parents in a natural place and developing an understanding of the world around them. Intergenerational experiences were a critical component of this place-based education.

FIGURE 3.2 Children's observational drawing using charcoal

Source: © Janette Leibhardt.

This case study demonstrates how the cross-curriculum priority of sustainability could be developed for early years classes. By spending time in a natural space and going on 'an adventure' children are able to experience the natural world first hand and develop an affinity with the environment (Sobel, 2008; Wilson, 2008). They kept to the track, learnt more about the plants and the animals and ensured that the place was left better then when they arrived; this included taking their own and other people's litter back to school. Through such activities young children start to show care and respect for the environment. Such time in the bush could also lend itself to developing Indigenous perspectives, by inviting local elders to be part of the experience to share their Dreaming stories and explain how plants can be used as both a food source and for medicines.

1. Think about the place of the outdoor environment in science teaching and learning. How can you include more science outdoor experiences in your practice?
2. There is much preparation required to have annual day events for parents and children as described in Case study 3.3. What are the advantages to educators, parents and children of such events?
3. What other science activities could be included in such a day in the bush?

REFLECTION

Conclusion

This chapter focused on providing an overview of the Australian Curriculum: Science and it showed the importance of weaving the three strands of Science Understanding, Science Inquiry Skills and Science as Human Endeavour into learning experiences. Three case studies were used to demonstrate how experienced teachers, with a passion for science, incorporated experiential learning into their classroom. They also showed how and where the general capabilities and cross-curriculum priorities were evident.

Acknowledgement

I would like to acknowledge the contribution Marianne Nicholas and Janette Leibhardt made to this chapter. Both generously shared their wisdom, experience and knowledge of teaching in early years science.

3 References

Australian Curriculum, Assessment and Reporting Authority (ACARA). (2014a). Australian Curriculum, 'Science – Content Structure', www.australiancurriculum.edu.au/science/content-structure, accessed 1 October 2014.

—— (2014b). Australian Curriculum, 'Science – General Capabilities', www.australiancurriculum .edu.au/science/content-structure, accessed 1 October 2014.

—— (2014c). Australian Curriculum, 'Science – Rationale', www.australiancurriculum.edu.au/ science/rationale, accessed 1 October 2014.

—— (2014d). Australian Curriculum, 'Science – Science across Foundation to Year 12', www .australiancurriculum.edu.au/science/science-across-foundation-to-year-12, accessed 1 October 2014.

Australian Government. (2014). *Review of the National Curriculum: Final Report*, Canberra: Department of Education, docs.education.gov.au/system/files/doc/other/review_of_the_ national_curriculum_final_report.pdf, accessed 1 October 2014.

Bonney, R., Cooper, C. B., Dickinson, J., Kelling, S., Phillips, T., Rosenberg, K. & Shirk, J. (2009). Citizen science: A developing tool for expanding science knowledge and scientific literacy, *BioScience*, 59(11), 977–84.

Clarke, P. (2013). *Education for Sustainability: Becoming Naturally Smart*, Abingdon, UK: Routledge.

Department of Education, Employment and Workplace Relations (DEEWR). (2009). *Belonging, Being and Becoming: The Early Years Learning Framework for Australia*, Canberra: Commonwealth of Australia.

Louv, R. (2008). *Last Child in the Woods: Saving Our Children from Nature-Deficit Disorder*, Chapel Hill, NC: Algonquin Books.

—— (2011). *The Nature Principle Human Restoration and the End of Nature-Deficit Disorder*, Chapel Hill, NC: Algonquin Books.

Ministerial Council on Education, Employment, Training and Youth Affairs (MCEETYA). (2008). *Melbourne Declaration on Educational Goals for Young Australians*. Canberra: MCEETYA.

National Curriculum Board. (2009). *Shape of the Australian Curriculum: Science*, Canberra: Commonwealth of Australia.

Paige, K., Lawes, H., Matjec, P., Stewart, V., Taylor, C., Lloyd, D., Roetman, P., Zeegers Y. & Daniels, C. (2010). 'It feels like real science': How 'Operation Magpie' enriched my classroom, *Teaching Science*, 56(4), 18–41.

Paige, K., Lloyd, D., Zeegers, Y., Roetman, P., Daniels, C., Hoekman, B., Linnell, L., George, L. & Szilassy, D. (2012). Connecting teachers and students to the natural world through Operation Spider: An aspirations citizen science project, *Teaching Science*, 58(1), 13–21.

Smith, G. (2002). Place-based education, *Phi Delta Kappan*, 83(8), 584–95.

Sobel, D. (2008). *Childhood and Nature: Design Principles for Educators*, Portland, Maine: Stenhouse Publishers.

Sterling, S. (2001). *Sustainable Education: Re-visioning Learning and Change*, Totnes, UK: Green Books for the Schumacher Society.

Wilson, R. (2008). *Nature and Young Children: Encouraging Creative Play and Learning in Natural Environments*, Abingdon, UK: Routledge.

Woodhouse, J. & Knapp, C. (2000). *Place-Based Curriculum and Instruction*, ERIC Document Reproduction Service No. EDO-RC–00–6.

Learning theories related to early childhood science education

Coral Campbell

Children attempt to make sense of, and to understand, the various situations and phenomena with which they interact. This is science in its purest and simplest sense – allowing children to gain an understanding of the world around them. Children's understanding is based on the range of experiences and interactions they have and the cognitive development of 'concepts' that help to explain the phenomena, to them at least.

There are many theories about how children (and, indeed, adults) learn science and the factors that affect learning in young children. This chapter describes and discusses accepted theories of children's development and the range of influences upon science learning.

OBJECTIVES

At the end of this chapter you will be able to:

- recognise the factors underpinning children's cognitive development

- describe a range of learning theories that relate specifically to how children develop science understandings

- describe the importance of affective factors and motivation in children's learning

- distinguish between everyday concepts and science concepts in children's learning of science

- recognise the importance of alternative conceptions in restricting children's learning in science.

Children's cognitive development

The term **cognitive development** is used to describe a child's development of cognition or conceptual knowledge and understanding. When considering cognitive development, Johnston and Nahmad-Williams (2009) indicate 10 aspects of importance:

Cognitive development – the development of conceptual understanding.

- memory
- abstraction – the ability to form general concepts
- logic – being able to reason
- problem-solving
- intelligence – a measure of thinking ability
- reasoning – providing evidence for a belief
- thinking – using the mind
- knowledge – belief about something that is known
- understanding – to comprehend something
- metacognition – to understand one's own thought processes.

When we discuss cognitive development we are really talking about the development of one or more of the above aspects. Sometimes the development can occur singly, but often these aspects are inter-related. Some aspects occur before others and some take a longer period to develop.

Johnston (2014) described these aspects of cognitive development within the broader frame of children's development, indicating how young children's capabilities are defined across time. For example, very young children (birth–2 years) acquire language, start to order things in their world and in their own thinking, develop sensory awareness, show interest in small objects and develop social behavior. These capabilities not only allow greater involvement in science exploration, but can enhance it. Across the next few years of development (3–4 years old), children's cognition develops further and they are able to make links between ideas, and to reason. Practical experiences are crucial to developing science cognition further to enable children to move away from everyday science (described later in this chapter), or intuitive thinking. As children develop further (5–8 years old), they start to develop abstract

FIGURE 4.1   Investigating the principles of 'balance'

ideas. They can begin to combine ideas mentally, rather than needing to use concrete materials. Their mental schemas become more complex as they incorporate multiple experiences into cognitive mental models.

In a National Forum on Early Childhood Science, Mathematics and Technology Education, held in the United States in 1998, children's cognitive and conceptual developments were discussed in depth. Seminal studies (Gelman, 1998; Lind, 1998) were presented about the influence of how we think of young children as science learners. Gelman (1998) reported that children used concepts as tools for organising their experience. Their early concepts were not necessarily concrete or perceptually based, and pre-school children were capable of reasoning about non-obvious and abstract concepts. Gelman also observed that children's concepts reflected emerging theories about the world and were not uniform across content areas or across individuals or tasks. In her concluding statement to the forum, Gelman (1998) stated that since children's cognition was more sophisticated than previously thought, it was important early childhood educators engaged with children's cognitive development and, in particular, with the conceptual development and emerging theories about young children. Further research by Gelman (2009) highlights the social nature of cognitive development, particularly in very young children.

At the same forum, Lind (1998) discussed how concepts used in science developed from early infancy, as babies explored the world with their senses. It is a common sight to see young babies discover the joy of dropping something from a height, performing the same task over and over again as they develop their naïve concept of gravity. Babies and toddlers develop concepts of space and the relationship of their body to the space around them (spacial sense). They learn about weight as they pick up objects and about shape, texture and materials as they touch new surfaces. They quickly learn about time sequences and how time is arranged in their lives.

As children grow, they learn to sort and categorise objects according to their own interests. They explore volume, ratio and weight as they play in the sandpit or with water. During this exploration, children are developing their own understandings and concepts based on these experiences.

FIGURE 4.2   Sinking the balloon

Theories of learning

Catherwood (1999) observed that the development of children's abilities incorporates factors of children's knowledge, interest and learning context. She stated, 'It is generally the case that no one theory or model predominates and Piagetian perspectives are now taken to be just one mirror on the multi-faceted world of children's cognition' (p. 24). However, we need to acknowledge that the early theorists and their theories have influenced current practice in early childhood. Apart from Piaget's theory of cognitive development (Piaget, 1950) which drew attention to understandings of how children move from everyday (intuitive) ideas to more scientifically correct ones, Montessori's study of children with special needs (Montessori, 1994) highlighted that all children explored the world around them as young scientists, repeatedly testing their ideas to develop understandings.

There are many theories of learning, and all could be considered when viewing the young children as learners. Many theories consider the immediate environment and its influence on the learner. For example, ecological systems theory considers how the person accommodates the setting in which she or he lives and how the relationship with these settings impacts upon learning (Bronfenbrenner, 1989). The theory of social dynamics (Durlauf & Young, 2001) refers to how the group behaves as a result of the interaction of individuals within the group and the group's behaviours. The basis for social dynamics theory is that individuals are influenced by and influence other's behavior. Both theories involve the learner and his or her interaction with the social environment.

Another theory, situated cognition, defines learning as the knowledge and skills obtained in contexts that reflect the ways in which they will be used in real life. Supporting a situated cognition theory, Lave and Wenger (1991) described learning as an integral part of generative social practice in the lived-in world. They suggest that learning is in part creative, social and within real contexts.

When considering early childhood, the theory of situated cognition makes sense as children's learning can be considered creative or co-creative, it often takes place in social situations or through interactions with others, and it often mimics the real world. In order to encourage or enhance learning, practitioners need to create an environment that approximates as closely as possible the context in which children's new ideas and behaviours will be applied. Understanding is promoted with specific relationship to the situations in which the learning occurs. In particular, in science education, children will contextualise their understanding, believing one thing to be true in one situation, and another to be true in a different situation. This generation of two concepts rather than one is a common feature of children's learning in science.

Knowledge generated in early childhood settings (pre-school or early school) is fundamentally a response to, and a product of, that situation. Put simply, all learning is context-bound and cannot be separated from the social/cultural framework within which it was generated. For educators, the implication is that links must be made between the learning situations of the experiences of children and within the broader community – between pre-school, school and home or the wider world. This is particularly relevant in science education.

> Social cognition is at the heart of children's ability to get along with other people and to see things from their point of view. The basis of this crucial ability lies in the development of theory of mind. (Astington & Edward, 2010, p. 1)

The theory of mind (Astington & Edward, 2010) suggests that a child is able to understand that the people he or she mixes with have their own beliefs and desires, and their own intentions. This tends to happen at around 3 years of age, and at this point the child is able to recognise that the person she or he is playing with has their own ways of doing things. The child is more likely to be able to sustain a 'relationship' when interacting with others. Understanding theory of mind provides the educator with an understanding of children's abilities to play with others, to work collaboratively, to be empathetic and to co-learn.

In relation to enhancing children's learning, an educator with strong 'theory of mind' capabilities would be able to understand where the child's learning is at, whether she or he is confused or fully engaged. This provides the educator with valuable information about whether strategies for children's learning are working or not.

Constructivism

An individual's construction of understanding or meaning is based on the person's own experiences and attempts to make sense of those experiences. This is termed the constructivist theory – the construction of meaning from an experience or a set of circumstances. Jean Piaget (1950) theorised that individuals can and do form their own understandings based on their experiences, and that they are able to develop these understandings when given more experiences that link with prior experiences. He termed these mental structures 'schemas': learners formed mental representations and operations (combinations of schemas) since these determined their understandings of experiences and phenomena. Piaget specified particular stages of cognitive development that continue to be of interest in education, although further research has added to and re-defined his original theories (McInerney & McInerney, 1998).

There have, in fact, been interpretations of personal constructivism that promote a pure form of 'discovery learning', in which the educator never tells children anything, but simply organises enabling activities and deflects questions as the responsibility of the learner. Recent research (Kirschner, 2006; Klahr, 2004) has indicated that children do not necessarily learn much by this approach. Mayer (2004) reported that guided discovery was much more effective than a pure discovery process in helping children to learn. In fact, Mayer (2004) stated that 'learning involves cognitive activity rather than behavioural activity, instructional guidance rather than pure discovery, and curricular focus rather than unstructured exploration' (p. 1). Without adequate support, children's understandings may be naïve at best and incorrect at worst.

The main principles of the constructivist theory (adapted from Campbell & Tytler, 2007) state that:

- learning involves the active construction of meaning
- meanings are constructed by learners from what they see or hear and are influenced by prior knowledge (this prior knowledge can assist or hinder new learning)

- children, from when they are born, seek to construct meaning about their world, and this process continues throughout their lives
- learners have the final responsibility for their own learning (thus, an educator can never learn for a child, and teaching is never more than the promotion of opportunities and support for learning)
- learners often develop their own understandings that are alternative to a scientific understanding and are difficult to change.

Domain-specific theories

Most **learning theories** are what could be termed domain-general, and imply that cognitively, children have broad mental structures which are developed over time, with exposure to a range of experiences. There is an assumption that abstract thought is not developed in young children and that some mathematics and science experiences are not appropriate because of the need for abstract thought. However, most early childhood educators will know, through their own experience, that this is a broad generalisation, and that many young children are capable of abstraction of ideas. Gelman and Brenneman (2004) discuss how the demonstration of non-verbal concepts in very young children and abstract conceptual abilities in pre-schoolers have led to the idea of domain-specific rational–constructivist theories. Domain-specific theorists promote the idea that there are innate, domain-specific mental structures which can underpin and aid learning in some knowledge areas. They postulate that domain-relevant inputs can assist in the acquisition of domain-specific knowledge and understanding. Domain-specific concepts can link to other concepts, for example – language (see also Chapter 6 on 'Approaches to enhance science learning'), which allows children to generalise from what is known to what is not known. For example, if a child knows some of the characteristics of animals, and is told that a worm is an animal, they generalise that a worm can eat, breathe and move.

> **Learning theories** – theories which attempt to explain how people/children learn.

Gelman and Brenneman (2004, p. 152) state, 'A domain-specific, constructivist description of mental structure (and learning) has implications for the development of educational experiences about scientific material. The connectedness of concepts in the head and in the world implies that learning experiences should be conceptually linked as well.' This has implications for approaches to science learning in early childhood and will be discussed further in Chapter 6.

Shifting towards a sociocultural perspective

In more recent times, there has been much greater interest in exploring learning as a social or cultural phenomenon, with a shift in focus from individual understanding to the ways in which environments support effective learning. A social constructivist position focuses attention on the social processes operating in the environment around a learner, by which an 'expert' other (adult or peer) promotes a community in which they all 'co-construct' knowledge. Psychologist Lev Vygotsky (1962) expanded Piaget's theories to include the social settings around and through which learning occurred. Vygotsky defined this as 'social constructivism' (and Piaget's theory as 'personal constructivism').

In social constructivism, the social interactions, particularly with an expert other, can aid and enhance children's learning. Vygotsky also postulated that language development was crucial for children's cognitive development as children were able to interact at the level of understanding with others. Social constructivism suggests greater involvement of an active educator. For Vygotsky, the culture and social interactions give the child the cognitive tools needed for development. The type and quality of social interactions affect the pattern and rate of development. Adults, such as parents and educators, are conduits for the tools of social interaction, including language, cultural history and social context. In today's society, electronic and digital technology providing information access are also included as tools of social interaction.

Zone of proximal development – the region between what a child is able to achieve alone and what he or she can achieve when interacting with more learned others, adults or other children.

Vygosky (1962) also described what he termed the **zone of proximal development**. This zone is considered the region between what a child is able to achieve alone and what he or she can achieve when interacting with adults who scaffold the learning. Children are able to achieve so much more with the help of an adult. Within a sociocultural environment, learning science becomes a shared experience (Driver et al., 1994) and the understandings developed are often shared among the children. The educator, along with other adults, is responsible for representing scientific culture and scientific ways of viewing and dealing with the world. In some ways, then, sociocultural constructivism places the educator as pivotal to children's learning, as compared to personal constructivism, which makes the individual responsible for his or her own learning.

Scott (1998) argued that the key to understanding effective science teaching and learning was discourse: the pattern of interactive talk during science experiences. In some cases the adult is the 'expert', at other times the child is given reign to express his or her views, with the adult or another child asking specific questions and seeking understanding from the child. The ability to shift between these different discourse modes is an important aspect of effective teaching.

In addition to the social constructivist perspectives there has been a growing interest in the fundamental role of language and culture in the construction of knowledge, and even in the way we think. These theoretical perspectives have become more broadly known as 'sociocultural', in which knowledge is a property of participation within a community. The science teaching and learning strategy that arises from this theoretical perspective is one that focuses on the language that develops in exploratory activities and talk, and how the educator's strategies might support high quality conceptual discussion in groups, or in the whole class. Effective teaching involves introducing activities and conversations that challenge perspectives and model the practices of science in seeking to interpret evidence, and to promote a rich way of looking at the world. This environment involves 'give and take' between the adult's and the children's perspectives. The educator is not necessarily seeking to gain strong conceptual understanding, but to move children's understanding a little closer to a scientifically correct understanding. Vygotsky (1987, p. 168) asserts that 'the development of scientific concepts begins with the verbal definition'. For educators, using the social environment and social interaction, and focusing on the relationships between word meanings in science, brings the science ideas to conscious awareness. Vygotsky (1987) believed that this moved a child into higher level thinking.

Affective factors

While much of the research in science education over the past 20 years has been focused on the cognitive aspects of science learning, educators are aware that if children are not happy and stable in their settings, they will not learn. Alsop and Watts (2003) stated that 'irrespective of how well pedagogical factors are designed' (p. 1046) children need to be comfortable for effective learning to occur. The general idea is that the cognitive process is not only supported but enhanced through positive **affective factors**. These factors are recognised as relating to student interest, motivation, attitudes, beliefs, self-confidence and self-efficacy. The role of the social context is extremely important in establishing these factors through relationships with educators, peers and other important connections. Children's identity, self-esteem and confidence are all key aspects of their development of what Day and Leitch (2001) called a 'personal and professional identity'. Children will fail to learn if they are bored, scared or disinterested in the topic, whereas enthusiasm, coupled with a belief in personal ability, can be a strong motivation for learning. Pintrich, Marx and Boyle (1993) reported that children's beliefs in their own abilities (self-efficacy) and the value they attributed to their learning tasks became significant predictors of understanding.

> **Affective factors** – interest, motivation, attitudes, beliefs, self-confidence and self-efficacy which influence learning; often called 'dispositions' for learning.

Motivation

> Young children are motivated to explore the world around them, and early science experiences can capitalize on this inclination. (French, 2004)

There is a general acceptance that for children to learn and change their personal constructs, there are other factors that come into play. Pintrich, Marx and Boyle (1993) indicated that 'motivation beliefs as well as ... contextual factors' (p. 167) contributed to the complexity of children's learning. The socially cognitive perspective on motivation discussed by Pintrich, Marx and Boyle (1993) suggested that children's motivational beliefs were highly context-specific. They commented that students who displayed prior conceptual understandings may not activate this knowledge when challenged in different situations (Pintrich, et al., 1993). Vosnaidou and colleagues (2001) suggested that learning occurred in a social and cultural context, and that in order for children to change their existing concepts, they must be motivated through the provision of an appropriate 'social and cultural environment' (p. 393), usually outside the narrow context of one setting.

Reasons that a child might have for choosing a task include the child's values, interests, goal orientation and how he or she rates the importance of the activity. In addition, the child needs to believe that he or she is capable of performing it, has some control over it and that the task is achievable. These factors will vary depending on the context, the chosen task and the effectiveness of the teaching. The level of engagement and willingness to persist in a given activity can be attributed to the child's motivation. Children make choices about whether to become cognitively engaged with the task at hand or not. If they become engaged and persist, then learning is likely to occur. If they do not become sufficiently involved in the learning task, then the best result is likely to be what is termed 'surface learning'. Pintrich and Schrauben (1992) provided empirical evidence to support the view that motivational beliefs can influence the process of conceptual change.

The provision of quality science learning experiences in early childhood helps children understand the world, develop science skills and, importantly, develop positive attitudes towards science learning. This provides a strong foundation for later learning in science and for development of scientific concepts (Eshach & Fried, 2005).

Play theory

Play experiences are part of every child's growth and development. Increasingly, play is being recognised as a powerful pedagogical tool through which to guide and enhance science learning (Fleer & Ridgeway, 2007). Play-based learning occurs when young children 'make meaning' through their exploration in a range of social situations. Interaction with peers, early childhood educators and significant others can stimulate children's curiosity to learn more and to ask questions. The role of the early childhood educator is to provide a physical environment that is rich in natural resources and, through guided participation, to help a child move past his or her own limitations of knowledge to develop deeper understandings. Vygotsky suggested that play was important for learning as it almost always created a zone of proximal development (Arthur et al., 2005). Play provides opportunities for problem-solving, abstract thinking, higher-order thinking, creativity, independent learning, research, exploration of complex issues and complex language, literacy and numeracy skills (Dockett & Fleer, 2002) – many of which are needed in learning science. When exploring their environment and undertaking their own science investigations, children engage in many types of play, including drama, symbolic play, exploratory play and constructive play (Chalufour & Worth, 2005). (See Chapter 7 for more information on play pedagogy in the early years.) As stated by Tucker (2005), 'Play is undoubtedly enjoyable for young children owing to the freedom it facilitates, the sense of ownership it affords and the self-esteem it promotes. Through play children can repeat, rehearse and refine skills, displaying what they do know and practising what they are beginning to understand' (p. 5). The early childhood educator must 'acknowledge the importance of play as a platform for learning and practising the basic process skills of science' (Howitt, Morris & Colville, 2007, p. 234).

MAKING BUTTER FROM CREAM

An early childhood educator wished to introduce more science into the children's schedule so she decided to have them make butter from cream. Sitting all the children in a circle, she discussed with them what she had in her hands and proceeded to drop some marbles into the cream. She asked the children to predict what might happen if they were to shake the bottle for a while. Several answers were provided: the lid would come off, the marbles would have cream on them, but some of the children just shook their heads, acknowledging that they had no idea. As the jar was passed around, the teacher asked occasionally whether anyone noticed a difference in the jar, and took the lid off to show them what was happening. The task took 10–15 minutes, by which time the children were edgy and fidgeting. The teacher was obviously flustered by the children's lack of attention.

1. Which elements of a constructivist approach to expanding learning are evident in Case study 4.1?
2. What changes could the educator have made to provide a better learning experience, given the usual limitations of an early years setting?

Everyday concepts, science concepts and learning theories

Gelman (1998) stated that '[c]hildren's concepts reflect their emerging "theories" about the world. To the extent that children's theories are inaccurate, their conceptions are also biased' (p. 1). As children construct meaning from their own experiences, often they arrive at an understanding that is incomplete and unsubstantiated by multiple exposures. We often use the term 'everyday science' to describe how children have made sense of their world using only their own sensory and physical experiences. They explain their understandings in terms of what they know to happen in their everyday life. The term **everyday concepts** was introduced (Vygotsky, 1987, p. 119) to indicate how children's understandings were related to the world of experience in a direct but relatively *ad hoc* manner. He defined everyday concepts as different to scientific concepts (which are both more abstract and more general as they relate to other concepts in the same science area).

Everyday concepts – key ideas which are developed through experiences in the everyday world.

A recent expansion of Vygotsky's ideas of everyday **science concepts** comes from Hedges (2012) who has taken the idea of 'working theories', developed in the New Zealand early childhood curriculum, to highlight the possibility of a child having a networked theoretical construct. Working theories 'describe complex contributors to elements of children's thinking, inquiry and knowledge building' (Hedges, 2014, p. 35). The 'working theories' idea suggests that children develop theories about themselves, people, places and experiences in their lives. With time and greater experience, the working theories become more complex and more applicable for making sense of the world. Hedges (2012) suggested that when an 'everyday concept' is applied in different contexts, the child is developing his or her working theory. However, when the child is able to apply an everyday concept consistently, they are moving towards an understanding of the scientific concept. This research postulates that working theories are a mechanism used by children to advance their understandings. Children's working theories act 'as implicit mediators within children's active attempts in their own minds to extend and challenge their thinking' (Hedges, 2012, p. 146) – children connect, edit and extend their own understanding. Hedges links the explicit mediation occurring through a child's working theory with the conceptual development from everyday science concepts to scientific concepts. A child's everyday science understandings will alter how that child makes sense of a new science experience, and may lead to unintended learning outcomes of which the educator should be aware.

Science concepts – those key ideas which are generally accepted to be scientifically accurate at the time.

Children's alternative concepts

'Naïve concepts' is another term often used to describe the early concepts developed by children. The child analyses a new situation and is only able to base his or her understandings on the objective perceptual appearance. The child is unable to make meaning on any other level. Everyday science concepts and naïve concepts are considered pre-theoretical, developed through the sensory aspect of the experience rather than from a systematic, analytical viewpoint. A term often used in the past, and still used by some educators, is 'misconception'. This term implies that the child has a wrong idea, or an incorrect development of a science understanding. This term is no longer used as it implies a judgement of the child and an inability to recognise that the concept a child develops is not only in line with the child's experience, but in that particular set of experiences also explains the experience adequately to the child. A preferred term is **alternative concept**, which is commonly used to describe the situation whereby a child has arrived at his or her own understanding, based on the child's own experience. The alternative concept held by the child may or may not bear a relationship to the scientifically accepted concept. The alternative concept may arise out of the child's association of the idea with common language or everyday science, from confusion or lack of knowledge.

Alternative concepts (conceptions) – ideas which are alternative to main science concepts; they could be partially correct.

Research has found some interesting aspects of alternative concepts that have an impact on children's future learning and, therefore, educators should be aware of these. Alternative concepts (adapted from Skamp, 2004, p. 5):

- cut across age, ability, gender and cultural boundaries, and are often found to be similar, irrespective of these factors
- are influenced by everyday experiences including direct observation, peer culture, language, teachers' explanations and resource materials
- are context-specific (children may use different ideas to explain the same scientific phenomenon, if they occur in different contexts)
- are implicit and tacit to children's thinking (children may not be aware that there are other ways to explain something)
- are held tenaciously and are resistant to change by transmissive teaching approaches (unintended learning outcomes are often a consequence of alternative concepts)
- are similar to those ideas held by scientists of a century ago.

As children are exposed to increasing sets of experiences, and through the interactions of social learning, they may start to develop concepts that bear some relationship to the scientifically accepted view. Within this framework, children may develop partial conceptual understanding. What they know or understand of a concept is correct, but incomplete.

If we think of a continuum between a scientifically correct idea and a child's developing understanding, then a partial concept can be mapped anywhere along that continuum (see Figure 4.3). The squiggly line represents the fact that the pathway between the alternative concept and the science concept is not linear and that children will often move forwards, but also backwards, before they gain understanding.

Other experiences

Alternative concept

Science concept

Partial concept

Other experiences

Conceptual understanding continuum

FIGURE 4.3 A continuum of conceptual understanding

Case Study 4.2

THE DROPPED TOY

Linc (8 months old) was sitting in his high chair, while Nanna was trying to feed him. In expressing his need to be autonomous, Linc was trying to take the spoon from Nanna's hand as she was attempting to feed him. To distract him, Nanna gave him a small plastic toy to play with. After only a minute of playing, the toy dropped to the floor. Nanna returned it to Linc. Immediately he dropped it again, but this time leant over to see where it went. While still feeding him, Nanna returned the toy to him over and over again, only to have it dropped each time. Every time it was dropped, Linc observed where it had landed. In this simple feeding session, Linc was investigating the phenomenon of gravity and learning that the toy always fell to the ground. He also learnt that Nanna always picked it up for him!

1. Consider what other simple activities young children (birth–3 years) participate in which highlight science learning.
2. When a child plays with moving toys, what science is being explored?

REFLECTION

Practical task

ENRICHMENT ACTIVITIES

After considering Case study 4.2, devise a set of five enrichment activities or rich resources for young babies 6–12 months old. Introduce a new resource or activity on a daily basis. Comment on responses from children.

EXPLAINING ALTERNATIVE CONCEPTS OF AIR RESISTANCE

Working in a 5-year-old Foundation class, the educator was showing children what happens when a horizontal sheet of paper is allowed to fall through the air. Most children were able to predict that it would 'waft' down (not their words). Then the educator scrunched a piece of A4 paper up into a little ball and asked for the children's predictions on how the paper would fall, letting it go alongside a flat sheet. Again, most knew it would travel straight down, faster than the wafting paper. When asked why the scrunched-up paper fell faster, the children all cried out that it was heavier. The educator tried to reason with them, reminding them that both sheets of paper were the same size to begin with. This caused some consternation until one child, thinking through the entire episode, was able to say quite confidently that the scrunched-up paper had 'more words on it' and was therefore heavier!

REFLECTION

1. Consider Case study 4.3 and where the children are in relation to everyday concepts and science concepts.
2. What could the educator do next to challenge the alternative concepts the children held?

EXPLAINING ALTERNATIVE CONCEPTS OF CONDENSATION

Children in Year 2 (8-year-olds) were investigating evaporation and condensation. The educator placed a container filled with ice water in front of a group of children and asked them to feel the outside of the container. 'Oh, it's wet!', they said. When asked why there was water on the outside of the container, children explained that it had seeped through the sides of the glass container. One child believed that it had crept up the inside and dribbled down the outside. To challenge this understanding, the educator removed the container and refilled it with fresh iced water, coloured with red food dye. This time children felt the water on the outside with a tissue and determined that the water was not coloured. The educator asked the question again, 'Where did the water come from?' The children were unsure until one child explained patiently to the teacher that the water had come through the sides of the glass, as it had done previously, and the glass had filtered out the colour!

Consider Case study 4.4 and the following questions:

1. Consider the range of alternative conceptions the children expressed in Case study 4.4. What could the educator do next to challenge the alternative concepts the children held?

2. What extra understandings do the children need to be able to make sense of condensation?

REFLECTION

Conclusion

This chapter discussed contemporary theories on cognition and how children learn, particularly in science. The ecological theory, theory of mind, social dynamics theory, constructivism, sociocultural theory, play theory, motivation and other affective factors were highlighted as aspects of children's learning. The importance of understanding children's alternative conceptions was also discussed. Knowing how the theories relate to cognition allows educators to better understand how children are learning and what can be done to enhance learning opportunities.

Alsop, S. & Watts, M. (2003). Science education and affect, *International Journal of Science Education*, 25(9), 1043–7;

Arthur, L., Beecher, B., Death, E., Dockett, S. & Farmer, S. (2005). *Programming and Planning in Early Childhood Settings*, Melbourne: Thomson.

Astington, J. W. & Edward, M. J. (2010). The development of theory of mind in early childhood, in R. E. Tremblay, R. G. Barr, R. DeV. Peters & M. Boivin (eds), *Encyclopedia on Early Childhood Development*, Montreal, Quebec: Centre of Excellence for Early Childhood Development, 1–6, www.child-encyclopedia.com/documents/astington-edwardngxp.pdf.

Bronfenbrenner, U. (1989). Ecological systems theory, *Annals of Child Development*, 6, 187–24.

Campbell, C. & Tytler, R. (2007). Student science conceptions and views of learning, in G. Venville & V. Dawson (eds), *The Art of Teaching Primary Science*, Sydney: Allen & Unwin.

Catherwood, D. (1999). New views on the young brain: Offerings from developmental psychology to early childhood education, *Contemporary Issues in Early Childhood*, 1(1), 23–35.

Chalufour, I. & Worth, K. (2005). *Exploring Water with Young Children*, St Paul, MN: Educational Development Center Inc., Red Leaf Press.

Day, C. & Leitch, R. (2001). Teachers' and teacher educators' lives: The role of emotion, *Teaching and Teacher Education*, 17, 403–15.

Dockett, S. & Fleer, M. (2002). *Play and Pedagogy in Early Childhood: Bending the Rules*, Melbourne: Thomson.

Driver, R., Asoko, H., Leach, J., Mortimer, E. & Scott, P. (1994). Constructing scientific knowledge in the classroom, *Educational Researcher*, 23(7), 5–12.

Durlauf, S. & Young, P. (2001). *Social Dynamics*. Cambridge, MA: MIT Press.

Eshach, H. & Fried M. N. (2005). Should science be taught in early childhood? *Journal of Science Education and Technology*, 14(3), 315–36.

Fleer, M. & Ridgeway, A. (2007). Learning science through play, in M. Fleer (ed.), *Young Children: Thinking About the Scientific World*, Canberra: Early Childhood Australia Inc.

French, L. (2004). Science as the center of a coherent, integrated early childhood curriculum. *Early Childhood Research Quarterly*, 19(1), 138.

Gelman, S. (1998). Concept development in pre-school children, paper presented to the Forum on Early Childhood Science, Mathematics and Technology Education, Washington, DC, Project 2061, American Assocation for the Advancement of Science.

—— (2009). Learning from others: Children's construction of concepts, *Annual Review of Psychology*, 60, 115–40.

Gelman, S. & Brenneman, K. (2004). Science learning pathways for young children, *Early Childhood Research Quarterly*, 19(1), 150–8.

Hedges, H. (2012). Vygotsky's phases of everyday concept development and the notion of children's 'working theories', *Learning, Culture and Social Interaction*, 1, 143–52.

—— (2014). Young children's 'working theories': Building and connecting understandings, *Journal of Early Childhood Research*, 12(1), 35–49.

Howitt, C., Morris, M. & Colville, M. (2007). Science teaching and learning in the early childhood years, in V. Dawson & G. Venville (eds), *The Art of Teaching Primary Science*, Sydney: Allen & Unwin, 233–47.

Johnston, J. (2014). *Emergent Science, Teaching Science from Birth to 8*. London and New York: Routledge.

Johnston, J. & Nahmad-Williams, L. (2009). *Early Childhood Studies*, England: Pearson Education.

Kirschner, P. A. (2006). Why minimal guidance during instruction does not work: An analysis of the failure of constructivist, discovery, problem-based, experiential, and inquiry-based teaching, *Educational Psychologist*, 41(2), 75–86.

Klahr, D. (2004). The equivalence of learning paths in early science instruction: Effects of direct instruction and discovery learning, www.psychology.nottingham.ac.uk, accessed 30 October 2009.

Lave, J. & Wenger, E. (1991). *Situated Learning: Legitimate Peripheral Participation*, Cambridge: Cambridge University Press.

Lind, K. (1998). Science in early childhood: Developing and acquiring fundamental concepts and skills, paper presented to the Forum on Early Childhood Science, Mathematics and Technology Education, Washington, DC, Project 2061, American Assocation for the Advancement of Science.

Mayer, R. (2004). Should there be a three-strikes rule against pure discovery learning? The case for guided methods of instruction, *American Psychologist*, 59(1), 14–19.

McInerney, D. & McInerney, V. (1998). *Educational Psychology: Constructing Learning*, 2nd edn, Sydney: Prentice Hall.

Montessori, M. (1994). *From Childhood to Adolescence*. Oxford: ABC-Clio, 7–16.

Piaget, J. (1950). *The Psychology of Intelligence*, London: Routledge & Kegan Paul.

Pintrich, P., Marx, R. & Boyle, R. (1993). Beyond cold conceptual change: The role of motivational beliefs and classroom contextual factors in the process of conceptual change, *Review of Educational Research*, 63(2), 167–99.

Pintrich, P. & Schrauben, B. (1992). Students' motivational beliefs and their cognitive engagement in classroom academic tasks, in D. Schunk & J. Meece (eds), *Student Perceptions in the Classroom: Causes and Consequences*, Hillsdale, NJ: Erlbaum, 149–83.

Scott, P. (1998). Teacher talk and meaning making in science classrooms: A Vygotskian analysis and review, *Studies in Science Education*, 32, 45–80.

Skamp, K. (2004). *Teaching Primary Science Constructively*, 3rd edn, Melbourne: Cengage Learning.

Tucker, K. (2005). *Mathematics Through Play in the Early Years*, London: Paul Chapman Publishing, Sage Publications.

Vosnaidou, S., Ioannides, C., Dimitrakopoulou, A. & Papademetriou, E. (2001). Designing learning environments to promote conceptual change in science, *Learning and Instruction*, 11, 381–419.

Vygotsky, L. (1962). *Thought and Language*, Cambridge, MA: MIT Press.

—— (1987). Thinking and speech, in R. W. Reiber and A. S. Carton (eds), *The Collected Works of L. S. Vygotsky, Vol 1: Problems of General Psychology*, (trans. N. Minick), New York: Plenum.

PART 2

How can I enhance children's learning of science?

Approaches to enhance science learning

5

Coral Campbell and Kate Chealuck

This chapter links theory with practice by discussing the range of approaches that can be used with young children to enhance their learning. It discusses the interactivity of approaches that educators use with children and settings. Whether it is through the processes of science, such as the development of observation, or through the skillful questioning of the educator, the approach used should enhance opportunities for children's learning.

Considering the range of learning theories presented in Chapter 4, how does an educator make sense of the multitude of theoretical perspectives available and translate these into a practice that aids children's learning? One way is to consider the strong messages coming from all theories: children construct their own understanding, learning is enhanced through social interaction and the educator is pivotal to children's learning.

If we think about these messages and in particular the ideas relating to domain-specific constructivist learning, we acknowledge that there are specific mental schemas relating to science understanding which can be aided through the actions and inputs from the educator. In particular, science learning can be enhanced and promoted by an educator who uses science-related ideas, language and experiences with children. As science-specific skills, language and concepts can often be linked (illustrated by the worm as animal idea from Chapter 4, for example), an educator who teaches with an understanding of science can draw on the connections to make them apparent to the children.

OBJECTIVES

At the end of this chapter you will be able to:

- recognise a range of formal and informal approaches which enhance children's science learning
- demonstrate the need to scaffold children's explorations and how this can be achieved
- use effective questioning for focusing and enhancing children's science learning
- describe ways that educators can enhance science learning through targeted exploration
- recognise the science skills, processes and knowledge that can be acquired by young children.

The importance of prior knowledge

The acceptance of constructivist theory (in its many variations) has led to a number of approaches that are used to enhance children's learning or understanding in science. Because children construct meaning from experience, the educator needs to expand their experiential base, not only to introduce new experiences but also to build on children's prior experiences. The educator should initially determine what children already know before attempting to provide new experiences. In that way the new experience will be linked with children's previous **schema**, creating a new schema and a more complex or sophisticated understanding. This aligns with the idea of Gelman and Brenneman (2004) in relation to the connectedness of ideas in a child's mind and how it can be linked to the current experience of the child.

Schema – a mental construct which connects ideas in a child's mind.

Child-instigated versus teacher-instigated activities

Child-instigated – play or activity which the child has initiated.

There is a general belief that children's explorations should be **child-instigated**. However, a vast number of explorations would not be attempted if everything was left to children. In particular, some children (just as some adults) work within their level of comfort and rarely challenge themselves. The natural breadth of young children's experience is limited, related to age and family involvement, and exposure to new things is always of interest to their enquiring minds. Thus, an effective early childhood educator should aim to expand children's experiences by introducing activities that would normally be outside of children's opportunities. Examples of this include: magnetism activities, simple electricity (e.g. play dough circuits), simple chemistry reactions, and incursions involving unusual animals (snakes and lizards).

Approaches to enhance children's science learning

Intentional teaching

Intentional teaching – the deliberate decisions and actions of an educator to enhance children's learning.

Current research supports the idea that educators should be purposeful and thoughtful in the way they provide experiences to children and in the way they interact with them (DEEWR, 2009; Epstein, 2007). The term **intentional teaching** has been used to describe the deliberate decisions and actions of an educator in the way they approach children's learning. However, intentional teaching is not a 'formal' teaching approach and is not intended to mimic a school-structured approach; rather, it is recognised as educators enhancing children's learning through play in a purposeful way. Houghton (2013, p. 10) identifies that educators 'need to be intentional in fostering children's skills to discover and explore what they can do themselves'. In science, as in any other learning within the pre-school, intentional teaching is characterised by 'educators taking the lead in deliberately and purposefully initiating and selecting a specific aspect of learning to focus on' (Margetts & Raban, 2011, p. 55).

For an educator, it is important to recognise the science in regular activities such as making play dough, exploring small animals in the garden, floating and sinking play, gardening and many other child-instigated explorations. Intentional teaching may be demonstrated when the educator reads a story (for example, *The Very Hungry Caterpillar*) in response to a child's investigation of caterpillars in the garden. It may be as simple as asking a child a question while they are observing the caterpillar's movements in the garden. Also see Chapter 14 'Intentional teaching of science'.

Supporting science learning for all ages

Educators frequently ask how they can 'teach' science to a baby. Rather than thinking of science in this restricted 'curriculum' way, educators should think about science as developing an understanding of the world. Babies need exposure to new experiences, new materials and the opportunities to explore new ideas. This exposure provides them with the basis for constructing meaning. Thus, an educator should be looking for ways to enrich the learning opportunities for babies to investigate new materials or phenomena using their senses.

With toddlers, there are greater opportunities to expose children to new experiences and introduce them to a phenomenon which may not exist in their home environments. As their language is developing rapidly at this time, it is appropriate to introduce the language of science alongside their 'everyday' language. Children need to be able to follow their own investigations, while being scaffolded by educators to achieve success.

Pre-schoolers can investigate their own ideas and educators provide them with scaffolding to follow a simple process or inquiry. They can enhance their learning through the opportunity to discuss and revisit their explorations. They can also evaluate the findings of their investigations, leading to new explorations.

Case Study 5.1

TO BOUNCE OR NOT!

Lincoln (18 months) is obsessed with balls! At the moment his favourite game is to fill a plastic tub with a variety of balls – a basketball, netball, soccer ball, tennis ball, 'bouncy' balls and some soft, spongy balls. He drags the tub to the table where he proceeds to throw each ball onto the table and watch what happens to them. 'Uh oh!' he exclaims as the big round, hard balls roll off the table and the small 'bouncy' balls bounce off the edge. He looks perplexed when the soft spongy balls don't roll but stay on the tabletop where they land, and lifts his hands in an 'I don't know' gesture. Lincoln is experiencing how the material from which the ball is made affects how the ball bounces: the hard balls bounce while the soft balls don't.

Consider Case study 5.1 and the following questions:

1. How could the educator extend the science learning described in Case study 5.1?
2. What other everyday types of material could children under 2 years of age explore?

REFLECTION

Formal and informal approaches to enhance children's science learning

As discussed in Chapter 4, children's understandings are often different or naïve in science. Thus, the educator should challenge those understandings by introducing **discrepant experiences** that encourage children to re-think their understanding. Further, educators should provide rich and varied experiences and promote, through discussion or questioning, more appropriate understanding of the scientific concepts.

Discrepant experiences – experiences which disagree with a child's current thinking and that encourage children to re-think their understanding.

Knowledge of the constructivist theory has led to the development of a number of 'teaching' approaches that foster learning in science (and other areas). Despite variations, the salient points include probing children to determine prior understanding; using effective questions to highlight children's thinking; and scaffolding children's learning through dialogue, activities and focused discussion. Much of the educator involvement with children's learning is dependent on effective communication and the importance of the introduction of science terminology is now acknowledged (Gelman, 2004). In addition, awareness of children's capability for abstract thought implies that a scientific process, such as inquiry, can also be introduced with success with young learners.

In helping children to construct their own knowledge, educators may facilitate children's science experiences through a range of more formally recognised approaches. These include a process skills approach, guided discovery learning, interactive approach, inquiry learning approach, problem-based learning approach and project approach. Each of these is described below.

A process skills approach

Process skills approach – an approach whereby the educator assists children to develop science skills.

In a **process skills approach**, the educator assists children to develop science skills. In essence, while building science knowledge, we also want children to develop the skills and processes to be able to confidently undertake their own investigations. In the process skills approach the educator focuses on a particular scientific skill or some combination of process skills. Process skills in the early years include observing, communicating, comparing, classifying, measuring and using tools, predicting and inferring. A summary of these process skills is presented in Table 5.1. Generic skills such as collaborating, counting, estimating, generalising, recording, and problem-solving are also important to consider in the teaching and learning of science (Beaumont, 2010).

In assisting children to learn the skills of science, the educator is emphasising the nature of science and how scientists work. However, this is only one small part of learning in science and should always be complemented with other approaches.

Discovery approach – children 'discovering' knowledge and understanding through their own investigations. A guided discovery approach involves the educator assisting the child.

The guided discovery approach and scaffolded learning

Originally, the **discovery approach** was adopted by pre-school centres (and primary schools) as the most natural way for a child to investigate things of interest. Children attempt to make sense of their world through their

Process skill	Example
TABLE 5.1 SUMMARY OF THE SCIENCE PROCESS SKILLS APPROPRIATE TO THE EARLY YEARS	
Observing	Using the senses to gain information. This is an extremely important skill that educators can enhance in young children. Close and accurate observation is crucial in following through with an investigation.
Communicating	Describing an object or event in simple terms, through oral, written, pictorial or graphic modes.
Comparing	Looking for similarities and differences between objects and events.
Classifying	Grouping objects into two or more meaningful categories based on one property. This also involves sorting, matching, grouping and naming colours and objects.
Measuring and using appropriate tools	Selecting appropriate tools for measuring a range of objects. With young children, these tools are usually informal – such as a piece of rope, string, or body parts.
Predicting	Beginning to predict the possible outcomes of actions and events based on prior knowledge.
Inferring	Beginning to suggest reasonable explanations based on observations.

own play explorations and, if a constructivist approach to learning is accepted, children build their own understandings from their own experiences. However, children are limited in how far the discovery can aid understanding. Interaction with peers and adults provides additional stimulus to extend understanding further. Eshach (2006) commented that ' … assuming children are able to understand complex concepts and are able, to some extent, to connect theory and evidence, educators should, in our view, expose children to situations in which those abilities may find fertile ground to grow' (p. 17). Being a co-investigator with the child or asking effective questions that encourage further explorations provides children with the opportunity to extend their own investigations while they experience the science of their own world.

In undertaking their own investigation, or even through everyday play, children are often exposed to science experiences. This is termed **incidental science** or part of an **emergent curriculum**; that is, curriculum arising from children's own investigations (Johnston, 2014; Dockett & Fleer, 2002, p. 199). There is considerable opportunity for an educator to guide children's learning through focused questioning and positive interactions (called **scaffolding**) at this point and time of interest. For this reason, it is crucial that early childhood educators have a basic understanding of science in the world. Educators who are attuned may recognise the science in spontaneous events and can make use of these to develop deeper understandings in children. In light of the literature on emergent curriculum in which educators need to respond to the children's questions and learning needs 'on the spot', it is evident that some early childhood educators would not be prepared if

Incidental science – occurs when children are exposed to science experiences during their own investigation, or through everyday play.

Emergent curriculum – curriculum arising from children's own investigations.

Scaffolding – adult guiding and supporting the child's learning via focused questions and positive interactions.

their own background knowledge of science is insufficient (Campbell & Jobling, 2009). Dockett and Fleer (2002) described the role of adults as 'one of focussed observation and responding to the play that occurs in ways that extend and enhance learning' (p. 198).

Interactive approach and inquiry learning

Interactive approach – children are actively engaged in learning science; children's question(s) lead the explorations and the educator's role is to provide resources and guide/scaffold the explorations.

The **interactive approach** to learning recognises that children have legitimate questions of their own to which they would like to find answers. In an interactive approach, the children's question(s) lead the explorations and the educator's role is to provide resources and guide/scaffold the explorations. The educator supports the development of the children's ideas, asks focused questions, suggests alternative ways of thinking and helps develop children's responses. The extent of support offered by the educator is dependent upon the complexity of the investigation, the age of the children and the available resources, which may include educator knowledge. An interactive approach relies strongly on the ability of the educator to be flexible, to be able to help children with knowledge or where to locate it and to be able to take a 'helper' position with regard to children's learning.

Inquiry approach – children undertaking investigations to answer their own questions, through phases: engagement, exploration, explanation, elaboration and evaluation.

An **inquiry approach** is the most current approach to learning science and relates to children undertaking investigations to answer their own questions. It is said to follow a number of phases: engagement, exploration, explanation, elaboration and evaluation. With very young children, the engagement phase arises from the children's own interest in a particular item or phenomenon. Alternatively, the educator can use this engagement phase to determine the child's prior understandings. The exploration phase is one that comes most naturally to children; however, as early childhood educators we can also introduce children to other explorations (or educator-instigated experiences) through providing additional materials and further scaffolding of the exploration. Through the guided exploration, encouraging children to ask their own questions, focusing their observations or asking specific questions, early childhood educators can help children develop their own scientifically enhanced explanations. Through providing other activities, children can be extended to transfer their new knowledge to different contexts (elaboration). Finally, again through scaffolding, children can be encouraged to share their

FIGURE 5.1   Scaffolding learning

understandings with others and present their learning through discussion, role play, drawings or other communication mechanisms. While these may seem to be higher-order processes, we should never underestimate the capabilities of young children. With appropriate help, young children are quite capable of following through on an inquiry approach, particularly in the 5–8-year age group.

Problem-based learning

In **problem-based learning**, the educator provides a problem to children, usually in small groups, and gives them time to try to solve it. It is a child-centred approach. With young children, the educator works with the children to help find out facts, generate ideas and assist the learning. Children may challenge each others' ideas and the educator helps to resolve issues. The process continues as new information is added to existing facts and more thinking occurs. Solving the problem is not the most important aspect; rather, it is the learning process through child-directed inquiry that is most important. Effective problems are those that engage children's interest and motivate them to probe for deeper understanding of science concepts. Educators take a small role during problem-based learning – they stimulate learning by asking effective questions and offering support. With more practice, children become better able to direct their own learning and identify what they need to find out to solve their problem.

> **Problem-based learning** – a child-centred approach where the educator provides a problem to children and gives them time to try to solve it.

There are usually five steps in a problem-based approach:

1. The problem is presented to the group by the educator, who may use stimulus pictures to help children remember what to focus on.
2. Children talk about what they already know.
3. Children brainstorm their ideas and identify the broad problem.
4. Children identify what else they need to learn in order to prove or disprove their ideas.
5. Children share their findings with others.

Educators can generate ideas for problem-based learning from a wide range of resources: stories, television, children's games, or news articles. Problem-based learning can enrich children's normal learning experiences by providing them with challenge and stimulation not normally available in their learning setting. The problem-based learning situation should align with the educator's desired learning outcomes or with the theme existing in the centre.

Project-based learning

In this approach, children are involved collaboratively in a particular project which requires problem solving around a specific need. The project might be something as simple as children devising a means of reminding themselves to wash their hands after using the toilet. It could be that they are building a cubby house from materials they find outside. In attempting to solve a problem which is directly related to their own lives, children become active participants in their own learning and the generators of ideas to move the project forward. A typical science-related project involves children investigating some science ideas as part of the completion of the project. For example, children who are constructing temporary homes for small animals from the garden will need to investigate what the animal's normal habitat looks like and what food is required. **Project-based learning** promotes critical and higher-order thinking, along with analytical and creative thinking. In the Australian Curriculum, project-based learning is linked with 'Design & Creative Technology', a preliminary process to engineering in later years.

> **Project-based learning** – children work collaboratively to problem-solve around a specific need.

Strategies to enhance science learning

Strategies are different to approaches; a strategy is a way of doing something within a broader approach. Strategies for enhancing science learning are varied and in most instances can be applied across all of the informal and formal approaches. Remembering that early childhood educators generally follow a play-based learning philosophy, some of the strategies accepted in early primary school are not necessarily applicable in an early childhood centre.

Strategies which could be used include, but are not limited to, the following:

- direct instruction – instructing children in how to carry out a science exploration or experience
- demonstrations – showing children a science phenomenon which may be too difficult (or dangerous) for them to undertake
- questioning – see below for detail on questioning
- interactive – any strategy where children are actively contributing, such as brain-storming, co-learning, cooperative play, peer discussion, role plays, conferencing or using children's questions
- indirect instruction – scaffolding, inquiry, problem solving
- autonomous or child-directed – project-based, play, exploration tables
- experiential – hands-on activities, exploration tables, construction or model building, multi-modal, representational activities.

Information related to targeted exploration, children talking and children exploring is presented below as additional strategies for enhancing science learning.

Targeted exploration

Children explore the world around them at all times, trying to make sense of their own experiences. When we are aware of children's interest in a particular science area, it might be the time for a **targeted exploration**. We need to be aware of what children can achieve by themselves, and what might be realistic in terms of broadening their range of experiences and opportunities. A topic might be introduced in response to children's questions or through a related story or event. For example, when there is any major environmental disaster captured in the national news, children want to know more. The educator may be able to set up a tornado in a plastic bottle to show the movement of tornadoes, or show how clouds

> **Targeted exploration** – educators provide resources to support children's interest in a particular science area, or focus.

are formed in bottles. Simple activities or demonstrations in which children participate can provide additional experiences from which they build their understandings.

We have mentioned that children need scaffolding to be able to shift their initial naïve beliefs to more scientifically appropriate ideas. Asking questions is one way to focus children's observations and open their eyes and minds to further possibilities. For example, a child may be watching a snail move and comment on how slow it is. A simple, focused observation would be to ask the child to see whether the snail moves faster over other surfaces. Another example occurs when a child comments on how soap bubbles move through the air; the teacher can ask whether the bubbles have different shapes.

Children talking

Recent research has indicated the power and value of children's talk with adults and peers (Eshach, 2006; Sfard, 2000). It is during these discussions or share-time that children may tend to adjust their thinking or the talk process may help children clarify their own ideas. Such discussions may reveal to children that often there can be more than one idea or answer. It lets children know that it is alright to have a different response. In shared talking, children contribute to the discussion and extend their own thinking when challenged with alternative ideas. However, when engaging children in talk, an adult should allow time for children to 'gather' their thoughts and then put these into words that the adult can understand. Sometimes children have never had to order their thoughts in such a way as to make them understandable to others. Patience is required.

Group discussions add another dimension. Not all children will feel comfortable contributing in a group situation, but it can be the opportunity to introduce new vocabulary and draw out the more timid children by having them repeat the new words. This will provide them with a successful interchange and make the next discussion less fearful. The quantity and quality of adult–child shared talking supports children's learning and appears to be directly related to improved cognitive outcomes for children. As indicated by Koralek and Colker (2003), talking with children about what they were doing not only 'involved the children in a conversation, but also offered them the relevant vocabulary and modelled ways of thinking about and talking about their experiences' (p. 6).

Children exploring

From the first moment they enter the world, children start to explore. You can see it when a child learns to move a hand or arm deliberately. Each movement is practised over and over, and each time there is wonder in the child's eyes at the discovery he or she has made. Dropping items onto the floor from a height is an investigation that produces several observations – the object often leaves the sight of the child, a sound follows the dropping, the object can re-appear. Slightly older children discover that they can 'hide' and re-appear, thereby establishing a constancy about the people and the objects in the immediate environment.

When children explore, they are usually following their own interests or that of one of their peer group. They use all five of their senses (sight, hearing, touch, taste and smell) to work out what it is they have encountered. Their curiosity encourages

FIGURE 5.2 Free use of materials can lead to unintended learning outcomes, as indicated by a child building a tower from a range of materials

investigation to solve problems or to make connections between what is known and what is unknown. Through their explorations, children play with objects, materials and ideas to extend or develop new understandings.

As children explore, they ask questions for further exploration or to seek ideas from others (peer group or adult). Educators can assist this through their scaffolding and through providing additional resources and experiences. As the educator observes children's explorations, the use of shared conversations and focused questions can provide a direction or alternative direction for children's inquiry.

Children require sustained periods of time for their explorations and their investigations. They need to be able to think about what they have seen or experienced. They need time to try it all again and to solve any problems that arise. Opportunities should be provided for children to involve others in their explorations or to work alone, with minimal interference. Scaffolding should never be deemed to be interference if undertaken professionally with consideration for children's cognitive development.

Probing for understanding

There are several ways in which an educator can elicit children's prior and current understandings such as questioning, using children's drawings and representational challenges, using the 'interview about instances' strategy, and through puppets.

Effective questioning as part of the scaffolding practice

Effective questioning – asking the right question at the right time.

There are many recognised ways to provide support for children undertaking their own investigation. **Effective questioning**, asking the right question at the right time, is a skill that takes time to develop. It takes practice to ask an open-ended question that requires children to think along a particular path. Using questions effectively can draw children's attention to a particular focus, or open their minds to other possibilities. Simplistically, the question stems 'Who?', 'Why?', 'How?', 'If?', 'Where?', 'What if?' and 'What do you think?' linked to a science idea can provide the stimulus for conversations, further investigations or deeper thinking. Questions that promote hypothetical, tentative and exploratory talk are productive, open-ended and usually centered on children in some way (Department of Education and Training, 2003).

There are many ways to use effective questions in early years settings (adapted from Department of Education and Training, 2003):

- as a stimulus for an exploration – this is particularly strong if the question was generated by children

- using a question to stimulate a prediction before children undertake an activity or exploration – 'What do you think will happen?'

- finding out what children already know – 'Why do you think the bubble floated?'

- to promote reasoning – 'Why does the snail have those long stalks on its head?'

- productive questions encourage children's investigation and discussion
    - attention-focusing questions – 'Have you noticed ... ?'
    - measuring and counting questions – 'How many ... ?', 'How long ... ?'
    - comparison questions – 'How are these different or the same?'
    - action questions – 'What happens when ... ?'
    - problem-posing questions – 'How can you make ... ?', 'Can you find a way to ... ?'

- person-centred questions focus on the children's ideas and hence tend to reveal their alternative conceptions and why these are held – 'What do *you* think ... ?' and 'What can *you* see ... ?' are typical starting stems

- questions can be used to promote thinking and action; such questions might focus on finding out children's ideas (prior knowledge) or be used to develop their ideas
    - questions that focus on identifying children's prior knowledge are person-centred and specific – 'How do you think the sound of the siren travels from over there to your ear?'
    - questions designed to develop ideas encourage children to think of ways they could test their ideas – 'If you think that the piece of wood is too large to float, how could you test that to see if it is true?'

- questions can also be used to develop processing skills; such questions can be categorised as
    - observing – 'What do you see ... ?'
    - hypothesising – 'Why do you think that happened?'
    - predicting – 'What do you think will happen if ... ?'
    - investigating – 'What do you want to do to find out?'
    - interpreting and drawing conclusions – 'What did you find out?'
    - communicating – 'How can you show this to others so they can understand?' or 'What else will you need to use (materials)?'

LAUNDRY BASKET RIDES

Four-year-old Mason happily pushes his friend around the centre in a plastic laundry basket. On the tiles, the basket slides around the corners and moves easily causing both boys to laugh and whoop. As soon as Mason tries to push the basket over the carpet, however, it slows to stopping. 'It's not working now', he complains. 'It's very hard! I need some help.' The educator helps Mason pull the basket (still with his friend in it) back onto the tiles. 'I don't need you now!', he shouts as he again picks up the pace and slides the basket around easily. Mason is learning that the surface of the floor makes a large difference to the amount of effort he has to exert to move the basket and his friend.

REFLECTION

1. What key science ideas are being enabled through the play described in Case study 5.2?
2. How could the educator enhance this experience further while still keeping in the spirit of play and without interfering?
3. Develop a question from the types outlined earlier in the chapter which could stimulate further discussion with the children in relation to the key science ideas.
4. Is there another play activity which could help reinforce the learnings?

Children's drawings and representational challenges

Ainsworth, Prain and Tytler (2011) suggested five reasons why drawing should be encouraged in science education: to enhance engagement, to learn to represent in science, to reason in science, as a learning strategy and to communicate. Drawings provide an accessible way for children to express their ideas about a science phenomenon. Annotated drawings include words, stated by the child but generally written by the educator, that explain what is happening in the drawing. Annotated drawings provide children with the opportunity to include more detail than what is possible in a simple drawing, while also compensating for young children's limited graphic skills in their drawing (Naylor, Keogh & Goldsworthy, 2004).

Children tend to draw what they understand. By asking children to describe their artwork, their prior understandings can become clearer. The educator can ask children to describe what is happening in the artwork, and may focus on one aspect of it.

Children's drawings form one aspect of a **representational construction** or response to a science idea. Basically a representational construction strategy involves providing children with multiple ways to see, experience or interact with a key science idea. For example, an educator wishing children to engage with the idea of the human body may provide books on the human body, bones to investigate, drawing material – sketch a skeleton, a medical focus on nurses and doctors, as well as songs on the

Representational construction – strategy which involves providing children with multiple ways to see, experience or interact with a key science idea.

body (recognising body parts, e.g. 'Heads, Shoulders, Knees and Toes'). Hubber (2014) states that understanding a key science concept is much more than simply remembering words, it includes the range of experiences which link with the words to create a complex mental schema. Accurate science representations, demonstrated by the educator or developed by the child, form part of the mental schema. Similarly, providing children with the means to represent their science ideas in multiple ways allows them to more effectively communicate what they understand.

Interview about instances

This is a simple technique that relies on an educator presenting a picture or artefact to a child and asking a number of focused questions to draw out the child's understandings (White & Gunstone, 1992). It is a non-threatening way to determine quite specific information about a child's conceptual understanding of a particular science

FIGURE 5.3 A simple piece of artwork can illustrate a child's attempt to understand shape, form and/or colour

theme or phenomenon. An educator should encourage answers that relate to the concepts being probed, and that can be done in the following ways:

1. Begin with a focus question that requires application of the concept to be investigated, without forcing the child into an explicit definition. This indirect approach is usually quite productive because it allows the child to discuss her or his understanding. It can also help the instructor to gain an idea of how the child might apply the implicit concept.

2. The child should not be forced into a specific response to each artefact. If the child does not have an understanding of the concept that allows her or him to talk about a specific instance, do not force the child to choose. This lack of understanding is an important piece of the child's 'conceptual framework'.

3. Allow 'wait time' of at least 3 to 5 seconds to give the child time to interpret the question. Be prepared to re-word the question or to repeat it in simpler terms.

4. Use prediction interviews – these require children to predict a possible outcome of a situation. This type of interview indicates whether a child can apply his or her own meaning to the situation.

5. Use sorting interviews – children are presented with pictures or items and asked to sort them according to a particular instruction or their own classification. As the child sorts, he or she is asked to talk about what they are doing.

6. Use problem-solving interviews – similar to the sorting interview, the child is presented with a problem and with the physical means to solve the problem. The child is asked to think aloud while attempting to solve the problem. Understanding the child's conceptual framework remains the overarching goal in conducting the interview.

EXPLORING FLOATING

The educator was working with a small group of children (6 years old) and had them sitting on the floor in a circle. In the centre of the floor was a large clear container filled with water and next to the container were about 10 items of various materials. The teacher wanted the children to explore what floated and what sank, but also wanted to engage them with the idea that the material that an object is made of, and possibly its shape, can affect its ability to float. Her prior experience with children made her aware that young children often believe that small things float while large things sink (two alternative concepts). She started off with a general discussion to tune them into the activity and to gain an understanding of what they thought floating was. One child answered, 'When things are on the top of the water' and the others chorused their agreement. Another child added, 'When they go to the bottom, they have sanked.'

Each child was then selected to trial an object by placing it in the water. Before this, children had to predict what they thought would happen to the item – float or sink? This raised many interesting comments from the children and provided the educator with some ideas of their prior learning. As they moved through the objects, the educator drew children's attention to the material the object was made of. However, they still persisted with the belief that light things float and heavy things sink. Some also expressed the belief that small things float and big things sink. To challenge the children's understandings, the educator introduced two pieces of wood – a match and a stick. The children thought the stick would sink because it was heavy, but that the match would float because it was light. When both floated, they were astounded. The educator discussed the material of the items, until one child commented that they were both wood. She repeated the activity with two pieces of metal – a paper clip and a metal toy. This time, the children were not as confident predicting that the small item would float and the large one would sink. When both sank, the educator again asked the children what material the objects were made of. When they determined that they were metal, the children started to realise that what the object was made of could determine whether it floated. At that point the educator left the children to finish off their own further explorations.

REFLECTION

Consider Case study 5.3 and the following questions:
1. What questions did the educator ask in Case study 5.3? List them.
2. This is an educator-directed activity to determine children's prior knowledge. What follow-up activity could be provided which would allow further development of children's understandings?

Using puppets to determine children's prior knowledge in science

One way of determining children's prior understandings in science is to use puppetry to question them about certain aspects. Children love playing with puppets. Research in the United Kingdom has shown just how useful puppets can be in gaining information of children's science understandings. Puppets can be used to:

- ask the children questions, thereby gauging their understanding or naïve concepts in science
- help children plan an investigation – the puppet becomes the 'learned other'
- answer some questions – it is less intimidating than adults
- ask the teacher for some ideas on how to decide what to do
- ask the children for help – the children become the 'expert'.

'The Puppets Project' (Naylor et al., 2007) used puppets to assist 4–8-year-old children in learning science. Results from this research found that nearly all of the children were highly engaged and motivated when puppets were used. Children listened more, became more involved in the discussion and more engaged in conversation with puppets. Many children who did not normally speak became more willing to share their ideas with the puppets. The children were found to give fuller explanations of their understandings so that the puppet would understand better. Children's science talk was also found to involve more reasoning and children talked more readily about scientific problems with the puppets. Higher-order thinking skills (such as explanation and justification) were promoted and improved. This allowed educators to observe and document a range of science skills that may be difficult to see in other science explorations.

Like any resource, puppets should not be over-used. However, research has indicated that children react positively to puppets and, apart from their other applications at pre-school for imaginative play, they can be used to expand and enhance children's understandings in many areas of science as well as provide an educator with many opportunities to document science learning.

When using puppets to engage children in science, there are a number of practical elements which should be employed to gain maximum benefit from the experience. When planning the puppet dialogue, you need to be fully prepared. Simple things to do include:

- think about a character when you are using a puppet – it should suit your personality and teaching style
- introduce your puppet to the children – children will then know what to call the puppet
- allow the puppet to show a range of emotions and have a life outside the 'lesson' (avoid stereotyping)
- having the puppet make eye contact with individual children as it speaks to them (i.e. turn its head to face the child speaking)
- avoid having the puppet make lengthy speeches – simple sentences promote responses.

Discuss with children some ground rules (not too many) so that everyone has the opportunity to talk. Remember that most of us can, at times, have overlapping conversations. The idea is that all children feel that their ideas are equally valuable; all children who want to share ideas can do so. When ready, your puppet can be used as a stimulus for talk. For example, have your puppet present a science problem to the children. Some examples of how to do this are:

1. Being muddled and asking the children for ideas, e.g. puppet says, 'I don't understand why the feather is floating. Can someone explain, please?'
2. Presenting a range of ideas children have been overheard discussing, e.g. puppet says, 'Robbie said the car travels in a straight line if its wheels are straight.'
3. Disagreeing with the educator's ideas, e.g. puppet says, 'You're wrong – the very hungry caterpillar turns into a moth, not a butterfly!'
4. Using puppets to help children solve a problem, e.g. puppet says, 'Help me with this. What can I do?'

Conclusion

This chapter discussed various teaching approaches early childhood educators can use to advance children's learning in science. It presented practical strategies for helping children to learn in science: intentional teaching, probing children's prior understandings, scaffolding learning, effective questioning, and science explorations. Finally, it referred to the underlying beliefs that are at the heart of children's learning: children construct knowledge from their own experiences, educators are able to scaffold that learning, and social situations enhance learning opportunities.

Practical task

USING PUPPETS TO INTRODUCE SCIENCE CONCEPTS

At an early childhood centre, you have been asked to use puppets to introduce children to the ideas surrounding life cycles. How would you do this? Provide an outline of your approach, indicating what character the puppet will take on, the role of the educator with the puppet and how the puppetry will introduce the topic (e.g. being muddled or asking the children for help).

1. What science concepts or key ideas will the puppet introduce?
2. What other props might you use?
3. After the introduction using the puppet, how will you engage children in further explorations?

5 References

Ainsworth, S., Prain, V. & Tytler, R. (2011). Drawing to learn science, *Science*, 333, 1096–7.

Beaumont, L. (2010). Developing the adult–child interaction inventory: A methodological study, unpublished manuscript, The Boston Children's Museum, Boston, MA, www.informalscience.org/research/wiki/adult-interactions-in-a-science-museum, accessed 10 August 2014.

Campbell, C. & Jobling, W. (2009). Science professional development for early childhood educator – some identified issues, paper presented to the 11th New Zealand Early Childhood Research Conference.

Department of Education, Employment and Workplace Relations (DEEWR). (2009). *Belonging, Being & Becoming. The Early Years Learning Framework for Australia*, Canberra: Commonwealth of Australia.

Department of Education and Training, Victoria. (2003). *Questioning Categories*, report prepared by Deakin University, Victoria.

Dockett, S. & Fleer, M. (2002). *Play and Pedagogy in Early Childhood: Bending the Rules*, Melbourne: Thomson.

Epstein, A. S. (2007). *The Intentional Teacher: Choosing the Best Strategies for Young Children's Learning*, Washington DC: NAEYC.

Eshach, H. (2006). *Science Literacy in Primary School and Pre-schools*, Dordrecht: Springer.

Gelman, R. & Brennerman, K. (2004). Science learning pathways for young children, *Early Childhood Research Quarterly*, 119, 150–8.

Gelman, S. (2004) Psychological essentialism in children, *Trends in Cognitive Sciences*, 8(9), 404–9. DOI: dx.doi.org/10.1016/j.tics.2004.07.001.

Houghton, A. (2013). *Intentional Teaching: Promoting Purposeful Practice in Early Childhood Settings*, Melbourne: Teaching Solutions.

Hubber, P. J. (2014). Representation construction: A directed inquiry pedagogy for science education, in P. Blessinger & J. M. Carfora (eds), *Inquiry-based Learning for Faculty and Institutional Development: A Conceptual and Practical Resource for Educators (Volume 1)*, Bingley, UK: Emerald Group Publishing Limited, 201–21.

Johnston, J. (2014). *Emergent Science: Teaching Science from Birth to 8*. London and New York: Routledge.

Koralek, D. & Colker, L. (2003). *Spotlight on Young Children and Science*, US: National Association for the Education of Young Children.

Margetts, K. & Raban, B. (2011). *Principles and Practices for Driving the EYLF*, Melbourne: Teaching Solutions.

Naylor, S., Keogh, B., Downing, B., Maloney, J. & Simon, S. (2007). The Puppets Project: Using puppets to promote engagement and talk in science, in R. Pinto & D. Couso (eds), *Contributions from Science Education Research*, Dordrecht: Springer, 289–96.

Naylor, S., Keogh, B. & Goldsworthy, A. (2004). *Active Assessment: Thinking Learning and Assessment in Science*, Oxon: Millgate House Publishers.

Sfard, A. (2000). Steering discourse between metaphor and rigor: Using focal analysis to investigate the emergence of mathematical objects, *Journal for Research in Mathematics Education*, 31(3), 296–327.

White, R. & Gunstone, R. (1992). *Probing Understanding*, New York: The Falmer Press.

6 Teaching science inclusively with a special focus on Indigenous learning

Kate Chealuck and Coral Campbell

This chapter will investigate science learning from the viewpoint of inclusive practices, which acknowledge cultural perspectives and Indigenous science knowledge.

The authors acknowledge that they are not Aboriginal or Torres Strait Islanders but have sought guidance from Indigenous associates to ensure that the representation is factual and truthful with due respect for Indigenous peoples.

OBJECTIVES

At the end of this chapter you will be able to:

- discuss the principles of inclusive teaching in relation to science learning

- describe ways in which educators can be more inclusive in their teaching, specifically with respect to science

- describe Indigenous learning in sciences, particularly in an early childhood context

- outline the relationship between Indigenous learning and inclusive practices.

Inclusive practice

The Melbourne Declaration on Educational Goals for Young Australians (MCEETYA, 2008, p. 7) indicates that all students must have access to high quality schooling that is free from discrimination based on gender, language, sexual orientation, pregnancy, culture, ethnicity, religion, health or disability, socioeconomic background or geographic location.

Social justice and equity are important elements of early childhood education, where there is an emphasis on including all children in educational settings. Accordingly, this emphasis has been instrumental in changing both policy and practice to meet the needs of a diverse range of learners. In particular, people who were often discriminated against and segregated in the past on the grounds of their religion, race, ethnicity, sexuality, disability or gender are a central focus of this educational reform.

Australia is a diverse country. There are over 400 languages spoken and 16 per cent of the population has English as a second language (ABS, 2010). Approximately eight per cent of children have a disability. Differences in socioeconomic status, family structure, living conditions, health and the outer limits of 'normal' appearance are additional factors that add to this diversity. This highlights that children in early childhood settings have a range of different backgrounds and different life experiences.

A core value of early childhood centres is the care of all children in their centres, but with particular emphasis on the child as an individual. Being focused on individual needs and stages of development of young children, rather than age-related development, provides many opportunities for inclusivity. In recognising that families and educators have different backgrounds and expectations, there is a need for all groups to work at the negotiation and creation of collaborative relationships to promote practice which is of benefit to young children.

Within a centre or a school, **inclusive practices** require a committed approach by all staff members with the development of policies and the adoption of common practices. Staff should have positive attitudes to children with **diverse needs** along with a shared understanding of the best way to deal with the learning needs of these children.

> **Inclusive practices** – education practices in which all children are supported to be involved in all aspects of learning.
>
> **Diverse needs** – various different and possibly multiform requirements.

Inclusive principles have been developed in most state jurisdictions to guide educational provision. The principles (adapted from the Department of Education and Training, Queensland) include, but are not limited to, the requirement to:

- provide high quality education for all students
- respond constructively to the needs of educationally disadvantaged or marginalised students
- view difference as a resource to support learning
- ensure that all school community members feel safe and free from discrimination, bias and harassment
- promote locally negotiated responses to student, family and community needs through effective community engagement processes and cross-agency collaboration
- ensure that inclusive education practices are embedded in all state school policies and initiatives.

The nature of science in society: incorporating inclusive practices

In general, it is acknowledged that science affects society in many different ways, but, equally importantly, society affects the directions of science. Social and cultural issues and the thinking associated with them may be shaped by scientific issues and influences. Infusing early childhood policy and practice with inclusive practices ensures that the voices of children from diverse groups are considered. Representing science in the broadest sense of the nature of science in society and how it relates to the child, the family and the community, enables children from diverse groups to see themselves reflected in the nature of science in society. In particular, the nature of science in early childhood relates to children answering questions of interest to them. As indicated by Worth (2010), 'The content of science for young children is a sophisticated interplay among concepts, scientific reasoning, the nature of science, and doing science.' To illustrate this, the following example is described.

A child asked the educator questions about a specific breed of small parrot found only in the local area. In conversations at home, the child's parents had been discussing the local protest in response to an industry development near the parrots' breeding ground. The child asked why people were getting angry and why the parrot could only live there. The educator was unable to answer all the child's questions, but together they searched on the internet to find answers. The child's interest then started to focus on the birds that were present in the outside environment of the centre. With guidance from the educator, the child observed the birds in the outside space over five days, using pictures of local common birds downloaded from the internet. The child constructed a journal where she drew the birds she saw and recorded how many she saw in a day. She observed the birds' activities, raising questions about certain behaviours. At the end of the week, she had completed her inquiry and had recorded her observations in a journal which she took home. During this time, the child was engaged in her own inquiry into a social – science interest while she observed and documented animal (bird) behaviours.

Societal stereotyping disadvantages science learning for students with diverse needs

The image of science is equated with stereotypical Western masculine characteristics such as domination, objectivity, logic, independence, rationality (Skamp, 2001.) Schinske, Cardenas and Kaliangara (2015), in a review of past research, found that holding certain stereotypes of science and scientists could affect children's interest and persistence in science. When children describe scientists, they tend to mostly draw men in white coats with test tubes in pockets, performing explosive experiments. The men usually have beards and glasses. Although this image of science is slowly changing, there remains a societal expectation that science is a predominantly male field.

The effect of this stereotypical image of science, even among very young children, is that diverse groups can be marginalised from science. Such groups include gifted and talented children, gender groups, sociocultural groups (including migrant and refugee children) and special needs children (those with medical, behavioural, developmental, learning or mental health issues).

Gifted and talented children

One group of children which is often not considered when thinking about inclusivity are the gifted and talented. However, these children need support to ensure that they receive developmentally appropriate programs regardless of social or cultural background. If given specific support, gifted children have the potential to excel in areas such as language, problem-solving, physical or interpersonal skills. These students require support in some of the following ways:

- multi-level and multi-dimensional approaches to address differences in the rate, depth and pace of learning
- individual projects – at their own ability level
- enrichment activities
- enhanced cognitive expectations through higher-order thinking skills.

Aspects of gender

There is significant research around the idea that gendered roles start to develop in young children from birth. In early childhood, young children's attitudes tend to follow that of their parents and their experiences that are also largely governed by their closest relationships with family and friends. The gendered role of parents can develop children's gendered roles. If male children are never expected to help with household tasks such as cooking, but have the opportunity to 'build' things with their father, stereotyping can occur. If children only ever see men in the role of a scientist on television or in videos, then they will accept these as 'normal'. Research by Campbell, Bachmann and Sprung (2006) into young children's prior experience with science activities, has shown that at the start of the kinder year, 66 per cent of 4-year-old boys compared to 51 per cent of 4-year-old girls said they 'do science'. However, by the end of the year at pre-school, the research found that all children believe they 'do science'. The pre-school teacher, who actively worked to engage all children in science, was able to change the opportunities for children to engage in science-related activities. Gendered attitudes to science fluctuate across primary school, with research indicating the girls tend to have a more positive attitude to science, although experiences still varied depending on their external exposure. Essentially, most research into gender has found that children's access to science learning depends on the involvement of the educator and how he or she promotes science to all children in an inclusive way.

Sociocultural groups

Sociocultural groups include those who may be disadvantaged due to their social situation: low economic situation, poverty, lack of education, or those from different cultural backgrounds. Socially disadvantaged children may lack the support at home, and they may have lower expectations or reduced experiences in the broader world. Culturally diverse children

YOUNG CHILDREN DEMONSTRATING RACIAL AND GENDERED BEHAVIOUR

Two educators, Tracey and Miriam, were both challenged by explicitly gendered and racial behaviour (name-calling and bullying based on colour and gender) from young 4–5-year-old children in their early learning centre. They had expectations that young children would not have developed such prejudices; however, they found their expectations to be false. The educators commented that 'issues of race, gender and culture directly impact children's learning' (Freeburn & Giugni, 2008, p. 1).

REFLECTION

Reflect on instances where you have experienced racial or gendered behaviour:

1. Have you observed any gendered behaviour in early childhood centres you have attended? How did the educator deal with them?
2. Were your experiences of learning science at school affected by gender or race?

may exhibit both cultural differences and language differences which might impact on their learning. Educators, however, can be inclusive of sociocultural diversity by offering opportunities for children and parents (communities) to share their experiences and cultural stories with respect and acknowledgement of difference. Being respectful and open to difference can lead to an enriched understanding at pre-school and school. In particular, Harlan and Rivkin (2012) indicate that parental expectations in some cultural groups actually improve the possibility of their child succeeding at science and mathematics. Early childhood educators can harness this expectation when offering experiences to different groups.

Cultural perspective – interpreting a situation through the viewpoint of an individual's or group's characteristics and knowledge.

Increasingly, the importance of teachers being culturally inclusive and acknowledging **cultural perspectives** are being recognised and promoted. Socioculturally inclusive attributes and practices are found throughout the curriculum, policy documents and the Australian Professional Standards for Teachers. Inclusive teachers are able to understand, interact and communicate effectively, and with sensitivity, with people from different backgrounds, and apply their sociocultural competence in practice every day (Perso & Hayward 2015).

Experiences children have in the home (i.e. home culture) also affect the way they consider and interact with science. Children who are exposed to living things in the garden will generally have an appreciation and 'care' for them when compared to children for whom all spiders are perceived as 'scary' and are killed when they appear in their homes.

Adopting critical equity practices in early childhood science

There are a number of practical steps educators can do to present an inclusive 'science within society' image. For example, materials, such as books and videos, can be changed to reflect wider society values of diversity, communication, **divergent thinking**, cooperation and concern. For most of the routines in an early learning centre, where play is a large component of the learning environment, children from diverse backgrounds will learn at their own pace through the experiences involved.

Divergent thinking – thinking that is spontaneous and free-flowing.

Steps to adopting equity in practice include:

- recognise individual difference in all interactions with children – educators attempt to provide children with learning opportunities based on each child's need
- balance interactions between all groups – educators spread their time evenly so that no child feels disadvantaged
- have similar expectations for all groups – the educator's expectations should always be for optimum effort and achievement from every child, regardless of the diverse group to which they belong
- build confidence and self-esteem – the educator values the language and experiences of all children to build their self-assurance.
- challenging the image of science – educators need to challenge the image of science by using examples of science in diverse settings with diverse groups
  - providing role models which include diverse groups – educators should provide images of scientists from all cultures and diverse groups (visiting scientists who are not Caucasian as well as female scientists)
  - challenge non-inclusive assumptions and behaviour – educators need to challenge children's biases (or that of their parents) and model appropriate behaviours
  - provide opportunities for negotiation – educators need to encourage and value every child's input
  - vary teaching strategies – educators use strategies which allow for different learning preferences and participation of all learners
  - improve access of equipment and equitable distribution of resources – educators ensure that all children have equal access. (Campbell, 2012)

Introducing a range of measures to remove or minimise the effects of inequitable practices, enables children to participate equally in all that the centre and the educators offer in science experiences.

MODIFYING OUR APPROACH

When teaching children from diverse backgrounds it is sometimes appropriate to change the teaching approach to more appropriately cater for them. For example, expecting a child from a non-English speaking background to understand instructions immediately is not acknowledging that they may not have the same language understanding or ear for English language intonations as children from an English-speaking background. Strategies which could be adopted include slowing speech down, using simple language and gestures that model the required actions, introducing non-language-based communication tools (icons or drawings) and ensuring that the child fully comprehends what is said.

REFLECTION

Consider what other adaptations may be required for working with children from diverse backgrounds:

1. What could you do when providing science information to a child with short-term auditory problems?
2. How can you adapt an exploratory table for a child in a wheelchair?
3. How can you ensure that your science activity is inclusive of all your cultural groups?

In science, it is always important to start from children's own experience, as it is accepted that a child constructs new knowledge by linking new experiences with old and by building on prior knowledge. This has benefits in terms of inclusivity due to the fact that when starting from children's own experiences the educator is demonstrating that they place a value on that experience. When an educator starts from a child's own experiences and interests it is much easier to motivate the child to develop further explorations and curiosities about the world. Using a constructivist approach and inclusive strategies, such as a child-centred approach, the educator allows children to develop their own understanding, their capacity to learn and enhances their decision-making skills.

Inclusive practices in science also involve the enabling of effective communication through active listening and engagement and through positive reinforcement of effort and achievement. Recent research (Harlan & Rivkin, 2012) has highlighted that discussions with adults or peers can enhance science learning through the development of shared meaning. With diverse groups of students, this approach allows them to participate. A number of mechanisms are identified which can improve communication. These include:

- talking, discussing, brain-storming – allowing children's input into all aspects of discussion (this involves using a non-threatening approach which encourages children to participate, accepting that children might like to just listen sometimes)
- learning the language of science – this empowers children to engage in discussions using the right words and with the same base line

- peer tutoring, cross-age interactions – children learn from each other in less threatening or intimidating situations
- interactive teaching – using children's questions to guide explorations
- effective questioning – asking children questions to focus their thinking, enhance their thought processes and to provide the educator with additional information about the learners' understandings
- offering other means of communication such as drawing to support children's attempts at verbal communication.

Using these approaches, the educator is valuing the child's own language and making attempts to include children using their own language or representations which are understandable to a non-English speaker.

Applying generalised practices in science activities and explorations

Science is considered important for all children as it is an approach to thinking and behaving which incorporates aspects of motor, behavioural, sensory, communication and mental functioning (Harlan & Rivkin, 2012). Through a collaborative approach, children's opportunities for personal interactions are enhanced. Children from diverse backgrounds can contribute to the opportunities involved in exploration and investigations. Working at their own level, children come into an activity from a point of their own understanding, they develop further through participation in the activity, and exit the learning experience with knowledge that relates to their needs.

At a practical level, there are many simple strategies educators can use to make the materials and environment more accessible to children so that all can contribute:

- placing material on a table for a child in a wheelchair
- using tongs for children with limited fine motor control
- forewarning students of things to come – effectively repeating some introductory instructions (those with limited language skills can hear/see the information clearly and can be more prepared to engage)
- using visual material for children with limited aural or language skills
- ensuring that the educator is in the line of sight of a child with limited hearing, modelling the task for children to observe before doing
- using a ramped task (one of less or more complexity) or scaffolding for a difficult activity/exploration.

The key to working with children from diverse backgrounds is variation and complexity – keeping instructions, materials or tasks more varied and with increasing complexity so that all can participate.

Practices which are more inclusive in science usually tap into children's individual experiences embracing a broad range of 'ways of doing' things. These can lead to a more comprehensive and creative approach to science explorations that use:

- communication media – photography, videos, newspapers, magazines, computers (many young children are adept at using digital technologies and these can be used in an early childhood setting to enhance the science learning through online research or digital recording of an exploration; videos and photographs of items, events or places can stimulate a child's curiosity to try to learn more about a particular subject)

- games – games can often provide a different way of looking at something (i.e. a simple categorising game can help children group animals according to visible characteristics)

- cartoons and humour – young children enjoy humour and a cartoon can represent a science idea in a visual manner, allowing children to understand the basic concept

- role plays, acting and drama – ideas can be reinforced through role play, acting or children creating their own drama around their understandings (one which has been used with very young children is the acting out of the planting and growth of a seed, with the main characters being the farmer, the seed, the Sun and the rain; most children love to participate and are happy to take their turn as one of the characters)

- creative drawing, design, construction – there is a level of cognitive involvement in creative drawing and construction (a child involved in these activities can often convey quite complex ideas through other representations)

- creative writing, storytelling – storytelling or creative writing can provide a child with opportunity to 'tell their story' in ways that they can understand (in particular, valuing a child's prior experience through encouraging storytelling is an inclusive practice and links with Indigenous cultural practices discussed later).

Within the context of a child's world, science is demonstrated as a human activity. It is accepted that all children are capable and interested in exploring and understanding their world. Educators can achieve this connection to the child's world through:

- valuing inquiry-based learning – using children's own questions to guide their own investigations

- looking at historical perspectives – talking about how people managed in the past, how science exploration has impacted on human life

- visits and visitors show that science is 'outside' the pre-school centre and is valued by others

- awareness of science in a broader context – using local news items to highlight the science in the wider world

- values – particularly relevant with environmental issues and children developing their own values about the place of science within the debate on solving world problems

- social implications of science and technology – discussion on how science has helped or hindered personal lives.

In helping children to develop a range of practical skills, educators can enhance the skills of those children who haven't had the opportunity to learn them at home.

- These skills could include:
- helping to solve problems in a practical way with hands-on explorations

- providing a tinkering table so that children can pull things apart and (maybe) put them together again

- demystifying the use of modern technologies by allowing children access to a range of technologies available in the early years.

Cultural understandings: the importance of Indigenous knowledge

Indigenous knowledge is a term which refers to the systems of understanding generated at the level of community. It is used by Indigenous people in settings as the basis for local level decision-making, but can extend much further than local boundaries. Semali and Kincheloe (2011, p. 3) comment that Indigenous knowledge arises when residents of an area 'come to understand themselves in relation to their natural environment'. Indigenous knowledge arises through Aboriginal people's relationality and connection with land and relates to their ways of knowing, ways of doing and ways of being. Embedded in culture, it is significantly different to the modern understanding of science knowledge. It should also be understood that there is no single 'Indigenous knowledge system' – no 'one size fits all' (Rigney, 2010). Diversity exists within the broader Indigenous communities where Indigenous languages are different and knowledge systems are generated across different regions. A knowledge system is a cluster of understandings related to content, components or types of knowledge that are defined by the user who assigns value to it. It can evolve and adapt and is subject to variations of the user. In relation to appropriate educational approaches, educators should seek out local Indigenous elders to gain understanding of the local knowledge system.

> **Indigenous knowledge –** systems of understanding generated at the level of community, embedded in culture and related to ways of knowing, ways of doing and ways of being.

Aboriginal and Torres Strait Islander culture

Aboriginal identity is about relationships, connections and obligations to people ('kinship') and/or place (Country). Perso and Hayward (2015) state that 'Aboriginal and Torres Strait Islander identity is about ancestry and "country" of origin; about seeing oneself as Aboriginal. It is not about skin colour, DNA or bloodlines' (p. 7).

Relationships are extremely important in Aboriginal and Torres Strait Islander cultures so it is essential that educators build strong relationships with children and their families. This can be achieved by showing interest in knowing them, knowing about them and their extended family, meeting the families and caregivers. It is most important to allow time for children to trust and respect the educator (Perso & Hayward 2015, p. 32).

Indigenous science

Indigenous science knowledge is the oldest system of knowledge in the world, spanning at least 50 000 years. It has been refined through multiple exposures and interpretations, based on multiple experiences. It is a system of science knowledge which is intertwined with Indigenous belief systems and ways of knowing.

> **Indigenous science knowledge –** based on close observation, experiences and interpretation of the natural world.

Indigenous science understandings relate to knowledge arising from a focus on land, knowledge of the environment, weather, circular time (where time exists in a circular pattern and the individual is in the centre of time-circles), traditional tools and their development and purposes. These science understandings are based on close observation, experiences and interpretations of events which have been passed down through generations and are focused on specialised understandings of the world: Earth, space, living things, environments and weather, and patterns.

In more recent times, researchers have tried to elaborate the differences and similarities between science derived through Indigenous environments and those developed in the Western world. Baker, Rayner and Wolowic (2011) comment that Indigenous science has evolved through human experience with the natural world and is characterised by:

- knowledge of the metaphysical (spiritual) world
- a view of nature as interconnected and interdependent (note – modern Western science, such as ecology, is coming into agreement with this view)
- rooted in local places and community needs
- derived through direct interaction with the natural world
- assumed responsibility for maintaining harmonious relationships among people, nature, all life, and the spiritual realm.

Western science is:

- discipline-based (e.g. biology, chemistry, physics)
- limited to knowledge of the physical world
- focused on the search for knowledge that is universally valid as a fundamental goal
- based on knowledge frequently obtained through *in situ* experiments that limit the complexity of natural environments by controlling variables and placing phenomena of interest into controlled environments (field studies, using observational methods in most biological environments)
- concentrated on the ideal of value-free research for the objective and unbiased search for knowledge which it holds in high regard.

While Western science studies the individual parts of the natural world to try to understand it, Indigenous science understanding is developed in a more holistic way by observing the connection across the parts (The Living Knowledge Project, 2008). This juxtapositioning of the two science knowledge systems allows cross-overs and natural links to be made.

Early childhood science is similar to the way in which Indigenous science knowledge arose. Both incorporate a need or want for the understanding of the surrounding world, experiencing of scientific phenomena, undertaking inquiries and developing everyday science understandings based on experiences. In particular, Indigenous science knowledge relates strongly to the practices of inquiry science as children observe, interpret and apply their observation to other situations.

Social protocols

Within the classroom, cultural differences have implications that are important for teaching science. Differences in children's language and behaviour may result in unintended interpretations of misbehaviour or disrespect. Aboriginal and Torres Strait Islander children might avoid eye contact, which may be interpreted as rudeness or disinterest. They may be reluctant to engage in debate or arguments and may sit silent in the face of questioning, which could be interpreted as not knowing the answer, or rudeness. Instead, consider that these behaviours may be signs of respect or politeness, or a means to avoid giving offence – it might be culturally inappropriate to challenge or question a teacher or elder person (Alberta Education, 2005).

Cultural differences in social protocols and how language is used may also be about respect and politeness. According to the Government of Western Australia (2012), this may include:

- who has the right to talk and when
- the types of topics that can be discussed
- the types of questions that can be asked and answered
- the time taken to respond
- the type of response given
- the use of body language.

An educator with the knowledge of social protocols will be able to develop respectful working relationships with Aboriginal children, their families and communities to work together towards enhancing children's learning.

WORKING WITH ABORIGINAL AND TORRES STRAIT ISLANDER PRE-SERVICE TEACHERS

While questioning in science education classes is common to determine prior understandings and challenge non-scientific ideas, it came as a shock that it was unintentionally causing anger and distress to some Aboriginal and Torres Strait Islander students in my class. In discussing this further with them, I realised that singling out or individually asking students to answer questions they may not know the answer to had resulted in them feeling 'shame' – a high form of embarrassment that could damage teacher–student relationships and impact on learning.

Shame in Aboriginal culture is debilitating and connected to avoidance. Shame influences self-confidence and self-esteem and can dominate how many Aboriginal children think, talk and behave in the classroom (Basaraba, 2017).

Considering that it is imperative to teacher–student relationships that everything is done to avoid shaming someone else:

1. What could you do, in this case, to help students 'save face' or diffuse any embarrassment experienced so that the student can regain their composure quickly?
2. What could you do to keep your relationship with the students intact?
3. How else might you ascertain the understandings of Indigenous students?

REFLECTION

Aboriginal and Torres Strait Islander pedagogy

Aboriginal children bring different knowledge to the early childhood centre or classroom. It is important to share that knowledge with other children, which adds value to their knowledge (Perso & Hayward, 2015). Inviting local elders to share their traditional scientific knowledges can help bridge the cultural gaps between what may be interpreted as the two distinct and separate knowledge systems of Western science and Indigenous science knowledge.

Science education lends itself to the learning needs and pedagogies of different people. The importance of observation, discovery and exploration is emphasised in both Western science and Indigenous knowledge systems. Inquiry and discovery learning enables a balance between teacher direction and children's autonomy that is also important to Aboriginal cultures. Collaborative work enables and enhances relationships with others, and representations and visual symbols draw on forms of non-verbal communication that follow cultural protocols.

One example of an Aboriginal pedagogy framework that can be utilised in science education is Yunkaporta's (2007–2009) *8Ways: Aboriginal Ways of Learning and Pedagogy*. This recommends using Aboriginal processes and protocols rather than Aboriginal content to enable a culturally inclusive classroom environment. The framework allows teachers to remain focused on curriculum content while integrating Aboriginal perspectives and practices into everyday teaching. Yunkaporta states that the framework was intended to be a 'culturally safe point of entry for teachers to begin engaging with Aboriginal knowledge and cross-cultural dialogue in the community' (2007–2009, p. 8). These protocols can enhance learning for all children.

The framework, as shown in Figure 6.1, interconnects eight pedagogies that link to cultural protocols, including narrative storytelling, visual learning, hands-on practices, the use of symbols and metaphors, land-based learning, modelling and connecting to community.

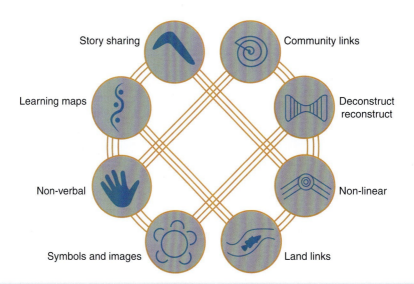

FIGURE 6.1 *8Ways* Aboriginal pedagogy framework

Source: Yunkaporta, 2007–2009, p. 10.

USING THE *8WAYS* FRAMEWORK

Yunkaporta (2007–2009) used the *8Ways* Aboriginal pedagogy framework to develop learning experiences for children about space and the universe. The *8Ways* were utilised in the following programs of learning:

1. A learning map was created with children to describe the topic and the intended learning outcomes. This was visualised and discussed with the children along with how they might share what they learn with their families and communities at the end of the program.

2. Stories were shared about experiences with and understandings of the topic – the educator shared family stories of watching the stars and recognising the constellations with her father, and listening to her mother recount the Moon landing from 1969. Children shared their stories in pairs and small groups, verbalising to the whole group only if they wished. A traditional custodian of the land, from the local cooperative, was invited to the class to share cultural stories about the universe and make more explicit cultural links.

3. Hands-on activities were provided for children to interact with independently and in groups. Some of these activities were first modelled for children, promoting the Aboriginal protocol of 'watch first, then do' (deconstruct/reconstruct). There were opportunities in activities for non-verbal learning and reflection, as well as verbal. Activities contained many representations and visual symbols of space artefacts and objects. Children could repeat activities if they were interested, encouraging the non-linear process of repetition and returning to concepts. Children also went outside to connect to their local environment (land links) to investigate the Moon and the Sun.

4. Children were encouraged to create their own visual images and symbols to communicate their understandings and represent their learning in a variety of ways, such as drawing, painting and making models.

5. Children were encouraged to 'try it a new way' (non-linear) and apply their understandings to new situations, such as tracking and tracing shadows to show the movement of the Sun. They were encouraged to connect with home and go outside to look up at the sky at night.

Consider the *8Ways* framework provided in Case study 6.4:

1. Would you feel comfortable incorporating the *8Ways* into your practice? Why or why not?
2. How many of these processes (e.g. story sharing) do you already incorporate in your teaching?
3. How might you utilise these processes in planning learning experiences?

REFLECTION

Bush kinders

Bush kinders provide opportunities for children to foster connections to land and culture and use nature to make cultural links to both Western science concepts as well as Indigenous science knowledge. Inviting local community involvement from traditional custodians or family members can also help build these links through oral stories, and using nature to build tools and traditional artefacts. Bush kinders can be highly culturally inclusive and can cater to culturally inclusive learning needs (Perso & Hayward, 2015): incorporating observation and imitation, personal trial and error, real life experiences, context-specific skill building, relationship building, spontaneous learning, and collaborative problem-solving, as well as the *8Ways* pedagogy discussed earlier. Bush kinders also facilitate cultural protocols such as 'study nature but do no harm', make links to totems and build a sense of belonging and respect for the environment. See Chapter 12 for further information about bush kinders.

COOLART BUSH KINDER

This bush kinder commenced in 2010 and exists as a partnership between Somers Pre-school and Parks Victoria. A particular feature of this bush kinder approach is the inclusion of the local Boon Wurrung people whereby a traditional custodian accompanies the children, introducing them to Aboriginal culture, plants and animals, singing, dancing, using tools and enacting stories.

The educator commented that the bush kinder approach had been particularly worthwhile for one boy on the autism spectrum. 'Our relaxed program of tree climbing, running and building with natural materials allowed him to show his strengths and skills, both on his own and with his friends' (Julie Georgiou, educator).

REFLECTION

Consider Case study 6.5 and the following questions:
1. How does the inclusion of a traditional custodian assist in developing the children's respect for inclusivity?
2. How could the educator build on this practice back at the centre?

Principles of inclusivity

Various principles of inclusive practice in working with Aboriginal and Torres Strait Islander peoples/children have been identified:

- respecting and recognising difference as important
- collaborative practice with children, parents and other teachers
- developing relationships with children, family and community members
- working with children's strengths
- consideration for individual difference.

When considering inclusive teaching practices with Aboriginal and Torres Strait Islander children, educators are also considering individual difference and building values related to equity and social justice.

A close look at these principles will allow the educator to see that these are widely applicable. They are not only principles to consider when teaching children with diverse needs, but they also strongly resonate with the general practices surrounding early childhood science learning.

Conclusion

This chapter has provided insight in relation to inclusive teaching practices in early childhood science education. Inclusive pedagogies were discussed and illustrated through case studies and stories of appropriate teaching and learning. Science education in early childhood centres has the ability to bridge the diversity gap and allow science learning to occur from the child's own perspective and strength, celebrating the diverse learning needs of the young children in their care. The chapter concluded with some practical examples of ways in which educators can adapt their practice to have an inclusive cultural focus when working with Australian Aboriginal and Torres Strait Islander children and their families.

Acknowledgement of country

The authors acknowledge and pay respect to the traditional custodians of this land. We pay our respects to elders past, present and emerging, for they hold the memories, the traditions, the culture and hopes of Aboriginal and Torres Strait Islander peoples across the nation.

Alberta Education. (2005). *Our Words, Our Ways: Teaching First Nations, Metis and Inuit Learners*, Edmonton: Canada, Alberta Education Aboriginal Services Branch, education.alberta.ca/media/563982/our-words-our-ways.pdf, accessed 19 April 2017.

Australian Bureau of Statistics. (ABS). (2010). *Yearbook Chapter, 2009–10: Characteristics of the Population*, cat. no. 1301.0, www.abs.gov.au/AUSSTATS/abs@.nsf/Lookup/1301.0Feature+Article 7012009–10, accessed 8 January 2018.

Baker, J., Rayner., A. & Wolowic, J. (2011). *A Primer for Science Teachers*, Native Science, ctabobandung.files.wordpress.com/2011/11/ns-primer.pdf, accessed 1 May 2017.

Basaraba, D. (2017). Written communication on cultural protocols, 2 June 2017.

Campbell, C. (2012) Catering for children's differing needs in early childhood science education. In Campbell, C. & Jobling, W. (eds) *Science in Early Childhood*. Melbourne: Cambridge University Press, 131–47.

Campbell, P., Bachmann, K. & Sprung, B. (2006). Children and Fun Science: The impact of playtime is science on young children – Executive summary of Research Report for Academy for Educational Development.

Department of Education and Training, Queensland, *Inclusive Education Policy Statement*, Queensland Government, education.qld.gov.au/schools/inclusive, accessed 30 June 2017.

Freeburn, T. & Giugni, M. (2008) 'Girls can't be Batman!': Gender, Aboriginality and multiculturalism in early childhood education, *Every Child*, 14(1), 32–3.

Georgiou, G. (2016). Coolart bush kinder and its kids continue to thrive, Parks Victoria, parkweb.vic.gov.au/about-us/news/coolart-bush-kinder-and-its-kids-continue-to-thrive.

Government of Western Australia. (2012). *Tracks to Two-Way Learning: Focus Area 9*, Department of Education and Department of Training and Workforce Development, Government of Western Australia, tle.westone.wa.gov.au/content/file/f161442e-265e-4ff7-aee5-ed805d10c81d/1/tracks.zip/content/docs/Focus_Area_9.pdf, accessed 19 April 2017.

Harlan, J. & Rivkin, M. (2012). *Science Experiences for the Early Childhood Years: An Integrated Affective Approach*, New Jersey: Pearson.

The Living Knowledge Project. (2008). Incorporating Indigenous knowledge into your teaching, livingknowledge.anu.edu.au/html/educators /index, accessed 19 April 2017.

Ministerial Council on Education, Employment, Trading and Youth Affairs (MCEETYA). (2008). *Melbourne Declaration for Educational Goals for Young Australians*, www.curriculum.edu.au/verve/_resources/national_declaration_on_the_educational_goals_for_young_australians.pdf.

Perso, T. & Hayward, C. (2015). *Teaching Indigenous Students: Cultural Awareness and Classroom Strategies for Improving Outcomes*, Sydney: Allen & Unwin.

Rigney, L-I. (2010). Indigenous education: The challenge of change, *Every Child*, 16(4), www.earlychildhoodaustralia.org.au/our-publications/every-child-magazine/every-child-index/every-child-vol-16-4-2010/indigenous-education-challenge-change-free-article.

Schinske, J., Cardenas, M. & Kaliangara, J. (2015). Uncovering scientist stereotypes and their relationships with student race and student success in a diverse, community college setting, *Life Science Education*, 14(3), www.ncbi.nlm.nih.gov/pmc/articles/pmc4710393.

Semali, L. & Kincheloe, J. (eds) (2011). *What is Indigenous Knowledge? Voices from the academy*, New York: Routledge.

Skamp, K. (ed.) (2001) *Teaching Primary Science Constructively*, South Melbourne: Cengage.

Worth, K. (2010). Science in early childhood classrooms: Content and process. *STEM in Early Childhood (Seed) Collected papers*. Early Childhood Research and Practice: Beyond this issue (online).

Yunkaporta, T. (2007–2009). Draft Report for DET on Indigenous Research Project conducted by Tyson Yunkaporta, Aboriginal Education Consultant, in Western NSW Region Schools, 2007–2009: Aboriginal Pedagogies at the Cultural Interface, 8ways.wikispaces.com/file/view/draft+reprot.doc, accessed 1 May 2017.

7 Using play pedagogy in early years science education

Jane Johnston and Coral Campbell

Play is an important developmental tool, rather than just an informal aspect of childhood. While children's actions are purposeful activities that help them make sense of their world (Ebbeck & Waniganayake, 2010), they are often misconstrued as messing about without purpose. This chapter addresses the theoretical aspects of play and describes how play supports child development. It discusses play in both the pre-school and school setting and play pedagogies to support science education.

OBJECTIVES

At the end of this chapter you will be able to:

- describe the importance of play in young children's understanding of science concepts

- describe different play pedagogies that support the development of scientific understanding in young children

- outline the role of the teacher in supporting play pedagogies in science education.

The importance of play

The importance of **play** is assured through the work of many theorists. Froebel (1826) felt that 'play is the purest, most spiritual activity of man' (p. 3). He put his ideas about play into practice by creating the first schools for pre-school children, which he called 'kindergarten' (children's garden). These kindergartens stressed the natural growth of children through action or play, with the emphasis on pedagogies that encouraged and guided. Froebel also developed a range of practical resources to support children's play, which he called 'gifts', and educational activities, which he called 'occupations'. Many of the practical educational resources used today originated or were developed from Froebel's ideas.

> **Play** – anything (activity) which is fun, and is instigated by the child.

Rousseau (1911), in his work *Emile*, believed that children should be allowed to develop through play free from the restrictions imposed by society, and that early pedagogies should provide a balance between individual freedom and happiness and control from society. Most importantly, Rousseau stressed the importance of personalised learning, emphasising that adults and the context should accommodate the individual child rather than the child be expected to change to suit the adult or context. **Child-centred learning** and **experiential learning**, central to both play and scientific development, are legacies of Rousseau's theories.

> **Child-centred learning** – approach which encourages children to take responsibility about what they will learn and explore.
>
> **Experiential learning** – learning through 'doing' and thinking about (reflecting) on the experiences.

Piaget looked at the development of play in children and identified four different types (Dockett & Fleer, 2002; Piaget, 1976): **functional play** involving the repeated use of objects or actions, **constructive play** involving the manipulation of objects to build or construct something, pretend or **symbolic play** where imaginary situations replace real ones, and **rule-governed play** that is used in games. In all play, Piaget regarded children as having an active physical and mental role (Dockett & Fleer, 2002).

> **Functional play** – involves the repeated use of objects or actions.
>
> **Constructive play** – involves the manipulation of objects to build or construct something.
>
> **Symbolic play** – imaginary situations replace real ones.
>
> **Rule-governed play** – play that is used in games.

Vygotsky (1962) emphasised the importance of language in learning and the social situation in which both language and learning occur. Vygotsky's social constructivist theories stated that learning is enhanced by social interaction and that social learning leads to cognitive development (Vygotsky & Cole, 1978). He postulated that learning is accelerated through interactions with more capable 'others' and that scaffolded instruction is an effective way to enhance children's learning. Vygotsky believed that symbolic play in young children promoted cognitive, emotional and social development (Ebbeck & Waniganayake, 2010).

The work of these theorists is relevant today for early years science education as they link to many of the main principles of effective science learning and teaching with young children. These principles include:

- child-centred and tailored to meet individual needs
- practical and exploratory, so that children develop skills
- motivating, so that children develop important scientific attitudes
- creative and challenging, so that children develop conceptual understanding

Play pedagogies – strategies which promote learning through play; a systematic approach to the practice of learning and teaching through children's play.

- relevant, so that children can make links between science and everyday life and play with purpose
- social, so that children develop socially and linguistically.

Throughout this chapter, we consider how these principles can be incorporated into **play pedagogies** so that young children develop in an holistic way, supported by knowledgeable professionals and in an exciting context so that scientific development equates with fun.

Types of play and how they support child development

Scientific development involves children developing specific and general understandings, process and social skills, attitudes, language and vocabulary. As such, the development of science understandings in very young children is very similar to the overall holistic development of children. This section discusses how play supports scientific development in an holistic way.

The distinction between work and play is difficult to define in the early years. Children consider any 'work' that is fun to be 'play', while adults may not value 'play' (Moylett, 2010) as contributing to children's development. There is also a misapprehension among some adults that structured, teacher-led activities are play activities (CLS, 2013), or that we can direct or control play (Russell, 2010). There are many types of play, with Table 7.1

FIGURE 7.1   2-year-old Nate with a puppet, demonstrating imaginative play

TABLE 7.1 TYPES OF PLAY AND HOW THEY SUPPORT CHILDREN'S DEVELOPMENT

Type of play	Definition	How play supports children's development
Solitary play	Characteristic of early childhood, where the child plays alone.	Social development (independence). Emotional development (perseverance).
Parallel play	Children play alongside others and may imitate behaviours. Often develops from solitary play.	Skills development (through imitation). Social awareness.
Cooperative and collaborative play	In cooperative play children play and cooperate with others as they play. In collaborative play, the children have common aims and work together to achieve these. Cooperative and collaborative play in middle childhood is seen once children are socially aware.	Social development (cooperation, collaboration). Emotional development (tolerance, respect for others' ideas). Cognitive development (language development, sharing of knowledge).
Epistemic play	Children bring existing knowledge to their play.	Cognitive development (knowledge and understanding, language development).
Symbolic play	Children use objects in their play in ways that they were not designed for.	Creative development (use of imagination). Cognitive development (developing knowledge).
Imaginative play	Children use their imagination in their play, creating imaginary scenarios or using objects in creative imaginary ways. Imaginative play can lead to ludic play.	Creative development (use of imagination), Social and emotional development (as children re-enact scenarios). Cognitive development (knowledge and understanding, language).
Ludic (fantasy) play	Children imagine that they are others, such as fantasy characters or animals	Creative development (use of imagination). Social and emotional development (when playing with others). Cognitive development (knowledge and understanding, language).
Socio-dramatic role play	Children re-enact stories.	Creative development (use of imagination). Social and emotional development (when playing with others). Cognitive development (knowledge and understanding, language).
Exploratory play	Children explore objects and phenomena in their play, bringing existing ideas to their play and developing new ideas.	Cognitive development (knowledge and understanding, language). Skill development (observation, prediction, hypothesis, interpretation).

describing some of these. As shown in Table 7.1, play is more than one type of activity and each type of play can support children's holistic development.

Free play occurs when the play, or part of the play, is child-initiated, with the child selecting the resources and deciding what to do. For example, when a child takes a paint brush and bucket of water and decides to 'paint' the outdoor shed, she is exploring the evaporation of water in completely self-initiated play. Most forms of play involve the teacher in some way, as described below, so that free play may be an element of the play rather than the total play.

Solitary play (Johnston & Nahmad-Williams, 2010) is characteristic of early childhood play, before children learn to play with others. It involves children playing alone without social contact, and can help children to begin to be independent and to persevere at tasks they may find difficult. Young children may spend long periods of time in the garden, sorting stones or making piles of stones, or moving them from one place to another. They may observe a moving toy and try to figure out how it works (Johnston, 2009). In this way, they make sense of the world around them and scientific phenomena that they encounter (Johnston 2014). It is important that practitioners allow children to play alone and not intervene or interact unless necessary, as this is a characteristic of creative practice (CLS, 2012).

Solitary play – the child plays alone.

Parallel play (Johnston & Nahmad-Williams, 2010) can lead from solitary play, and involves children playing alongside each other, with little or no social interaction. Sometimes children watch other children and imitate their play. As an example, two 3-year-old boys are playing in a sandpit. One, James, begins to use a spade to put sand into a sand wheel, making the wheel turn. The second boy, Freddie, watches for a while and then uses a bucket to pour sand into another sand wheel in the pit. After a while, Freddie takes a full bucket of sand over to James and pours sand into his sand wheel. James smiles and then takes another bucket and pours sand in, finding that this is easier than using a spade. In this parallel play the children are beginning to make causal links even if they cannot verbalise what they are thinking (CLS, 2012). The two boys then move away from parallel play towards a third kind of play, social or cooperative play.

Parallel play – children play alongside each other, but may not interact with each other in the play.

Cooperative play (Johnston & Nahmad-Williams, 2010) involves more sophisticated social development and is characteristic of middle and later childhood. Collaborative play is an extended form of more developed cooperative play, demanding enhanced social interaction. It involves children working towards a mutual aim. The more developed social play, involving cooperation and collaboration, can help children to develop understanding of rules (both social and within games) and the skill of negotiation (Johnston & Nahmad-Williams, 2010), understanding of the different scientific ideas held by others, as well as a sense of responsibility. Johnston (2011) found that cooperative play helps to develop the skill of observation through peer dialogue as well as interaction (see also Rogoff, 1995 and Robbins, 2005), and it plays a part in creative approaches (CLS, 2013).

Cooperative play – children play together with common aims.

Other types of play can lead to conceptual development, although that is not to say that social play cannot aid conceptual development. **Epistemic play** (Johnston & Nahmad-Williams, 2010) involves children using their existing knowledge in their play, and can support the development of knowledge and understanding along with language development (Johnston, 2011). The following case study highlights how different types of play can occur simultaneously, and each type contributes to children's development.

Epistemic play – children bring prior knowledge into their play.

THE PET SHOP

When 4-year-old children were playing in the 'pet shop' they had created in their classroom, they were using knowledge about caring for animals in their play: what animals eat, what care they need, and how long they live. In the role play, Meera sold a rabbit to a customer, explaining that it needed a hutch, a run, straw, food bowl and water bottle. She explained that the hutch needed to be cleaned out every day so that the rabbit had fresh bedding. Bobbie bought a dog from the shop. She explained that it was a sheep dog and that she was buying it for her farm to help round up the sheep. She then took the dog to her imaginary farm and, covering herself with a sheep rug, she 'became a sheep', while Joe chased her around the 'farm'. In this way the epistemic play became imaginative play (Johnston & Nahmad-Williams, 2010), imagining the farm, animals and events, and then **ludic play** (Piaget, 1976) or fantasy role play as Bobbie and Joe 'became' the sheep and the dog in their role play. Later, in the play, a large cardboard box became a dog kennel and then changed to become a trailer to carry the sheep to another part of the farm where the grass was better for the sheep to eat; typical of symbolic play (Piaget, 1976), whereby children substitute one object for another, pretending and imagining. Fran got the book *The Snow Lambs* (Gliori, 1995) and the three children (Bobbie, Joe and Fran) read the book and then decided to re-enact the story, each taking a role in the play (and swapping when they wanted to).

> **Ludic play** – children imagine that they are someone else.

When considering Case study 7.1, discuss the following:

1. How did the **socio-dramatic play** involve the children in exploring and sharing ideas about farming and the animals, interacting with each other and identifying how the characters felt at different stages of the story?
2. Can you identify what knowledge and skills were developed through this role-play activity?

Exploratory play (Johnston, 2005; 2014) is the type of play most often associated with scientific development, as it involves children using their senses to explore the world around them and supports cognitive development. Very young children do not necessarily exhibit exploratory play; sometimes their play does not lead to further exploration (Johnston, 2005). Further, some educators do not always appear to know how to support and encourage exploratory play (CLS, 2013). However, from about 6 years of age, exploratory play can lead to systematic investigations. In exploratory play, children are able to observe scientific phenomena and this can lead to exploration in which they discover aspects of the world around them and develop cognitively, socially, emotionally and physically. The *Creative Little Scientist Project* (CLS, 2012) identified in a comprehensive review of literature that inquiry-based science education (IBSE) and creative approaches (CA) had a number of synergies, one of which was play and exploration and that 'playful experimentation/exploration is inherent in all young children's activity, such exploration is at the core of IBSE and CA in the early years' (CLS, 2012, p. 46).

> **Socio-dramatic play** – re-enactment of a story.
>
> **Exploratory play** – children explore their surroundings and phenomena through their play.

Practical task

SEEING THE SCIENCE IN EVERYDAY ACTIVITIES

Consider the table below, which highlights some common play activities in pre-school. Complete the table.

Play activity	Science skills	Science knowledge and understandings	Science attitudes
Sand pit			
Construction area			
Water play			
Garden area			

Case Study 7.2

PLAY VERSUS SCAFFOLDING

Research by Backshall (2016) found that most children's play included science learning through participation in a range of play activities. Through documenting and measuring the incidence of the activities, she was able to draw conclusions relating to science learning and the educator participation.

Science area	Percentage of children's play	Percentage of educator's scaffolding
Physics (physical world)	45–66 %	25 %
Material world (chemistry)	9–17 %	10 %
Living world	14–32 %	60 %
Earth and beyond	3–14 %	5 %

REFLECTION

Consider the example in Case study 7.2 and comment on the implications of this for an educator's practice:

1. What might be the reasons for the observed differences in science play and scaffolding?
2. What can an educator do to enhance a more balanced approach?

Structured play in the early years curriculum

Most play in the pre-school and early school years curriculum is structured play (Johnston, 2014), where the educator is involved in the provision of time, space and a range of resources to support children's learning. The amount of educator involvement determines the amount of structure. Examples of how educators have developed different amounts of structured play are presented below:

1. Resources are selected by the educator and children are able to use them in their play and make decisions about the play in which they wish to engage. The resources help to structure the play and the scientific development. For example, if the materials include water and a collection of objects with which to collect and measure water, children will be more likely to explore 'volume' in their play.

2. Task-specific resources are selected by the educator. For example, children might be given some magnets and a collection of objects and asked to find out which magnet is the strongest. They can then be left to play with the magnets, with a specific purpose in mind. The children can choose to use the resources in any way they wish to solve the problem.

3. In educator-led activities, the educator works alongside the children to achieve a specific outcome. Here, the educator provides the materials, sets the task and explores with the children, modelling behaviours and suggesting ideas for new avenues of inquiry.

As demonstrated by these examples, structured play can provide opportunities for children to make decisions for themselves. Educators make professional decisions about how much structure is required, and how much support and guidance to provide the children.

Case Study 7.3

POST OFFICE

A post office had been set up in the classroom to support mathematical, language, social, scientific and technological development. The 5-year-old children were allowed to play in the post office at specified times and after other work had been completed. Six children were allowed to play in the post office at any one time. Hussein was wrapping parcels to send abroad, and he found that the paper he chose tore as he was wrapping the parcel. He explored the other paper in the post office and realised that the parcel needed to be wrapped in something thicker to protect it. He decided to find some card so he could make a box to protect the parcel but, at this point, the teacher announced that the children needed to move on to another structured activity.

Hussein's play at the post office allowed him to explore the different properties of materials, in this case the strength of different paper. In realising that the parcel needed to be wrapped in something thicker, he started to explore the use of card and the appropriateness of a box in order to protect the parcel. Through this structured experience, even though it was cut short, Hussein had started to develop his ideas about materials and their observable properties.

REFLECTION

When considering Case study 7.3, think of the following questions:

1. What science was Hussein learning in his play?
2. How would Hussein's scientific development be curtailed/enhanced by proscribing/ allowing the time spent in the play area?
3. What advantages/disadvantages are there to structured play?
4. How could you overcome the disadvantages of structured play and build upon the advantages?
5. How else could you support scientific development in post office role play?
6. How does Hussein meet the Foundation curriculum targets of the Australian Curriculum in relation to chemical sciences?

Some educators set up learning centres where children can move freely from one play area to another and decide how long they wish to spend at each activity. Educators may also set up the classroom so that children can freely move from indoor to outdoor play. In order for this to be effective, children and adults need to agree on shared rules, such as the maximum number of children at each activity, what resources are available/unavailable, as well as basic rules of health and safety in play. However, the rules should not adversely affect the quality of the play.

Post office role play, as in Case study 7.3, may begin indoors and then move outside for parcels and letters to be loaded on a tricycle and 'delivered' to addresses. The children can be encouraged to draw a map of their route, discuss the different terrain (muddy, sandy, grass, tarmac) and why the tricycle travelled better over some terrains than others. They could explore how the tricycle worked and whether a different vehicle travelled over the ground with greater ease. In this way, aspects of different materials (the different surfaces travelled) and forces (the way the tricycle worked or travelled over the different surfaces) could be developed, alongside physical, social and linguistic development.

Some role play lends itself to outside play, like a building site or a garden centre. As illustrated in Case study 7.4, some exploratory play activities are best set up outdoors (weather permitting) so that children have space and can make a mess.

TESTING BALLOONS

The water trough was placed outside the classroom and a range of objects were put on a table alongside it, to promote understanding of forces (objects that float and sink) and materials (objects that change in water – bubble, fizz, change colour – such as bath oils, colour-change bubble bath, or bath bombs). One group of 4-year-old children was fascinated by the air-filled, water-filled and ice balloons (balloons filled with water and then frozen) in the trough and decided to explore what would happen if they threw them or dropped them. The children told the educator they expected the air-filled balloon to fly away in the wind, the water-filled balloon to just drop to the ground, and the ice balloon to explode and leave a crater in the concrete floor.

(Consider: What would be your response to the children? How would you react to their suggestion to trial their predictions about the balloons?)

The educator helped the children to plan what they would do, so that no-one would get hurt, and they stood in a line and threw each balloon away from them. The children were very disappointed that the air-filled balloon did not fly away and that the ice balloon did not explode. However, they became very interested in the way the water-filled balloon made a 'splat' puddle on the floor and then this began to dry up in the sun.

REFLECTION

Based on Case study 7.4, consider the following:

1. How would you build on this interest to further develop the children's curiosity and scientific development?
2. Why is it important to start from the children's interests?
3. How could you encourage science from the children's interests in your own teaching?
4. How does this structured approach to play support the outcomes of the Early Years Learning Framework? In particular, consider Outcome 1 (children have a strong sense of identity), Outcome 4 (children are confident and involved learners) and Outcome 5 (children are effective communicators). Refer to Chapter 2 for a review of the EYLF.

The importance of play pedagogy in the first years of school

There is considerable research indicating that transition from pre-school to school settings is unsettling for young children, particularly those who are younger, less able, have special educational needs or who have English as a second language (Sanders et al., 2005; Timperley et al., 2003). The importance of a smooth transition was highlighted by Timperley and colleagues (2003), who stated that transition can have an immediate impact on children's stress and a long-term impact on their grades and retention. One reason for using play pedagogy in the early school setting is that young children are connecting with similar experiences from their pre-school days. Research by Sanders et al. (2005) identified that the biggest challenge to children was the move from a play-based approach to a more structured approach: 'The introduction of the full literacy hour and the daily mathematics lesson was identified as challenging because it was difficult to get young children to sit still and listen to the teacher' (p. iii). This was supported by Sena's research (cited in Johnston & Nahmad-Williams, 2010, p. 440), who stated that the two pedagogical approaches (child-centred and directed teaching) created barriers for children. She indicated that the pre-school approach was more skill-based, promoting learning through play, while early school was based on competency, with fewer play opportunities. Sena further indicated that it was important to have a balance between child-led and teacher-led activities. Siraj-Blatchford (2004, p. 713) also commented that ' … the most effective pre-school settings (in terms of intellectual, social and dispositional outcomes) achieve a balance between opportunities provided for children to benefit from teacher-initiated group work, and in the provision of freely chosen yet potentially instructive play activities.'

Internationally, the early years period is considered to occur between the ages of birth to 8 years of age, and this was recognised within the Victorian Early Years Learning and Development Framework (DEECD, 2009), which incorporated the transition-to-school process. Children in the 5–8-year age group are still developing dispositions for learning, and an early school curriculum which incorporates play pedagogy allows them to develop their thinking through a more open-ended, but guided approach. As children move across the first few years, they are becoming more complex in their thinking processes while being able to follow through on their own investigations. Inquiry approaches to science begin in primary schools, which support this learning, but play pedagogy, which allows greater child autonomy, allows children to transition to school in a less disruptive way. Weiland and Yoshikawa (2013) comment that children demonstrate long-term academic gains through participation in play-oriented early childhood classrooms.

Play pedagogies to support science education

Children's interest in the world around them usually begins with their observations, whereby they see, hear, smell or touch something that captures their interest and encourages them to explore. Kallery and Psillos (2002) found that observation formed only five per cent of classroom activities and was not generally made by the children, but by the teacher. Other research indicates that children's observation tends not to be used to initiate activities or motivate children to want to make inquiries (National Research Council of the National Academies, 2007). Interest and effective development are best where children are practically engaged in exploratory play (see, for example, BERA, 2003).

In planning play in the early years, educators should have an understanding of science experiences appropriate for the early years, young children's development, and the pedagogies that support early scientific learning (BERA, 2003; Johnston, 2005; Johnston, 2014; National Research Council of the National Academies, 2007) and promotes the need for scaffolding in play to facilitate scientific development. This structured support will also motivate and facilitate social and language development, alongside scientific conceptual understanding through questioning (Vygotsky & Cole, 1978) and co-construction of understandings (Siraj-Blatchford et al., 2002). Social interaction, especially where it involves practical exploration which builds upon previous knowledge, allows children to learn alongside peers and teachers.

It is also important that children are given sufficient time to observe, explore and discuss their emerging ideas with others, so that conceptual understanding can be developed through the creation of conceptual conflicts (Hand, 1988), debate and argument (Naylor, Keogh & Goldsworthy, 2004) and 'sustained shared thinking' (Siraj-Blatchford, 2009). Insufficient time can create frustration as children move from one sensory experience to another, and are not able to develop one aspect of their play or explore their own interests emerging from their play. However, if children are forced to remain in one play area just because the allotted time has not yet elapsed, they are likely to become bored.

Practical task

PLANNING PLAY ACTIVITIES

Plan some play activities for early years children that have a scientific focus. Specifically, plan your involvement in the learning through considering the following points:

1. How will you introduce the play?
2. How will you interact/support/guide/model during the play?
3. What questions will you ask to encourage scientific exploration?
4. How will you evaluate your part in the learning?

REFLECTION

In considering teacher involvement, think about the following:

1. What was the impact of your role on the children's scientific development?
2. How did having less teacher control over the activity affect scientific learning and behaviour?
3. How can you develop your role to support and extend scientific learning?

DIFFERENT PLAY PEDAGOGIES

Case Study 7.5

A scientific exploration day was set up for 60 children, consisting of two classes of 6 and 7-year-olds. The learning outcomes for the children, based on a topic of winter, were to describe the similarities and differences between a range of materials, to observe materials change when mixed, heated or cooled, and to make simple predictions based on their observations.

Although the two teachers planned together, they had very different ways of teaching. Nicola had been teaching for eight years and preferred a highly structured approach whereby she imparted knowledge to children to 'ensure' that they met the learning outcomes. Patrick was in his second year of teaching and preferred a play/exploratory-based approach, with the teacher facilitating learning rather than imparting knowledge. The classes included a large number of children with special educational needs, including autism and behavioural problems.

→

The children were told that they could move around from one activity to another, but that there should be no more than six children at any one activity. Nicola found this very difficult and organised the children into two groups of 15 children, rather than five groups of six children, and began to demonstrate one activity to one group, while a teaching assistant attempted to do the same with the other group. Patrick and his teaching assistant moved around the groups of children, encouraging, supporting and asking questions, and allowed the children to decide when they had completed one activity and were ready to move to another, providing there was space.

Within Nicola's class, there were incidents of poor behaviour as children wanted to observe and explore. Patrick's class was more motivated and behaviour was not an issue, even with children who had severe behavioural problems.

In Patrick's class there was one 7-year-old boy called John who had severe learning difficulties, being unable to read and write, and having work differentiated so it can be achieved at his level. John was particularly interested in one activity, which involved the children investigating whether woollen, cotton, rubber, furry or leather gloves kept ice-hands (ice-filled surgical gloves) cool or melted them, with a key question: 'What will happen if you put the different gloves on the ice hands?' John wanted to know how we got the ice into the glove. John told Patrick that ice comes from water that is very cold. Patrick helped John to fill up two gloves with water and asked John to tell him where they could put them to turn them into ice. John first suggested the freezer, so they put one into the freezer. John then noticed that it was very cold outside and that he had seen ice that morning. He then asked if he could put another glove outside. After 10 minutes he asked if he could check, but the gloves were still not frozen. John told Patrick that it needed more time to get really cold. A short while later John wanted to check again, and noticed that in the freezer the fingers were frozen but the palm of the glove was not. John told Patrick that it must be because the palm is thicker and the cold has not got to the middle yet. Eventually, the glove in the freezer had frozen so Patrick and John took it back to the classroom and compared it with the glove outside. Other children had now noticed this investigation, and it led to a whole-class discussion as to why this had happened. They discussed many possible reasons before another child, Lorna, told the class that it gets coldest outside at night because there is no Sun to warm us up. It was then suggested that they leave the glove outside overnight to see what would happen by morning, which they did, allowing the investigation to last beyond the normal allocated lesson. The children also went home and did the same investigation, bringing in their results the next day.

A few weeks later, Patrick was carrying out an investigation whereby the children held different foods in their hand to see how quickly they melted. The children started with a chocolate button and discovered that it melted very quickly. They then held a Smartie, and discovered that it did not melt as quickly. This led to a discussion in which John suggested that there was a thicker coating around the Smartie, stopping the heat getting in to melt the chocolate, and referred to the glove investigation, likening the coat on the glove to the Smartie.

The class discussion that followed then led to the discovery that when we put a thick coat on it does not warm us up but it stops our body heat escaping and stops the cold air getting in. This discovery put the learning into a real-life context. It was a wonderful discovery that had come from an independent, play-based activity and inspired the children to find out more information to extend their understanding.

Consider the following related to the two approaches described in Case study 7.5:

1. How do you think different groups of children would respond to the different pedagogical approaches?
2. With which approach do you feel most comfortable? Why?
3. Discuss the positive and negative aspects of the pedagogical approaches that the two educators used.

With the play approach followed in Case study 7.5, think about the following:

1. How did the play support and extend scientific learning for different children?
2. How could you accommodate more exploratory-based learning in your own planning?
3. How could you use a play approach in your classroom to achieve other scientific learning outcomes?

Conclusion

This chapter described the importance of play in children's science learning. It discussed the different play pedagogies that support children's development of scientific learning and the importance of play pedagogy in the transition from early childhood settings into school settings. Early school settings were discussed from the perspective of play pedagogy, with important points made about the use of play as a vehicle for science learning. Finally, examples of how play can be used in pre-school and school settings were used to illustrate the discussion.

Backshall, B. (2016). *A Culture for Science in Early Childhood Education: Where Cultures Meet Culture*, completed PhD thesis, Waikato University, New Zealand.

British Educational Research Association (BERA). Early Years Special Interest Group. (2003). *Early Years Research: Pedagogy, Curriculum and Adult Roles, Training and Professionalism*, Southwell, UK: BERA.

Creative Little Scientist (CLS). (2012). Conceptual Framework and Literature Reviews as addenda, www.creative-little-scientists.eu/content/deliverables, accessed 13 February 2014.

—— (2013). Report on Practices and Their Implications, www.creative-little-scientists.eu/content/deliverables, accessed 13 February 2014.

Department of Education and Early Childhood Development (DEECD). (2009). *Victorian Early Years Learning and Development Framework*, East Melbourne: Early Childhood Strategy Division.

Dockett, S. & Fleer, M. (2002). *Play and Pedagogy in Early Childhood: Bending the Rules*. Melbourne: Thomson.

Ebbeck, M. & Waniganayake, M. (2010). *Play in Early Childhood Education: Learning in Diverse Contexts*, Melbourne: Oxford University Press.

Froebel, F. (1826). *On the Education of Man*, Keilhau, Leipzig: Wienbrach.

Gliori, D. (1995). *The Snow Lambs*, London: Scholastic Publications.

Hand, B. (1988). Is conceptual conflict a viable teaching strategy? The students' viewpoint, *Australian Science Teachers Journal*, 34(4), 22–6.

Johnston, J. (2005). *Early Explorations in Science* (2nd edn), Maidenhead: Open University Press.

—— (2009). How does the skill of observation develop in young children? *International Journal of Science Education*, 31(18), 2511–25.

—— (2011). Children talking: Teachers supporting science, *Journal of Emergent Science*, 1(1), 14–22.

—— (2014). *Emergent Science: Teaching Science from Birth to 8*. Abingdon, Oxon: Routledge.

Johnston, J. & Nahmad-Williams, L. (2010). Developing imagination and imaginative play, in A. Compton, J. Johnston, L. Nahmad-Williams & K. Taylor (eds), *Creative Development*, London: Continuum.

Kallery, M. & Psillos, D. (2002). What happens in the early years' science classroom? The reality of teachers' curriculum implementation activities, *European Early Childhood Education Research Journal*, 10(2), 49–61.

Moylett, H. (2010). Supporting children's development and learning, in T. Bruce (ed.), *Early Childhood* (2nd edn), London: Sage.

National Research Council of the National Academies. (2007). *Taking Science to School*, Washington, DC: The National Academies Press.

Naylor, S., Keogh, B. & Goldsworthy, A. (2004). *Active Assessment: Thinking, Learning and Assessment in Science*, Sandbach, Cheshire: Millgate House.

Piaget, J. (1976). 'Mastery play' and 'symbolic play', in J. Bruner, A. Jolly & K. Sylva (eds), *Play – Its Role in Development and Evolution*, Middlesex: Penguin.

Robbins, J. (2005). 'Brown paper packages'? A sociocultural perspective on young children's ideas in science, *Research in Science Education*, 35(2), 151–72.

Rogoff, B. (1995). Observing sociocultural activity on three planes: Participatory appropriation, guided participation, and apprenticeship, in J. V. Wertsch, P. Del Rio & A. Alvarex (eds), *Sociocultural Studies of Mind*, Cambridge, UK: Cambridge University Press, 139–64.

Rousseau, J. J. (1911). *Emile* (trans. B. Foxley), London: J. M. Dent and Sons.

Russell, W. (2010). Playwork, in T. Bruce (ed.), *Early childhood* (2nd ed), London: Sage.

Sanders, D., White, G., Burge, B., Sharp, C., Eames, A., McEune, R. & Grayson, H. (2005). A Study of the Transition from Foundation Stage to Key Stage 1. SureStart, DfES Research Report SSU/2005/FR/013), London DfES.

Siraj-Blatchford, I. (2004). Educational disadvantage in the early years: How do we overcome it? Some lessons from research, *European Early Childhood Education Research Journal*, 12(2), 5–20.

—— (2009). Conceptualising progression in the pedagogy of play and sustained shared thinking in early childhood education: A Vygotskian perspective, *Educational & Child Psychology*, 26(2), 77–89.

Siraj-Blatchford, I., Sylva, K., Muttock, S., Gilden, R. & Bell, D. (2002). *Researching Effective Pedagogy in the Early Years*, Nottingham: DFES.

Timperley, H., McNaughton, S., Howie, L. & Robinson, V. (2003). Transitioning children for early childhood education to school: Teacher beliefs and transition practices, *Australian Journal of Early Childhood*, 28(2), 32–8.

Vygotsky, L. (1962). *Thought and Language*, Cambridge, MA: MIT Press.

Vygotsky, L. & Cole, M. (eds) (1978). *Mind in Society: The Development of Higher Psychological Processes*, Cambridge, MA: Harvard University Press.

Weiland, C. & Yoshikawa, H. (2013). Impacts of a pre-kindergarten program on children's mathematics, language, literacy, executive function, and emotional skills, *Child Development*, 84(6), 2112–30.

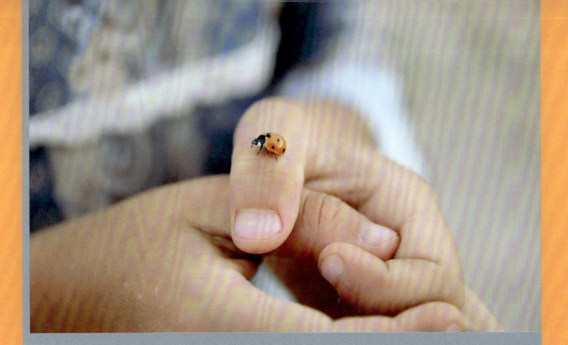

8

Enhancing young children's science identity through pedagogical practices

Elaine Blake and Christine Howitt

This chapter explores how young children's science identity can be enhanced when thoughtful pedagogy is provided by the educator. The first part of this chapter presents the definitions of science identity and pedagogy, followed by an exploration of the relationship between educator beliefs and what they teach. The second half of the chapter presents two case studies to illustrate pedagogical practices associated with learning and teaching of science with young children, using play as a medium. These two case studies are interpreted using the five learning outcomes of the Early Years Learning Framework (EYLF) to highlight young children's developing science identity.

OBJECTIVES

At the end of this chapter you will be able to:

- describe science identity

- describe pedagogy in terms of relationships and learning

- describe the relationship between beliefs and pedagogy

- relate young children's science experiences to the five learning outcomes specified in the Early Years Learning Framework to describe their developing science identity

- describe various pedagogical principles that enhance the science identity of young children.

Science identity in young children

Children build a strong sense of identity when positive experiences help them understand their contribution is significant and respected by others (DEEWR, 2009). **Science identity** refers to how children perceive whether they can do science and be successful at science, and how others perceive them at being able to do science (Fenichel & Schweingruber, 2010). Developing a science identity can be influenced by opportunity, social interactions with others and interacting with science resources. Recognition of belonging to a science community can also enhance science identity (Fenichel & Schweingruber, 2010). This sense of belonging to a science community comes from reflecting on past science events, engaging in current science activities, or imagining future science scenarios (Fenichel & Schweingruber, 2010). Further, educators play an important role in science participation and learning when they influence young children through opportunity, interests, habits and modelled scientific thinking to develop dispositions that reflect a science identity.

> **Science identity** – how children perceive whether they can do science and be successful at science, and how others perceive them at being able to do science.

Pedagogy

Broadly speaking, **pedagogy** is knowing what to teach and how to teach. Therefore, an educator's pedagogy guides teaching practice and children's learning. The EYLF describes pedagogy as 'early childhood educators' professional practice, especially those aspects that involve building and nurturing relationships, curriculum decision making, teaching and learning' (DEEWR, 2009, p. 9). Pedagogy looks different in different contexts, as there is no universal approach for an educator to teach or for children to learn. Thus, pedagogy should be considered as practice that adjusts for different cultural and contextual situations and for different children and their families (DECD, 2013).

> **Pedagogy** – knowing what to teach and how to teach.

The EYLF places **relationships** at the centre of effective pedagogy. This includes children's 'relationships with people, places and things' (DEEWR, 2009, p. 20). When educators establish respectful and caring relationships with children and their families, they work together to construct curriculum and learning experiences relevant to children's prior knowledge and interests, thus expanding a sense of belonging and identity through thoughtful pedagogy (DECD, 2013). Neuroscience acknowledges that children learn best in nurturing relationships where supportive and positive pedagogy is provided (Center on the Developing Child, 2007). Nurturing respectful relationships require educators to acknowledge children's rights, be responsive to their capabilities, provide challenges and learn together to better understand the world in which they live. Forming partnerships, interactions and activities with parents and the community allows children to acknowledge purposeful planned and unplanned events that reflect the rhythms and importance of relationships within their learning environment. (DECD, 2013; DEEWR, 2009).

> **Relationships** – the connection of children with people (educators and families), places and objects.

Pedagogies are the 'practices that are intended to promote children's learning' (DEEWR, 2009, p. 46). Therefore, collaborative curriculum decision-making will account for visible learning and a rich, stimulating environment where children can be themselves and 'seek to make meaning of the world' (DEEWR, 2009, p. 7). Flexible and individualised planning, responsive to children's needs, provides inclusive learning environments for deep extended play within established and flexible indoor and outdoor routines. These structures offer security and wellbeing for children to grow knowledge, form relationships and be actively engaged in their own learning (DECD, 2013; DEEWR, 2009).

The EYLF has defined **learning** as 'a natural process of exploration that children engage in from birth as they expand their intellectual, physical, social, emotional and creative capacities' (DEEWR, 2009, p. 46). Learning and teaching science in the early years requires an understanding of a range of educational theories, the implications of current research and being perceptive about learning that occurs in consistently changing contexts.

> **Learning** – the process that children engage with in order to expand their intellectual, physical, social, emotional and creative capacities.

Acknowledging that children have diverse experiences, hold different perspectives and that they have accumulated a bank of knowledge and skills requires educators to be mindful about children's processes of learning, their families and cultures. Further, educators require a working knowledge of the content and intent of the EYLF, an ability to integrate literacy and numeracy, in a holistic manner, in to science-related learning, and an understanding of the place of intentional and incidental teaching, learning through play, active promotion of challenging experiences, creativity and thoughtful documentation (DECD, 2013).

The relationship between educator beliefs and pedagogy

Pedagogy is shaped by an educator's beliefs, values and reflections. What educators believe about children and how they learn will dictate what and how they teach. Choices and decisions about what and how to teach are constantly being made by educators. If they believe that children are active participants and decision-makers in their learning, then educators will develop learning experiences and establish a learning environment to reflect this. If educators believe that children are receptive to a wide range of experiences, then wide ranging experiences will be provided. What educators include or exclude from the

Practical task

THINKING ABOUT YOUR OWN PEDAGOGY

In thinking about your own pedagogy, consider the following:

1. What beliefs or theories shape your practice?
2. What practical aspects of pedagogy are effective in your practice, and why?
3. What have you excluded from your curriculum, and why?
4. Does what you say you believe match up with what you actually do? If not, why not?

curriculum will affect how children learn, develop and understand their world. Educators' professional judgements are central to the role of facilitating children's learning. Educators bring together professional knowledge and skills based on their understanding of children, families and communities; an awareness of how their beliefs and values impact on children's learning; personal styles; and past experiences. Educators also draw on their own creativity, intuition and imagination to improve and adjust their own practice (DEEWR, 2009).

Exploring pedagogical practice in developing young children's science identity

The following two case studies, adapted from Blake (2013), highlight effective **pedagogical practice** in developing young children's science identity through playful situations. Each case study is presented as a short vignette. This is followed by an interpretation of the case study from a science and pedagogical perspective. Finally, the case study is analysed using the five outcomes of the EYLF in order to illustrate the children's developing science identity.

> **Pedagogical practices** – the range of strategies used by an educator in the learning and teaching process.

WARM AND COLD CRAYONS

Crayon Boy (aged 3½ years) and the educator (E) were settled together at a table with a collection of paper, a box of pencils and a box of mostly well-used wax crayons. As Crayon Boy drew a picture of his nana's house and dog, he commented how some pencils and crayons did not work because 'when they get old there's no colour left'. He demonstrated this fact with blunt pencils and crayons that had been worn down to their paper case. Crayon Boy went on to explain, without encouragement, that the white crayon did not work because 'it kept its colour only for brown paper'. He proved this knowledge correct by producing a drawing in white crayon on brown paper. This was followed by a drawing with white crayon on white paper, with Crayon Boy announcing 'It's invisible!'

As the conversation turned to his nana's dog, Crayon Boy absentmindedly rubbed the palm of his hand along a thick orange crayon. He was asked what the crayon felt like.

Crayon Boy: Soft. And it's not cold now.
E: What was it like before?
Crayon Boy: It's hard. And cold.
E: Why isn't it cold now?
Crayon Boy: Ah, when you draw it gets warmed up. See? In the box are cold. Touch 'em. [Points for E to test.]

Crayon Boy handed E several chosen crayons from the box to test his idea.

E: So, when you draw, a crayon warms up, is that right?
Crayon Boy: Yes, this one [a blue crayon] was writing and it's not so cold.

→

→

E:	I don't think I can tell the difference.
Crayon Boy:	No. Blue's not good. I don't draw dogs with blue.
E:	What do you draw dogs with?
Crayon Boy:	This one. It's like Nana's dog [an orange crayon]. I reckon this one is a good one. See? [He began scribbling using the orange crayon he had been holding.]
Crayon Boy:	Try this one. This one works better now it's been drawing. See? It's not cold.
E:	How do you know it works better than the orange crayon in the box?
Crayon Boy:	Because I haven't used that one yet.

To prove his point, Crayon Boy demonstrated two orange crayons. The first crayon was 'cold' and had not been used before in this session. The second crayon that he had been using was 'warm' and made bolder colours.

Crayon Boy:	This one [cold crayon] is hard to draw with and this one [warm crayon] was a better colour. Look! You can do it. [Hands the warm crayon to E.]

REFLECTION

Consider Case study 8.1 and the following questions:

1. What prior knowledge did Crayon Boy have, and how did he acquire this knowledge?
2. How was E able to obtain this prior knowledge? Think of both the role of the educator and the role of the environment.
3. What pedagogical practices has E demonstrated? How did E extend Crayon Boy's thinking?
4. What is the everyday concept upon which this case study is based?

Interpretation of Case study 8.1

Although Crayon Boy had participated in the everyday activity of drawing with crayons, the scientific concept of change caused by the transference of heat was unknowingly tested and articulated. This occurred through the provision of appropriate resources in an environment that invited independent exploration of the tools. Having an interested adult encouraged Crayon Boy to share his information and extend his thinking, and resulted in his thoughtful participation. This case study highlights that when an adult listens intentionally to a child's interpretation of how things work, it gives that child's idea currency and leads them to greater confidence and understanding about their thought processes.

This case study also highlights why young children are seen as natural scientists. Crayon Boy observed differences, processed his ideas, tested them and reported his findings. He correctly articulated the differences between 'hard' and 'soft' and 'cold' and 'warm', and proved that the white wax crayon was ineffective on white paper. Further, he substantiated his information when he proved his theory to an audience.

Crayon Boy had incidentally discovered new knowledge and embedded his findings by testing them. He, therefore, improved his knowledge and explained his theory about why there are differences between warm and cold crayons. In doing so, he expanded his store of personal information, making it ready for further learning. Crayon Boy's knowledge base, confidence, oral language, demonstration skills and fine motor ability all increased as a result of this casual, undirected investigation.

Relating Case study 8.1 to the EYLF

What could have been interpreted as a child simply colouring in has been transformed into a story of a highly competent and capable 3½-year-old who has an emerging knowledge of science concepts and processes related to his personal experience of making crayons work better. A deeper analysis of this case study highlights many characteristics associated with the five learning outcomes provided under the EYLF. A summary of these characteristics, presented in Table 8.1, shows that having an interested adult prepared to take time to listen and respond to Crayon Boy's explanations gave him a developing sense of science identity and connectedness to his immediate world. His self-confidence and beliefs about how crayons work were readily communicated to the educator, indicating a willing and interested learner.

TABLE 8.1	SUMMARY OF THE MAIN CHARACTERISTICS OF CASE STUDY 8.1 – CONNECTION WITH EYLF OUTCOMES
EYLF outcome	**How this outcome was demonstrated**
1. Children have a strong sense of identity	Crayon Boy's identity is developed through his association with his nana and her dog. He is knowledgeable about crayons and how to make them work better, and is prepared to share this information with an interested adult. He expressed a range of thoughts and views, and was prepared to challenge the educator to test his ideas.
2. Children are connected with and contribute to their world	Crayon Boy readily expressed his opinion about the crayons and how they worked, and responded positively to the educator's presence and comments. His self-directed play included the educator who allowed him to investigate and explore new ideas when prompted to extend his understanding.
3. Children have a strong sense of wellbeing	Crayon Bay demonstrated trust and confidence as he shared his knowledge and experience with the educator. He took risks when challenging the educator to test his ideas, yet had self-belief and prior experiences to draw upon to develop new knowledge. He happily drew and shared his drawings with the educator.
4. Children are confident and involved learners	Crayon Boy was curious and enthusiastic about his knowledge of crayons, and eagerly sought to share this with the educator. He demonstrated problem-solving strategies and skill when demonstrating his view about why white crayons do not work on white paper. He confidently used various skills and strategies to better understand how crayons work. From these he made predictions and generalisations.
5. Children are effective communicators	Crayon Boy used verbal and non-verbal language and drawings to communicate his knowledge. His conversational language and explanations communicated thought processing and scientific ideas. The story his drawing told of his nana and her dog enabled him to express his ideas further, as did his practical demonstrations.

SOUNDING OFF

Sound Boy 1, Sound Boy 2 and Sound Girl (each aged between 3 and 4 years) were playing in the block corner of a classroom. These children added wooden and rubber mallets to their play, using them to strike blocks of different sizes and shapes. The class had recently been engaged in a series of music lessons that included the use of small mallets and objects to test sound. Sound Boy 2 noticed that by striking the hollow wooden blocks (as opposed to the solid blocks) a 'better' sound was produced. The children agreed that different-shaped blocks produced different sounds. Sound Boy 1 told his friends he was making different sounds with two blocks that were the same size and shape. Conversation was loud and comparisons about the sounds were discussed between the three children. Occasionally all three stopped talking and listened for differences in sound and pitch. In turn, they compared those differences as each child tried to prove or disprove opinions about the sound produced.

At 'pack away time', Sound Boy 1 remained with the two blocks that appeared identical in shape and size, yet produced a different pitch. He seemed engrossed in his work and continued to strike the blocks, one at a time, then to listen for results. Finally, Sound Boy 1 had to put his blocks away and join the rest of the class for a sharing circle.

The teacher asked the children what they had learnt. The following conversation, relating to the blocks, took place.

Sound Boy 1:	When I hit two of them with the gong they made different sounds.
Teacher:	What did you hit with the gong?
Sound Boy 1:	The blocks.
Teacher:	That was one big block and one small block, was it?
Sound Boy 1:	No. They are the same. The small ones.
Sound Girl:	They are both small but different.
Teacher:	What do you mean they are small but different? Do you mean size is different?
Sound Boy 2:	Yes. They are small but different.
Teacher:	How are they different?
Sound Boy 2:	At the top.
Sound Girl:	No. At the side. They are different at the side.
Sound Boy 2:	If you hold them like this, it's the top. [Uses hands to demonstrate without a block.]
Teacher:	Let's test Sound Boy 1's learning. Go and get the blocks and the gong. [While both blocks and a rubber mallet were retrieved by the three focus children, other members of the class were patiently curious and discussed the possibilities. They looked on, offered help and made comments that might help solve the problem.]
Teacher:	Those blocks look the same to me. How are they different?
Sound Boy 2:	See? The top.

Sound Girl:	No. The side. It's different on the side. See?
Teacher:	Let's all have a look. What do you think? [To children who had gathered around for a closer look.]
Chorus:	Same! Different! Hit it!

The children with the blocks demonstrated a slight difference in sound to their peers. They also correctly pointed out that although the blocks appeared to be the same size, they were in fact marginally different. This, they concluded, made the sound different.

REFLECTION

Consider Case study 8.2 and the following questions:

1. What prior knowledge did Sound Boy 1, Sound Boy 2 and Sound Girl have, and how did they acquire this knowledge?
2. Describe the role of the environment in assisting the children's learning.
3. What pedagogical practices has the teacher demonstrated? How did she demonstrate respect for the children as resourceful and successful learners?
4. What is the everyday concept on which this case study is based?

Interpretation of Case study 8.2

This case study provides an example of scientific concept learning through spontaneous play within a suitable learning environment. Learning was ultimately supported by an interested adult. During cooperative group investigations, the focus children transferred prior knowledge about sound and pitch to consolidate their understanding of previous lessons while further developing observational skills associated with aural and sight senses.

Spontaneous play, without hindrance, enabled these children to work like scientists as they used comparison, classification and explanation to develop their skills. They tested and defined ideas related to previous sound lessons and accidently expanded knowledge through discussion and investigation. This case study highlights that children learn effectively when the context makes sense to them.

FIGURE 8.1 Testing the sounds between a timber post and a rock

Transference of learning was demonstrated as these children, who had been studying sound during the previous two weeks, continued their music lessons according to their own agenda. By chance and meticulous testing they discovered that even the smallest change in the construction of like objects could change the pitch of sound produced when hit with a rubber mallet. Further, the opportunity offered by their teacher to test and report their ideas to peers provided exceptional pedagogy that included peer tutoring, oral language development, demonstration, perseverance and concentration. Teacher involvement at the end of this lesson legitimised children's learning by acknowledging their competent scientific inquiry and collaborative learning.

Relating Case study 8.2 to the EYLF

A summary of the main characteristics of this case study associated with the five outcomes from the EYLF is presented in Table 8.2. Through close observation these children are seen by their educator as capable and competent young scientists who have identified a problem and, as a group, tried to solve that problem. Enabling spontaneous play in an appropriate environment with adequate resources allowed these children to investigate their ideas

TABLE 8.2 SUMMARY OF THE MAIN CHARACTERISTICS OF CASE STUDY 8.2 – CONNECTION WITH EYLF OUTCOMES

EYLF outcome	How this outcome was demonstrated
1. Children have a strong sense of identity	The three focus children in the case study developed respectful working relationships with each other as they collaboratively discussed and tested their ideas. They responded to each other's comments with genuine interest and confidently explored and engaged the physical environment. Persistence was demonstrated as they tested the various blocks, expressed their thoughts and constructed views with each other, the teacher and the rest of the class.
2. Children are connected with and contribute to their world	The three focus children in the case study were cooperative in exploring different sounds and confidently expressed their opinions with each other. They brought prior experiences to their playful investigations and participated as a group to solve the problem and present their problem to the teacher and other children in their class. They explored, predicted and tested ideas, developed strategies to solve their problem and readily engaged with the larger group.
3. Children have a strong sense of wellbeing	Confident in each other's company the focus children made new discoveries then celebrated their own efforts and achievements with each other, the teacher and the class. They worked cooperatively and collaboratively over a sustained period of time. They engaged fine motor movement to develop their sense of sound while manipulating blocks and mallets with competence and skill.
4. Children are confident and involved learners	The three children demonstrated curiosity and enthusiasm as they investigated musical sounds, stayed on task and shared their knowledge with the teacher and other children. Through the medium of play they confidently investigated the science of sound with determination and concentration. They involved others in their learning and remained on task until their curiosity was satisfied.
5. Children are effective communicators	Both verbal and non-verbal communication was used as the children effectively interacted with each other, explored sounds and shared new knowledge. Their language communicated thought processes as they explained scientific ideas to the teacher and other children. Sound Boy 1 used demonstration to communicate his findings to the teacher and the class.

and satisfy their curiosity. Further, through respectful understanding by the educator, the children confidently communicated their findings to the rest of the class. Their emerging science identity was supported by the provision of time to explore a problem that they had identified.

Enhancing young children's science identity through pedagogical practices

Firm relationships and beliefs by early childhood educators echo wise pedagogy and respect for each child's ability, prior knowledge and experience. These two case studies indicate that children are constantly gaining new knowledge through their experiences and relationships as they satisfy their own curiosity. Young children are natural explorers and researchers. To benefit from their everyday scientific encounters they require facilitation, through educator's thoughtful pedagogy, to help them unravel the complex workings of their world.

These case studies highlight the everyday nature of early childhood science, and young children's emerging science identity. Crayon Boy's curiosity centred on the use of crayons, and why some crayons worked better than others. Through his many daily experiences with crayons, Crayon Boy had developed and tested his own theories. The three children in the second case study were extending their knowledge of sound as previously learned and through self-directed play they encountered and solved a problem as a team. Their curiosity and desire led them to share and explore different ideas about sound as they collaboratively tested and discussed theories.

Children's sense of identity is shaped by experiences and challenges that are motivated from within and encouraged by others who enable them to make choices and decisions. When children can discuss processes that have been used to solve their problems or answer their curiosity, present approaches or investigations they have undertaken in this process and explain their views, then their identity as an emerging scientist becomes visible.

These two case studies highlight the important role of educators in children's learning to bring science to the surface and assist identity development. In learning science, children require the assistance of more knowledgeable others to advance their cognitive understanding of experiences. With assistance, children more readily understand why things are the way they are and why things work the way they do (Fleer, 2005). Experiences using situations and objects that are familiar to children provide rich beginnings for their learning. It is from these everyday experiences that educators can introduce, highlight and support the development of scientific concepts (Fleer, 2007). Educators who use these pedagogical approaches legitimise children's points of view and assist their developing confidence, thought processes and growing science identity (Millikan, 2003). The role of a thoughtful educator is to observe, actively and respectfully listen, nudge curiosity, model behaviours, invite questions, develop conversations, wonder out loud, guide learning and challenge children's current conceptual understanding (Blake & Howitt, 2012; Forman, 2010; Millikan, 2003).

In both case studies, the competent action and perseverance of children was observed while they enhanced their scientific skills and developed their science identity. Those skills were amplified when the educator prepared the learning environments and assisted the children's investigations. The challenge for educators is to become aware of the everyday nature of science, and acknowledge children as capable and competent learners.

Conclusion

Rethinking pedagogy and beliefs about how young children acquire science skills and knowledge can assist educators to enhance children's science identity. Educators guide the progress of scientific concepts during the process of learning and teaching when they acknowledge and include children's prior knowledge and interests in curriculum development, while ensuring respectful relationships exist within the school community and learning environment. The two case studies presented in this chapter highlight children as highly capable and competent learners who, with the assistance of respectful educators, can describe and analyse their world through playful science experiences.

Blake, E. (2013). *A Socio-Cultural Study of Learning and Teaching Science in Early Learning Centres*, unpublished PhD thesis, Perth: Curtin University.

Blake, E. & Howitt, C. (2012). Science in early learning centres: Satisfying curiosity, guided play or lost opportunities, in K.C.D. Tan & M. Kim (eds), *Issues and Challenges in Science Education Research: Moving Forward*, Dordrecht: Springer, 281–99.

Center on the Developing Child (2007). *The Science of Early Childhood Development* (In Brief), www.developingchild.harvard.edu.

Department for Education and Child Development (DECD). (2013). Perspectives on pedagogy. Early Years Learning Framework, South Australia: DECD, www.decd.sa.gov.au/sites/g/files/net691/f/perspectives_on_pedagogy_early_years_learning_framework.pdf?v=1456704111.

Department of Education, Employment and Workplace Relations (DEEWR). (2009). *Belonging, Being and Becoming. The Early Years Learning Framework for Australia*, Canberra: Commonwealth of Australia.

Fenichel, M. & Schweingruber, H. A. (2010). Interest and motivation: Steps towards building a science identity, in M. Fenichel & H. A. Schweingruber (eds), *Surrounded by Science: Learning Science in Informal Environments*, Washington, DC: The National Academies Press, 81–101.

Fleer, M. (2005). Meaning-making science: Exploring the socio-cultural dimensions of early childhood teacher education, in K. Appleton (ed.), *Elementary Science Teacher Education: International Perspectives on Contemporary Issues and Practices*, Mahwah, NJ: Lawrence Erlbaum, 107–24.

—— (ed.) (2007). *Children's Thinking in Science: What Does Research Tell Us?*, Canberra: Early Childhood Australia.

Forman, G. E. (2010). When 2-year-olds and 3-year-olds think like scientists, *Early Childhood Research and Practice*, 12(2), ecrp.uiuc.edu/v12n2/forman.html.

Millikan, J. (2003). *Reflections: Reggio Emilia Principles within Australian Contexts*, Sydney: Pademelon Press.

9 STEM education in early childhood

Christine Preston

Science, Technology, Engineering and Mathematics (STEM) education is concerned with human endeavours that shape the world around us. The characteristic disciplines and thinking processes associated with STEM, especially when considered together, help children appreciate the ways in which curiosity, inventiveness and adaptability can be applied in everyday life. This chapter draws on current research into education and the applicability of STEM for early childhood education. Digital learning technologies in the context of STEM education are also discussed.

OBJECTIVES

At the end of this chapter you will be able to:

- explain what STEM education is and recognise the value of incorporating it into early years education

- identify ways in which STEM elements are incorporated in young children's play

- appreciate how STEM-related play can enhance young children's understanding of the world

- identify a range of situations that have potential for STEM learning experiences for young children

- describe how digital technologies can be used to enhance and document young children's STEM learning experiences.

Definition and importance of STEM education

There are various terms being used in relation to STEM, such as STEM education and STEM curriculum. These different terms can make it confusing to grasp the full meaning of STEM. Literally, STEM is an acronym for science, **technology**, mathematics and engineering. Practically, the term has been variously interpreted with the science and mathematics components often taking precedence. However, STEM education should actively include technology and engineering. What the 'T' for technology pertains to is also contentious. Technology is more than information and communication technology (ICT) or screen technology, a narrow but common focus. While computers, phones and iPads are useful technological tools, there are a myriad of non-digital **technologies** that are also useful; for example, wheels, gates, backpacks, pencils, lunch boxes and sticky tape (Lindeman & McKendry Anderson, 2015). The 'technology' component in STEM also relates to the design process and aligns closely with the recognised engineering process. While engineering, with its roots in problem solving and innovation, is not

Technology – a development of products, services, systems and environments, using various types of knowledge, to meet human needs and wants.

Technologies – materials, data, systems, components, tools and equipment used to create solutions for identified needs and opportunities, and the knowledge, understanding and skills used by people involved in the selection and use of these.

a formalised part of school curriculum in Australia, including engineering in school and pre-school education is advocated because it incorporates problem solving and is linked to innovation (Bybee, 2010). Engaging children in integrated rather than subject-specific units is said to develop general 'capabilities that include critical thinking, creativity, communication and self-direction' (Rosicka, 2016, p. 8). These capabilities are also encapsulated in the EYLF outcomes (DEEWR, 2009). For example:

Outcome 1 – children have a strong sense of identity

■ children develop their emerging autonomy, interdependence, resilience and sense of agency
  – be open to new challenges and discoveries
  – persist when faced with challenges and when first attempts are not successful.

Outcome 4 – children are confident and involved learners

■ children develop dispositions for learning such as curiosity, cooperation, confidence, creativity, commitment, enthusiasm, persistence, imagination and reflexivity
  – participate in a variety of rich and meaningful inquiry-based experiences
  – persevere and experience the satisfaction of achievement.

Outcome 5 – children are effective communicators

■ children interact verbally and non-verbally with others for a range of purposes
  – interact with others to explore ideas and concepts, clarify and challenge thinking, negotiate and share new understandings.

The purpose of STEM education in early childhood is to help children to explore and make sense of their world using child-relevant and appropriate contexts. The most appropriate definition of STEM for early childhood education is one that enables learning to remain reflective of children's interests. A more commonly adopted definition of STEM education for early childhood is: 'Teaching and learning between/among any two or more of the STEM subject areas and/or between a STEM subject and a non-STEM subject such as the Arts' (Rosicka, 2016, p. 5). Thus, educators are encouraged to see connections between the different disciplines, but do not have to connect all four disciplines.

Why teach STEM in early childhood

Science, mathematics and technology have been taught to young children as individual disciplines. Given the holistic nature of early childhood education, these disciplines are best taught in an integrated fashion. Engineering and design technology encompass the practical application of science, **digital technology** and mathematics and provide an authentic context for learning. This means that STEM education fits with the generalist model of early childhood education. In other words, it is appropriate for young children to learn about their world in an integrated rather than discipline-specific way. It is important to note that STEM education is a teaching and learning approach and is not part of the formal curriculum in Australia. STEM education is a way of contextualising learning that 'removes the traditional barriers separating the four disciplines and integrates them into real-world, rigorous, relevant learning experiences' (Vasquez, 2015, p. 11). Commencing STEM education in early childhood is argued to be important because early learning of concepts and skills are precursors for school achievement. Introducing STEM education at an early age also aims to counter gender-based stereotypes that affect career choices (Kazakoff, Sullivan & Bers, 2013). A universal argument for including STEM education across all ages is to facilitate the development of 21st century skills, sometimes called the 4Cs: creativity, critical thinking, collaboration and communication (P21, 2015). Table 9.1 provides definitions of these four skills.

These skills are important for encouraging active thinking and providing opportunities for children to develop into confident, capable learners in modern society.

> **Digital technology** – any technology controlled using digital instructions; computers, smartphones, digital cameras, printers and robots are all examples of digital technologies.

TABLE 9.1	DEFINITIONS OF THE 4C SKILLS
4C skill	**Definition**
Creativity	'the interaction among aptitude, process, and environment by which an individual or group produces a perceptible product that is both novel and useful as defined within a social context' (Plucker, Beghetto & Dow, cited in P21, n.d., a, p. 1).
Critical thinking	'the strategies we use to think in organized ways to analyze and solve problems' (P21, n.d., b, p. 1).
Collaboration	'as a process leading to other desired individual and group outcomes, such as successful problem solving and enhanced intellectual development' (P21, n.d., c, p. 1)
Communication	'effectively using oral, written, and nonverbal communication skills for multiple purposes (e.g., to inform, instruct, motivate, persuade, and share ideas); effective listening; using technology to communicate; and being able to evaluate the effectiveness of communication efforts – all within diverse contexts' (P21, n.d., d, p. 1).

Fostering creativity

Learning experiences where children design and build have great potential for supporting creativity. Science inquiry, design technology and engineering tasks enable children to both express their creativity and engage in creative processes (Hathcock et al., 2015). These authors use the term 'mini-c creativity' to mean 'constructing personal knowledge and understanding in a particular context' (p. 730). This refers to the ideas children use to make learning meaningful to *themselves* or intrapersonal creativity. Children's involvement in activites where they experience mini-c creativity can lead to higher levels of creative expression. 'Little-c creativity' involves the generation of possibile ideas (novel to the person or context) to solve real world problems or everyday creativity. 'Big-C creativity' involves ideas that make large-scale contributions to intellectual domain or creative genius. The teacher's role can be conceptualised as helping children to develop 'mini-c creative' experiences or ideas into 'little-c creative' expressions/products (Beghetto, 2007). Vital teaching strategies comprise listening to children's ideas, making clear task constraints, and providing many opportunities for ideas to be converted into products (Hathcock et al., 2015). The use of inquiry questions is emphasised as pivotal in scaffolding children's problem solving. This links with the role of Vygotsky's 'zone of proximal development' in enabling children to accomplish tasks that they could not complete on their own. Inquiry questions relate to creativity by encouraging children to think, analyse, develop and express their own ideas.

Elements of STEM in children's play

Following children's interests in early childhood means that STEM learning experiences could take a variety of forms. As noted earlier, STEM learning does not have to include all four disciplines. This avoids forcing the inclusion of one or more disciplines if they do not fit the learning situation. Similarly, STEM eductaion does not have to focus on problem solving or be project-based (Vasquez, 2015). The most important consideration is that the learning experiences are age-appropriate and relevant for children. The key principles of early childhood education (e.g. play-based, child-centred, open-ended exploration) remain paramount in STEM education. STEM education in early childhood becomes another approach for supporting young children's developmental learning. The STEM examples provided in this chapter involve situations and objects that children naturally engage with, highlighting that STEM is already a part of children's world.

Engineering in children's play

American researchers developed a framework that juxtaposes the characteristics of young children's learning with **engineering** education outcomes. Table 9.2 shows Bagiati and Evangelou's (2016) framework. There are several common elements between early education and engineering. For example, children are encouraged to learn cooperatively which is reflected in the dynamic, flexible work of resilient engineers. Children's innate desire to actively construct translates into the practical ingenuity of engineers.

Engineering – a practical application of scientific and mathematical understanding and principles as a part of the process of developing and maintaining solutions for an identified need or opportunity.

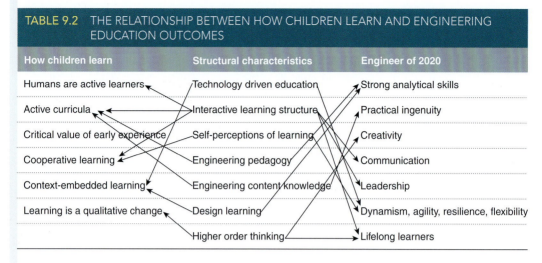

TABLE 9.2 THE RELATIONSHIP BETWEEN HOW CHILDREN LEARN AND ENGINEERING EDUCATION OUTCOMES

Source: Bagiati and Evangelou, 2016, p. 70.

Based on the argument proposed by these authors, STEM-based engineering activities have the potential to support children's learning behaviours.

These researchers observed the spontaneous play of a group (n = 18) of 3–5-year-old children with blocks and Lego over four months, in order to identify examples of engineering thinking and design behaviours of pre-schoolers. Questions concerning '*how* children construct with blocks, *why* they wish to construct, *what* they actually construct and ultimately *how they use* constructions' were of interest (Bagiati & Evangelou, 2016, p. 72). They concluded that the children's observed behaviours of needs identification, goal setting, thinking through problems, solution testing, repeating patterns, collaboration, ideas sharing, and design synthesis were comparable to the work of professional engineers. Although children's play could be mapped against the basic **design process** it was found to be spontaneous, materials-driven and adjusted to suit task needs (Bagiati & Evangelou, 2016).

Design process – a process that typically involves investigating and defining, generating and designing, producing and implementing, evaluating, and collaborating and managing to create a designed solution that considers social, cultural and environmental factors.

Technological literacy

Many young children are already technologically literate. Close observation of children in all types of learning contexts – independent play, adult-supported and adult-planned and led play – can identify evidence of technological know-how. A study of early childhood settings in New Zealand revealed 'well-developed technological knowledge and competence in instigating and carrying out technological tasks' (Mawson, 2013, p. 443). Children aged 3–4 years were observed and their play was classified as 'technological play' if there was evidence of 'clear intentions, plans and resource acquisition, an obvious process towards an appropriate solution and a way of evaluating success' (p. 445). Case studies included:

- boys creating a builder's yard to do builders' work
- girls making cars (equipped with seatbelts) to 'drive' to the shops and library
- children creating SCUBA gear (improved after a parent diver visit) and a dive boat
- an extended exploration of cows, farms and farming.

Mawson concluded that the children's play emulated technological practice. The children were observed 'establishing a purpose, planning and collecting appropriate resources and competently using tools and materals to achieve their desired outcome' (Mawson, 2013, p. 449). Notably, the settings had appropriate tools and materials available to children, which is more typical of early learning centres than school classrooms. Children also had time and freedom to revisit, modify and refine their products. The availability of resources and time have implications for the continuation of STEM learning experiences in the early school years. Some children may also require explicit instruction to develop specific skills, e.g. how to correctly hold and cut with scissors, to allow children's creativity to be fully expressed.

VACUUM CLEANING WITH MUM

Chloe (aged 2 years and 7 months) had a Hape® Butterfly Push Pal to use as a child-sized vacuum cleaner. Whenever her Mum vacuum cleaned the carpet, young Chloe would fetch the toy and work alongside her. Chloe pushed and pulled the toy back and forth in time with her Mum as she cleaned the carpet. This mother–daughter interaction is pictured in Figure 9.1. The smiles on their faces indicate this is an enjoyable time. This makes the task of cleaning enjoyable for Mum and provides a positive learning environment for the child.

FIGURE 9.1 Children learn about STEM in the home by modelling family members – as indicated by a child vacuuming with her Mum

Consider Case study 9.1 and the following questions:
1. What actions of the child indicate her interest in STEM learning around the home?
2. How could the conversation between Chloe and her mother enhance Chloe's understanding about the vacuum cleaner as a technological tool and how it helps people?
3. Where else might Chloe encounter vacuum cleaners being used?
4. How could you build on Chloe's home learning experiences in an early learning centre?

REFLECTION

Practical task

INTENTIONAL TEACHING WITH TECHNOLOGICAL DEVICES

Design a short intentional teaching activity around exploring a common technological device in the home, such as a vacuum cleaner. Consider the following in your planning:

1. Science – how a vacuum cleaner works and the health benefits from its use.
2. Technology – learning about the parts of the vacuum cleaner and thinking about how rugs/carpets were cleaned before vacuum cleaners were invented.
3. Engineering – design elements that make vacuum cleaners easy or comfortable for people to use and how technological products are tested.
4. Mathematics – relate to the actions of using a vacuum cleaner, size and shape of its components and how many times it can be used before emptying the dirt.

Using STEM education to enhance children's understanding of the world

Children growing up today encounter many technological products as part of their daily lives. A house without a television, for example, would be strange for most children. There are many examples of technological products that children use regularly without thinking about how they were made or how they work. Engaging children in exploration of common products, such as a pencil, torch, toy with moving parts that does not require batteries, scissors, tongs, stapler or a rubber band can help them learn about everyday items.

Involving children in design

Design is an important element of technology and engineering in STEM education. Design and technology 'involves problem finding and solving activities that are child-centred and focused' (Rogers & Wallace, 2000, p. 127). Design is a formal process that is characterised by explicit stages and pre-determined success criteria. The design process is often represented as a step-wise cycle to emphasise that it is iterative (it can be repeated). Regardless of the specific steps in the process, design incorporates problem-finding and solution-generating actions. Rogers and Wallace (2000) explain 'the act of design integrates different aspects of learning – the analytical and synthetic; the planning and tinkering; the detailed and the holistic; and the cognitive with the affective' (p. 128). The process should support children to be innovative, creative, resourceful and confident in their unique solutions. This is achieved by adopting an attitude of acceptance. There is no fixed way to approach tasks, and 'mistakes' are part of the process. Problems should be open-ended with a range of possible solutions.

Model – a representation that describes, simplifies, clarifies or provides an explanation of the workings, structure or relationships within an object, system or idea.

Young children's learning is very flexible. Expecting children to strictly follow even a simplified design process (draw a plan, make a **model**, work model creation), is unrealistic and inappropriate. A young child may swiftly develop a design plan in their head and be ready to construct. Enforcing a drawing phase could stifle their creative urge. Young children's drawn designs can be constrained by uncertainty about the purpose of the plan (why draw it), what it should look like (side view, top view) and their lack of drawing skills (inability to show what they imagine) (Rogers & Wallace, 2000, p. 134). Fleer (2016) highlights the role of teacher modelling of drawing and planning to develop these design skills. The act of drawing may help some children develop ideas when they are trying to decide what to construct. It is not essential for young children to complete every stage in the design process, or even to stick to the proposed order (Meeteren & Zan, 2010).

EXPLORING TORCHES

A group of 5-year-old children were looking at a collection of torches. The teacher had six different types of torches for the children to explore. In a small circle, the children passed all the torches around. They talked about what they liked about each torch, which was their favourite torch, and who had their own torch. The teacher guided the children to notice similarities and differences between the torches. She allowed the children to tell stories about when they had used a torch at home. The children turned the torches on and made light patterns on the ceiling. The teacher showed the children her torch, which was different from the others. She asked if the children could help her work out how to turn it on. This led to a search for the 'button' to press, which her torch did not have. Instead, it had a rectangular piece that slid forward. The children said this must be an old torch that was made before the 'button' part was invented. When the teacher tried to turn her torch on using the 'slide', it did not work. She wondered what was wrong. Some children told her to 'push it in', others said it must be broken. One child said she might have forgotten to put batteries in it.

REFLECTION

Consider Case study 9.2 and the following questions:
1. What makes this intentional teaching episode a STEM learning experience?
2. What could the educator do next to extend children's learning about torches?
3. Why are torches a good example of a technological product for children to explore?

MAKING A MODEL TORCH

The teacher asked her class of 5-year-old children if they thought it possible to make their own torch. What would they need to do this? Conversation pared down children's suggestions to the essential parts: a light bulb, batteries and something to join them together. Some children were surprised that a switch (button to turn it on) was not needed. Others were sceptical that a tube or case was also not required. The teacher explained that they were going to make a scientific model to help them understand how a torch works. The teacher had some special wires (Mag

Leads, see Preston, 2017) that could join to metal. She showed how one end 'stuck' to the class whiteboard. The teacher modelled where to attach the wire to the light bulb (on the screws). She highlighted a problem that the wire could stick anywhere on the battery and explained that it had to touch the ends of the battery. Pairs of children played with the materials to explore how to make the light work. Once one group made their light shine, much excitement ensued. Sharing of ideas, helping others and copying the arrangment of the parts assisted with the children's discoveries. Soon all the lights were working, with smiles all round, because the class had worked out for themselves how to make the light work. They also soon discovered that adding an extra battery made the light brighter. Some children also found that they could make the light flash by repeatedly clicking the batteries together and apart.

Consider Case study 9.3 and the following questions:

1. What teaching strategies were used to scaffold the children's torch making?
2. Why didn't the teacher use step-by-step instructions to make the light work?
3. How was this task developmentally appropriate for the 5-year-old children, given that electricity is part of the Year 6 science curriculum?

Case Study 9.4

DESIGNING A MULTI-PURPOSE TORCH

The teacher then challenged the class to make a multi-purpose torch. She outlined three design criteria needed: 1) it looks like a torch, 2) it can be easily carried around, and 3) it works as a reading light. The teacher showed the children the materials they could use (cardboard tubes, paper cups, masking tape, plastic containers, paddle pop sticks, bulb, battery, wires) and helped them think about the problem and possible solutions. The children worked in pairs to construct their torches. The teacher assisted with joining and assembly and made suggestions for problems that were difficult to solve. The children tested to see if their designs were successful. A class display was made of the completed designs. The teacher audio-recorded the children as they described special design elements of their torches and explained their purposes. The class talked about problems they encountered and how they were solved.

Consider Case study 9.4 and the following questions:

1. What STEM elements were involved in the multi-purpose torch design task?
2. How was digital technology used? What other ways could it have been used?

Recognising opportunities for STEM learning experiences

STEM learning experiences can arise in early childhood settings and classrooms in a number of different forms. They can be instigated by children or introduced by teachers based on children's interests or to align with formal curriculum. The key to appropriate and authentic STEM learning is to ensure that tasks are related to children's life experiences. While it can be easy to find a link to one or more of the STEM disciplines in almost any activity, adult input will usually strengthen the STEM learning capacity.

Play, creativity and invention

The relationship between play and invention that inspired a museum exhibit at the Smithsonian Institute in the United States (Smith, 2016) has implications for STEM learning experiences. The background research revealed similarities between children's play and the way inventors work. Literature from both invention and child development emphasises creativity. Creativity skills are developed through play, while inventiveness develops from the creative process. Certain types of children's play facilitate the development of creativity and resemble the playful approaches adopted by inventors (as shown in Table 9.3).

TABLE 9.3 RELATIONSHIPS BETWEEN CHILDREN'S PLAY AND INVENTORS' PLAYFUL APPROACHES

Children's play	Inventors' playful approaches
Exploratory play	Tinkering and experimenting with materials.
Play with puzzles, patterns and games	Problem-solving, including finding patterns and breaking patterns.
Symbolic or pretend play, including visual imagery	Simulation, modelling, and drawing analogies, spatial and visual thinking.
Social play	Brainstorming, role-playing and teamwork; subverting rules and diverging from norms.

Source: Smith, 2016, p. 249.

Inventors interviewed as part of the research agreed that play was integral to the inventive process because 'through play people develop creative habits of mind and hands-on skills' (Smith, 2016, p. 250). Inventors also spoke of the significance of informal education and interdisciplinary learning for enriching creative thinking. This suggests the value of STEM learning experiences for heightening children's creative abilities. The curiosity, imagination, zest for discovery and sense of wonder that children display as they try to determine how something works, or are busy constructing, is akin to the work of scientists, engineers, technologists, mathematicians and inventors.

Resourcing play

The type of play that young children engage in can be influenced by the materials provided in early learning settings. Meeteren and Zan (2010) argue that STEM and the design process already exist in high quality, constructivist early childhood programs. Identifying children's interests, posing developmentally appropriate problems and setting up learning centres with adaptable materials provides for the pursuit of learning aims with multiple solutions. Adding lengths of cove moulding and a variety of small objects to the block centre can stimulate children to build ramp structures. Inquiry can be prompted through broad questions, e.g. 'I wonder how we can get these objects to move?' Problems can become personalised by children's choice of materials (such as plastic eggs, small cars, blocks or marbles). Children's productive engagement in testing their design ideas and theories about force and motion can drive their learning. All aspects of STEM are encompassed by such learning situations. In particular, children's *practical* understanding of the science of force and motion can be developed as a precursor for later *conceptual* development (Meeteren & Zan, 2010).

STEM or STEAM

Some authors advocate combining arts-based strategies (e.g. dramatic play, drawing, painting and dancing) with STEM experiences and calling it STEAM. These authors suggest this affords greater communication potential arguing 'it is the arts that allow us to communicate the ideas we imagine' (Lindeman, Jabot & Berkley, 2014, p. 106). Effective early childhood teachers will make use of any, and all, strategies and experiences that support young children's learning and development. In that regard the STEM versus STEAM debate is rather moot. However, the definition adopted in this chapter does allow scope for such a merger. It does not matter if the term STEM or STEAM is used, so long as the science (and technology, engineering and mathematics) remains prominent. STEM education 'should be driven by engaging engineering problems, projects and challenges which are embedded in supporting science, mathematics, and technology skills, processes, and concepts' (Jolly, 2017, p. 31).

CHLOE'S CHAIR

Chloe's friend visited her with a bag full of plastic Lego-like blocks the size of house bricks. Chloe was instantly captivated and hurriedly helped empty the bag of blocks onto the lounge room floor. 'What shall we do with these blocks?', the adult friend asked. Chloe just smiled and started randomly arranging them. They played together for a while with the adult helping Chloe pull the blocks apart. Chloe quickly learnt how to make the blocks join together. The adult asked Chloe if she would like to use the blocks to make a chair. Chloe agreed. She made decisions about where to put the blocks with some guidance through conversation from the adult. For example, 'We need a higher part at the back, how can we make that?' 'If you place this lock across these two like that, it holds them together, it will make the chair stronger.' After the base was constructed together, Chloe continued to build the chair independently (Figure 9.2a)

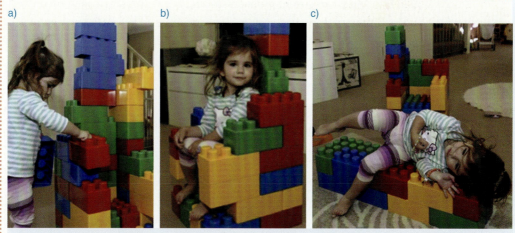

FIGURE 9.2 Chloe making her chair: a) Chloe placing blocks to construct a chair, b) Chloe is satisfied with her chair construction, c) Chloe's chair becomes a bed

Consider Case study 9.5 and the following questions:
1. Describe the role of the adult in this interaction.
2. As Chloe had not seen blocks like this before, could she have made a chair by herself?
3. When and why was it appropriate for the adult to withdraw her input to allow Chloe to continue free play with the blocks?

REFLECTION

In analysing the learning experience in Case study 9.5, various elements of STEM are apparent. The design process was loosely followed as the construction commenced with a goal, to make a chair. The product that was being constructed served a clear purpose, something to sit on. Chloe had a general idea about what the product should look like from her everyday experience with chairs. Mathematics learning was involved (although Chloe was not conscious of this) in the size, shape, number and symmetrical arrangement of the blocks and measurement. Area was also a factor relating to the size of the seat. This determined the final shape and usability of the chair. The iterative nature of the design process also became evident when the base of the chair had to be modified because Chloe could stand but not sit on the chair. The base was initally not big enough to fit Chloe's body. This design flaw was rectified by re-engineering the base. Science was encompassed in the properties of the material (durable plastic) that the blocks were made from as well as balance to ensure stability of the chair. Again, Chloe was not aware of these factors. Final product testing occurred as Chloe played with the chair that she was proud to have made. After a while, the novelty of the chair wore off and the blocks were remodelled into a bed (Figure 9.2c).

The sense of accomplishment, 'I made this!', is reflected in Chloe's body language (Figure 9.2b). This is an overt sign of the affective aspects of successful learning. It is this element of the STEM approach that contributes to the development of a child who feels capable in their ability to tinker and create. Through interacting with the blocks, Chloe has demonstrated that she can create, problem solve, make choices, evaluate, modify, use symmetry, and replicate a pattern. In this way, involvement in STEM-based play empowers children because this kind of activity provides opportunity and encourages such learning behaviours.

Practical task

OBSERVING STEM

1. Observe a group of children during their play time and note instances that could be categorised as science, technology, engineering and mathematics or a combination of these.
2. Analyse the knowledge that the children have brought to the play situation. What comprises their knowledge? What was the likely source of this knowledge?
3. List ways you could use the children's knowledge to extend these examples into STEM learning experiences.

The role of digital technologies in STEM learning experiences

Digital technologies – systems that handle digital data, including hardware and software, for specific purposes.

Computational thinking – a problem-solving method that involves various techniques and strategies that can be implemented by digital systems.

App – a software application with a very specific purpose designed to run on mobile devices (such as smartphones or tablets), through a web browser or on a personal computer.

There has been much rhetoric about the need for children to be exposed to computer programming or coding at a young age. Computer programming, the basis of all **digital technologies**, offers young children another avenue for creativity, plan execution, language development and problem-solving. Research into 'children's programming of animations, graphical models, games, and robots with age-appropriate materials allows them to learn and apply core computational thinking concepts' (Kazakoff, Sullivan & Bers, 2013, p. 246). In the Australian Curriculum: Technologies (ACARA, 2015), **computational thinking** is distinguished from **design thinking**, both of which are applied in digital technologies. While computational thinking draws on computing concepts, it is also 'a type of analytical thinking that can also be found in scientific thinking, mathematics thinking and engineering thinking' (Fleer, 2016, p. 135).

With the explosion of **apps** (short for 'applications') and recent emphasis on coding, there is a wide range of digital-based educational software designed for pre-schoolers. This presents a challenge for early childhood educators to detemine what constitutes appropriate and effective use of digital technologies. A critical consideration is whether engagement with a digital interface enhances children's learning over traditional instruction methods. Exemplary use of these technologies is when they enable children to experience learning in ways not previously possible.

Use of digital technologies by educators

An advantage of digital technologies for early childhood educators is the functionality in capturing significant moments when children are immersed in learning experiences. Spontaneous actions, candid expression of ideas, clever thinking, interesting observations and articulate explanations can be instantly captured by 'at-hand' electronic devices. These recordings can be replayed at the educators' convenience to use in assessment and monitoring of learning. They can also be replayed for the child or group to build on or discuss and reflect on the learning experience.

Tyler (2017) describes the potential use of iPads and specific apps for collecting assessment data in early primary classes to:

- increase children's engagement by recording in real time during investigations
- capture data from all children rather than one focus group
- provide more options to accurately document children's learning without the bias of literacy skills.

In the busy reality of early learning centres or early school classrooms, digital devices are being used in increasingly creative ways to support teaching and learning. The hands-on nature of STEM learning experiences means the digital devices are particularly useful for 'catching them doing'. Children can also learn *with* digital technologies and educators are continually finding new ways to do this.

Apps that have been developed for adults, rather than specifically for children, can also be used as stimulus for playful activities. A few examples that could be incorporated into STEM activities include:

- Bubble level – like a builder's spirit level that indicates whether a surface is horizontal (this can be introduced to help children evaluate structures they have built to improve their design)
- Dragon Dictation – spoken words are converted into digital text, a young child could describe a structure that they have designed and their spoken text could be placed alongside a photograph of the completed product
- Photobook – an educator can take photos of children as they design, create, produce and evaluate (the children could then select the photographs that they think best to show their creative process; they decide on the size of the book, the number of photos that will fit on each page, the layout and suitable captions, and the final product could be printed out or displayed on a digital bulletin board).

When considering which of the many available apps to use with pre-schoolers, educators should also be mindful of the diversity of learning needs of young children. Four useful principles to consider when providing experiences for all children are:

1. The child should be the source of the action.
2. The children should be able to see cause and effect relationships by changing the beginning action and seeing how it reflects on the outcome.
3. The outcome of changing the variable must be observable to the child.

4. The action and reaction must happen immediately for the child to see and make connections between the cause and effect (De Vries & Kohlberg, cited in Aronin & Floyd, 2013, p. 35).

WE SAW A CHICK HATCH

Early arrivers in Nicole's class of 5-year-olds ran straight to the incubator in the room to see if any more chicks had hatched overnight. The two children were avidly observing the new hatchlings when, by chance, a crack appeared in another egg. As none of the chicks had actually hatched during the school day, the children were very excited. They called the teacher over and she quickly grabbed her iPad and helped the children film the action. When all the children arrived, the teacher showed the recording to the class. The two children who took the video embellished the footage by relating their surprise and excitement in watching it happen.

Consider Case study 9.6 and the following questions:
1. How did the use of the iPad enhance the learning experience for the children?
2. What was advantageous about the use of this technology in this instance?
3. What other (non-digital) technology supported the richness of learning about living things for the children in the class?

Use of digital technologies by children

While digital technologies have advantages for early childhood educators, their potential is still being realised for direct use by children. Research is still emerging on the affordances of these technologies. Using interactive technologies just because they are available should be avoided. Digital technologies should be viewed as another tool for assisting children's learning. Like any other learning and teaching tool, their use must be evaluated and justified. For example, 'children playing with iPads to match one-to-one correspondence when this can be done with real items' (Lindeman, Jabot & Berkley, 2004, p. 99) is not an appropriate use of the technology. Teachers with a good working knowledge of digital technologies can guide children in using programs that facilitate creative expression and engage them in open-ended learning experiences.

A recent study of electronic books investigated the effectiveness of prompts built into touch screens on 4-year-old children's learning of biology concepts. The results showed that the use of the electronic book was just as effective in supporting understanding of camouflage as was the use of adult prompts (Strouse & Ganea, 2016, p. 1190). This result favoured children with a strong vocabulary. Children with lower vocabulary were better supported by adult-led prompting. The authors also noted that 'although electronic books are motivating because of their form, they may not motivate children to reflect and evaluate their conceptual theories in the same way as human interactions' (Strouse & Ganea,

2016, p. 1202). This reinforces the early childhood educators' role in deciding which tools to use according to desired learning goals and individual children's needs.

Robots and robotics

Robots are a technological invention that young children find fascinating. The fact that people can design and make machines that can perform human-like actions and tasks is intriguing. Incorporating robot technology into toys, making them programmable, brings robotics into the realm of children. The theme of 'Robots' is an appropriate STEM context for young children because it easily incorporates all four disciplines. Robots can also be explored in many different ways: read-aloud books, act out how a robot arm works, watch videos of robots in a chocolate factory, identify robots at home, and imagine futuristic robots (see *Robots Everywhere* in your future reading [Morgan & Ansberry, 2017]).

Codeable toys and computer programmable robotics designed for young children provide additional tools for early childhood educators to support children's development in different ways. For example, researchers hypothesised that sequencing of commands for robot programming uses similar processes to logical storytelling. Use of Lego WeDo robots with 4–5-year-old children resulted in a significant increase in sequencing ability (story card sorting) after a one-week intensive program. It was concluded that 'Robotics offers children and teachers a new and exciting way to tangibly interact with traditional early childhood curricular themes' (Kazakoff, Sullivan & Bers, 2013, p. 252).

Case Study 9.7

THEY CAN RECORD IT WITH THE IPAD

Some 6-year-old children decided they wanted to find out more about how balls bounce. One educator suggested a question they could investigate: 'What happens to the bounce height when a ball is dropped from different heights?' This teacher demonstrated how the children could use long blocks to standardise the drop height. She wondered out loud the best way to record the bounce height of the ball. The class educator suggested the children could record it using the iPads. Within minutes the children were using the camera function on the iPad to video the investigation. The children competently and confidently used the iPads. One group showed the educator how to use the iPad so they all could be recorded. This solved the problem of how to effectively measure the ball bounce height. A new set of skills were also developed as the technology was being applied in a different way. After the investigation, the class educator used the video to discuss and interpret the results on the investigation. Collectively, the children formed a generalisation to answer the original question.

Consider Case study 9.7 and the following questions:
1. How did the use of the iPad enhance the learning experience for the children?
2. What was advantageous about the use of this technology in this instance?

REFLECTION

Conclusion

This chapter highlighted how early childhood educators can foster the development of 21st century skills through STEM education, an integrated approach to teaching and learning about science, technology, engineering and mathematics. The characteristics and opportunities for STEM learning experiences in early childhood settings were described and emphasised with examples of familiar practice. The discerning use of digital technologies in the context of STEM was also discussed.

9 References

ACARA (2015). *The Australian Curriculum, Digital Technologies, Glossary*, 11, Australian Curriculum, Assessment and Reporting Authority (ACARA), Version 8.1. www.australiancurriculum .edu.au.

Aronin, S. & Floyd, K. (2013). Using an iPad in inclusive preschool classrooms to introduce STEM concepts, *Teaching Exceptional Children*, Mar/Apr, 34–9.

Bagiati, A. & Evangelou, D. (2016). Practicing engineering while building with blocks: Identifying engineering thinking, *European Early Childhood Education Research Journal*, 24(1), 67–85.

Beghetto, R. A. (2007). Ideational code-switching: Walking the talk about supporting student creativity in the classroom, *Roper Review*, 29(4), 265–70.

Bybee, R. (2010). Advancing STEM education: A 2020 vision, *Technology and Engineering Teacher*, September, 30–5.

Department of Education, Employment and Workplace Relations (DEEWR). (2009). *Belonging, Being & Becoming. The Early Years Learning Framework for Australia*, Canberra: Commonwealth of Australia.

Fleer, M. (2016). *Technologies for Children*. Melbourne: Cambridge University Press.

Hathcock, S., Dickerson, D., Eckhoff, A. & Katsioloudis, P. (2015). Scaffolding for creative product possibilities in a design-based STEM activity, *Research in Science Education*, 45, 727–48.

Jolly, A. (2017). *STEM by Design: Strategies and Activities for Grades 4–8*, New York: Routledge.

Kazakoff, E. R., Sullivan, A. & Bers, M. U. (2013). The effect of a classroom-based intensive robotics and programming workshop on sequencing ability in early childhood, *Early Childhood Education Journal*, 41, 245–55.

Lindeman, K. W., Jabot, M. & Berkley, M. T. (2014). The role of STEM (or STEAM) in the early childhood setting, in L. E. Cohen & S. Waite-Stupiansky (eds), *Learning Across the Early Childhood Curriculum* (*Advances in Early Education and Day Care*, 17) Emerald Group Publishing Limited, 95–114.

Lindeman, K. W. & McKendry Anderson, E. (2015). Using blocks to develop 21st Century Skills, *Young Children*, 36–43.

Mawson, W. B. (2013). Emergent technological literacy: What do children bring to school?, *International Journal of Design Education*, 23, 443–53.

Meeteren, B. V. & Zan, B. (2010). Revealing the work of young engineers in early childhood education, *Collected Papers from the SEED (STEM in Early Education and Development) Conference*, May 2010, Iowa: University of Northern Iowa.

Morgan, E. & Ansberry, K. (2017). *Picture-Perfect STEM Lessons, K–2: Using Children's Books to Inspire STEM Learning*, NSTA Press.

Partnership for 21st Century Learning (P21). (2015). *Framework for 21st Century Learning*, www.p21 .org/storage/documents/docs/P21_framework_0816.pdf.

—— (n.d., a). *What We Know About Creativity*, The 4Cs Research Series, Washington, DC: Partnership for 21st Century Skills.

—— (n.d., b). *What We Know About Critical Thinking*, The 4Cs Research Series, Washington, DC: Partnership for 21st Century Skills.

—— (n.d., c). *What We Know About Collaboration*, The 4Cs Research Series, Washington, DC: Partnership for 21st Century Skills.

—— (n.d., d). *What We Know About Communication*, The 4Cs Research Series, Washington, DC: Partnership for 21st Century Skills.

Preston, C. (2017). Try this: STEM torch design, *Teaching Science*, 63(3), 7–14.

Rogers, G. & Wallace, J. (2000). The Wheels of the Bus: Children designing in an early years classroom, *Research in Science & Technological Education*, 18(1), 127–36.

Rosicka, C. (2016). *From Concept to Classroom: Translating STEM Education Research into Practice*. Melbourne: Australian Council for Educational Research.

Smith, M. (2016). Playful invention, inventive play, *International Journal of Play*, 5(3), 244–61.

Strouse, G. A. & Ganea, P. A. (2016). Are prompts provided by electronic books as effective for teaching preschoolers a biological concept as those provided by adults?, *Early Education and Development*, 27(8), 1190–204.

Tyler, T. (2017). In the thick of it: Using tablets for recording and assessment, *Primary Science*, 147, 29–32.

Vasquez, J. (2015). STEM beyond the acronym, *Educational Leadership, December*, 10–5.

PART 3

How can I use the learning environment to enhance children's science understandings?

The science learning environment

Coral Campbell, Wendy Jobling and Christine Howitt

This chapter focuses on the ways in which educators can use indoor learning environments to support science learning in play-based contexts. Space, layout and materials are discussed in relation to the inside learning environment, with the use of materials highlighted through the potential they offer to enhance the curriculum. The place of cooking, the science discovery table, tinkering (also refer to Chapter 9, 'STEM education in early childhood') and construction are emphasised. Examples of science opportunities available in the indoor learning environment in relation to exploring materials and play equipment are presented.

OBJECTIVES

At the end of this chapter you will be able to:

- describe the importance of the learning environment for children's science learning

- describe how space and materials can support children's science learning in the indoor learning environment

- provide examples of science that can be explored by children through inside and built learning environments

- describe how digital technologies can be used to enhance and support young children's science explorations.

Learning environments

Learning environments – welcoming places that enrich the lives and identities of children and their families. Also known as 'places for childhood' or 'the third educator'.

Definitions of **learning environments** range from 'places for childhood' (Curtis & Carter, 2003) to 'the third educator' (Fraser, 2006) to 'wherever we are' (Williams-Siegfredsen, 2012). The definition from the Early Years Learning Framework states:

> Learning environments are welcoming spaces when they reflect and enrich the lives and identities of children and families participating in the setting and respond to their interests and needs. Environments that support learning are vibrant and flexible spaces that are responsive to the interests and abilities of each child. They cater for different learning capacities and learning styles and invite children and families to contribute ideas, interests and questions. (DEEWR, 2009, p. 15)

Learning environments are more than the physical space, as they include how time is structured and the roles that adults and children play (Greenman, 2007). Learning environments influence how children feel, think and behave, thus affecting their cognitive, linguistic, social, emotional and physical development. Every environment implies a set of values or beliefs about the people who use that space and the activities that take place within it (Curtis & Carter, 2003).

The learning environment includes both indoor and outdoor aspects. The arrangement of the learning environment is important in providing maximal learning opportunities. This arrangement should consider both space and materials: space to invite open-ended interactions, spontaneity and discovery; and materials to provoke interest, wonder and more complex thinking (Curtis & Carter, 2003). Through the development of appropriate learning environments, educators can assist children to investigate new objects, re-investigate familiar objects from a new perspective and construct new ideas about the world. Children are highly adaptable when it comes to using space creatively to test their own ideas. Educators can assist children through the making of creative spaces and the supply of appropriate materials and resources.

Supporting science learning through the physical environment

Along with the educator and program quality, the physical environment is a critical partner in children's learning. In discussing the indoor environment it is important to consider space, room layout and materials. Chaille and Britain (2003) comment that the physical space can contribute to children's learning of science from a social constructivist stance.

Characteristics of space

There are five characteristics of space that educators should consider when developing activities inside: flow, size and space, aesthetics, spatial variability and flexibility (Greenman, 2007). Flow refers to entries and exits and how children move from one point to another. It includes corridors between spaces and the routes that children take (planned or unplanned). Size and space refer to the scale of objects and people in the children's environment. Child-sized equipment and toys allow children to behave competently and to feel empowered. Aesthetics refers to the use of lighting, colours, art and display, texture, nature, sound and smell in the environment. Spatial variety provides children with places to be. These can be places to play in a group or places to be alone. Flexibility allows an environment to be transformed for a variety of uses. This can be done through play spaces at different levels, heights and angles. Large spaces can be turned into small spaces by screens, dividers, materials, boxes and pillows. There are a number of recognised principles (Chaille & Britain, 2003, p. 35) which can be applied when dealing with the physical space of a centre. The physical space should:

- allow for good traffic flow and easy movement (children's free movement encourages them to be independent and to facilitate play across areas and materials)
- allow for as much flexibility as possible in the use of the physical space (as children adapt their science play, the learning space should permit them to move things around to enhance this learning)
- allow for flexibility in the use of furniture (furniture which is not obviously prescribed for a single task permits children to re-imagine it in a novel way)
- encourage children's self-direction through the accessibility of materials (when materials are easily accessible to children, they are more comfortable and confident to choose for themselves without adult intervention)
- encourage creative problem-solving through reciprocity between learning areas (if children can move materials across spaces, their play is fluid and uninterrupted)
- provide materials which can be used in multiple ways (materials which can be re-purposed allow children to imagine differently and enhance creativity)
- allow children to create and maintain a social learning experience (facilitating children's play through making things as easy as practicable allows active exploration)
- allow for reasonable noise and movement (children's interactions produce noise, so restricting all noise will restrict creative play)
- enhance children's interactions through the provided resources (materials which encourage collaborative play improve children's learning opportunities)
- encourage social interaction (the way furniture is organised can encourage collaboration and cooperative play)
- encourage children's self direction through the way things are organised (the way materials and facilities are organised and available can aid or hinder the way children play).

Adapted from Chaille and Britain, 2003.

Room layout

Room layout is a reflection of the available space, children, program goals, educator's philosophy and available resources (Greenman, 2007). In developing a classroom layout, consideration should be given to the fixed spaces (doors, windows, sinks, lighting and toilets), different zones (wet area, dry area, quiet area, active area and transitional area), pathways, dividers, and nooks and crannies. Access to all activities and materials should be easy and free-flowing, allowing children the freedom to choose where they wish to play and what activity they will work on. Space should be allowed between activities so that children do not have to negotiate convoluted pathways or narrow corners.

In designing the room layout, consideration should be given to providing a range of activities. Along with the discovery table, learning spaces may incorporate a quiet reading area, a writing/drawing area, a construction area, a painting area and an imaginative play area (including dress-ups). For special teacher-directed activities, a free space may be needed to accommodate a range of activities. Low moveable dividers can create walled, inclusive spaces and provide the flexibility to move them at will, such as when a larger space is needed to accommodate more children or a larger activity. Physical indoor spaces can be changed, allowing children to use the space creatively and make use of materials found inside.

Materials

The materials found in an early childhood centre or in the lower classes of primary school usually fit into two categories – commercially available (purchased) or recycled (taken from another place and repurposed). Purchased materials include items bought to achieve a particular outcome, such as wooden or plastic blocks to facilitate construction activities, or plastic dinosaurs to enable play around prehistoric animals. Other purchased materials can be in the form of 'kits', such as a farm kit which includes a range of buildings, appropriate animals, tools and characters to make up the farm. In particular, general science equipment can include magnifying lenses, eyedroppers, mirrors, magnets – all of which facilitate science play.

In terms of the recycled materials, there are many types of materials which can facilitate more open-ended science play:

- containers – such as plastic (milk cartons) can be used to make terrariums, aquariums and other 'small animal' homes
- hardware items – such as hosing, plastic pipes and funnels, encourage material movement from one place to another and can be adapted to make musical instruments
- flashlights and torches – useful for an introduction to electricity
- toys, clocks and other small machines – good for a tinkering table or 'maker' space
- cardboard containers of all sizes can be adapted to a range of needs – dioramas, animal habitats
- pipe cleaners, straws, balloons, paper plates and cups, pieces of fabric – useful for construction activities and for material investigation activities
- any item which can be counted or sorted – such as buttons, lids or seeds can facilitate categorising and reasoning activities
- old clothes for dress-up and imaginative role play.

Materials have the possibility to enhance the curriculum. Children constantly use materials to learn about their world, explore their questions and represent their thinking (Curtis & Carter, 2008). Initially, children use materials to learn about their properties, trying to connect with their prior experiences. Once familiar with the materials, children will then use them with a specific purpose in mind. Curtis and Carter (2008) developed seven principles for using materials: select materials using an enhanced view of children (i.e. believe in the capabilities of the children), invent new possibilities for familiar materials, draw on the aesthetic qualities of materials, choose materials that can be transformed, provide real tools and quality materials, supply materials to extend children's interests, and layer materials to offer complexity.

'In any environment, both the degree of inventiveness and creativity, and the possibility of discovery, are directly proportional to the number and kinds of variables [materials or loose parts] in it' (Nicholson, 1972, p. 6). This **loose parts theory** suggests that when children are presented with a wide range of materials with no defined purpose, they will be more inventive in their play and will have infinite play opportunities for manipulating the materials in ever-changing ways. Loose parts, also known as open-ended materials, are items with no defined use that can be moved, carried, combined, redesigned, lined up and taken apart and put back together in multiple ways. Loose parts have no instructions; rather, they invite children to use their own imagination and creativity and develop their own play scripts. Loose parts can be natural or synthetic and include stones, stumps, sand, gravel, fabric, twigs, wood, pallets, balls, buckets, baskets, crates, boxes, logs, rope, tyres, shells and seedpods.

> **Loose parts theory** – this theory suggests that when children are presented with a wide range of materials with no defined purpose they will be more inventive in their play.

While loose parts enable creativity and invention, providing materials on their own to children does not necessarily teach scientific concepts. Fleer (2009) reported that where resources are introduced to children within an appropriate scientific framework, or teacher-led interactions are focused on scientific concepts, then science learning has more opportunity to occur. Fleer (2009) also noted that without adult guidance or a 'scientific framework for using materials in play-based contexts, children will generate their own imaginary, often non-scientific, narratives for making sense of the materials provided' (p. 1069). This implies that the best science learning opportunities will occur with discourse between children and adults while interacting with materials.

To encourage children to be self-directed, they require time along with free and easy access to activities and materials. Harlan and Rivkin (2008) observed that making available exploration time for young children was important in ensuring that children had sufficient opportunity to investigate and solve problems. However, if too many materials and choices are available, children can be overstimulated. This can lead to them 'flitting' between activities and not spending enough time on any single activity to allow for development or consolidation of ideas. Using materials sensibly and rotating them through activities means that children will be stimulated anew as the different materials are made available.

Organising materials to facilitate learning science through play

As material is collected for science learning, whether it is the various science-based kits, or the loose recycled materials, storage and appropriate organisation is required to allow for ease of access. Loose materials can be stored according to their properties or according to a science theme that they augment. For example, small containers may be placed together to allow for use in the collection of classified items, or shells may be placed together with rocks, magnifying lenses and other items for an exploration table around the theme of 'the sea'. Labelling is important both for the educator and the children. Use of coloured pictorial representation assists children to choose the most appropriate material for their play, and encourages them to return unused material to the right container. Children are very adept at organising things if given the right assistance.

Preparing science activities for teacher-led or child-instigated learning

In preparing activities, the educator should be aware of children's physical, emotional, social and cognitive needs and how best to meet these needs through the provided activities, resources and interactions. Some children will prefer an occasional, one-on-one interaction with the teacher, while others will prefer to work alone or in small peer groups. Allowing for all these possibilities will enhance children's learning. When developing activities, decisions have to be made about whether to use whole-group discussion (tuning in) or whether the activity can be left to children's 'discovery' with some educator guidance or focusing. Either way, planning is crucial so that the educator takes into account the purpose of the activity and the needs of the children. In particular, activities should be age-appropriate, open-ended and encouraging of some skill or knowledge development. Customised science learning experiences, based on children's demonstrated interests, should promote independence in actions and thinking; responsibility towards themselves, others and the objects they deal with; autonomy, reducing the need for adult intervention; involved engagement and active participation; enthusiasm and intrinsic motivation; and the development of conceptual understanding, problem-solving skills and creative thinking.

There are many common activities in early childhood centres that lend themselves appropriately to science learning. These include cooking, discovery/exploration table, play dough manipulation, and machines and construction activities.

Cooking

In any cooking activity, children are engaged in a number of science skills and processes. The selection of ingredients encourages children to discuss the function of each ingredient and its purpose in the cooking. Measuring allows for children to develop hand–eye coordination as well as the ability to read marks as communicating significance, such as volume. When children follow a recipe, they are learning that a process can lead to an end point or conclusion. In mixing, children see physical change occurring through their own application. In using tools such as mixers, egg beaters, spatulas, lifters and spoons, children engage in exploration of **forces**, levers and measuring devices. The final stage, cooking, provides children with experiences of a chemical change to a substance – the original materials are no longer retrievable. Other cookery investigations that promote science understanding of basic chemistry (mixing, dissolving, evaporation, condensation, melting, solidification, thawing and freezing) include making jelly from gelatine and fruit/flavouring, making butter from cream, making icecream and mixing flavoured drinks. The role of the educator is to ensure that the science is drawn out as part of the discussions and children's questions.

Force –
a force is a push or a pull. Children can experience this directly when using play equipment or when applying a push or a pull to shape materials.

CHOCOLATE POTATO CAKE

In an early learning centre for 3-year-olds one child discovered a potato when 'weeding' the vegetable patch during free play. This discovery filled many of the children with excitement and they joined the dig. The result was a harvest of many potatoes, which then led to a range of explorations and activities. A question was asked by the educator: 'What do you know about potatoes?'

On being asked to draw the potatoes, including different forms of potatoes, children explained their drawings as a 'A potato cookie with chocolate on it! This is a chocolate potato cake!'

The educator followed up on the children's idea that 'We should make a chocolate potato cake!' A recipe was found on the internet and a small group of children went into the kitchen to make the cake. They measured out the ingredients, mashed the potatoes, mixed the ingredients and licked the spoon. They then shared the cake with their peers and even the principal. The chocolate potato cake became the stuff of legend in the early learning centre. The children talked about it for weeks afterwards. It spawned a story book, a play, a podcast, mud play and further inquiry into recipes.

Case study 10.1 highlights how one child-initiated event led to many rich science learning experiences due to an educator who was prepared to follow the children's ideas. These science experiences included food coming from plants, observations for drawing potatoes, descriptions of potatoes, and physical and chemical changes associated with cooking, and the entire sequence of events resulted from one child weeding the garden.

1. What other science experiences could be included that relate to potatoes?
2. Discuss the importance of follow-up activities on the development of children's learning.

Science discovery table

The science discovery table is one way to provide children with materials not normally available to them. Children can investigate seeds, seed pods, leaves or bark as an extension of their outside explorations. They can use tools such as magnifying lenses, digital cameras, torches, magnets, wind-up toys and other moveable objects. The discovery table may provide objects that have a specific purpose, such as an egg slide, egg whisk, can-opener and other household implements. Construction items/kits and digital players (iPods or iPads) can provide children with the opportunity to explore the reason for such instruments and how they work. Building on this, objects can be provided for children to tinker with to find out how they work. Suitable objects can be simple toys that can be easily taken apart and put back together again. Avoid toys with small parts that could present safety issues and that may be beyond young children's fine motor skills. Manufactured materials, such as plastics, laminates, metals and timbers, can be examined more closely with greater attention to detail. Educators can encourage children to look closely at patterns, similarities, differences and changes in the science explorations.

DEVELOPING AWARENESS OF DIFFERENT ROCKS

To provide the 1–2-year-olds with experiences of different features and textures related to rocks, the educators placed large containers holding many different rocks on the discovery table. They then assisted the young children to select rocks according to their own classification, which related to colour, size and texture. They introduced the language, such as rough or smooth, to the children.

Consider Case study 10.2 and the following questions:
1. What other aspects of rocks could be incorporated into this investigation?
2. What other language could the educator use to expand children's understanding?

Play dough manipulation

As children work with play dough, they are shaping the dough to represent their ideas or understandings about something they are interested in. For example, it could be an animal with four legs or a boat with a strange shape. As the dough is manipulated, it is squeezed, rolled, pinched, pulled, pushed, stretched, rolled or twisted. All of these actions represent the force a child is exerting to alter the shape of the dough. They are not only experiencing the force they exert, but also the resistance of the material. If children are provided with the opportunity to work with clay or plasticine in addition to play dough, they start to understand the different properties of malleability as well as develop an appreciation of different surface textures of the different materials.

LAYERS OF POSSIBILITIES

To assist children to learn about texture, the educator provided the 2–4-year-old children with a range of household and natural materials to explore in play dough. She offered keys, screw-top lids, spanners, nuts, bolts and screws, along with shells, small pine cones, flowers and leaves. Observing how the children had interacted with these materials, the educator commented how delighted she was with the wide range of ways the children used the play dough. Some children flattened the play dough and positioned flowers or screws to form a pattern. Others took the new metal objects and explored the patterns they made in the play dough. Shells, pine cones and screw tops became the setting for adventure stories. The ends of the spanners were used to make rows of small play dough balls, which were then classified by size.

REFLECTION

Consider Case study 10.3 and the following questions:

1. Note how the educator used the play dough as a sensory base and then added layers of possibility with a range of familiar and new materials. What other materials could you use to expand the complexity of working with play dough to encourage scientific exploration?
2. What conversation could the educator have with the children to encourage them to explore with their senses and describe what they are doing?

Machines and construction

Machines in an early childhood environment refer to simple machines such as levers, wedges, screws, inclined planes, pulleys, and the wheel and axle. Scientifically, simple machines make work easier by allowing us to push or pull over increased distances. Children's play areas contain many examples of these simple machines. A slide is an example of an inclined plane; a pair of scissors shows us how wedges work; while every time children build ramps down which to run a car, they are demonstrating an awareness of an inclined plane as well as the mechanics of the wheel and axle.

Blocks of various shapes and sizes offer endless opportunities for children to design and construct. Research by Robbins and Jane (2008) indicated that block play can improve children's technological thinking; from planning through to designing, producing and evaluating their own constructions. This builds on earlier work by Fleer (2000) who found that young children (4–5 years old) are capable of developing their own **design briefs** and construction tasks.

Design brief – a concise statement clarifying a project task and defining a need or opportunity to be resolved after some analysis, investigation and research. It usually identifies users, criteria for success, constraints, available resources and timeframe for a project and may include possible consequences and impacts (ACARA, 2015).

Case Study 10.4

CONSTRUCTING A ROLLER-COASTER

The 5-year-old children had been learning about how the size and shape of an object influence how the object moves. Part of this discussion had included children's favourite show rides, such as the Ferris wheel, train rides and bumper cars. Many children said they wanted to go on a roller-coaster but their parents had told them they were not yet old enough. This started a two-week investigation by the children into different roller-coasters. They searched for different designs using the class computer and printed out their favourites. The children then each drew a picture of a roller-coaster they would like to make using the materials in the classroom, labelling their diagrams. The class voted on the 'best' five designs, with the children being split into groups to construct the roller-coasters.

One design used the materials from the block corner, which contained a 10 cm high table. Surrounding this table were blocks of different sizes and shapes, long cardboard tubes, small wooden spools, recycled boxes of different sizes, long strips of material, small plastic mirrors, plus an assortment of seed pods and small logs. The children initially followed the roller-coaster design, having the cardboard tubes angling from the table top to the floor. They then discussed the different heights of a roller-coaster and how this balance could be achieved in their

→

→ construction. Blocks and logs were used to create scaffolding of different heights on the table. Chairs were moved to the table so that cardboard tubes could go across, adding width to the roller-coaster. Children used the seed pods as the people and moved them over the roller-coaster.

The design of the roller-coaster became more elaborate daily as children thought of additional ways that materials could be connected and how the strips of material could be included. To capture the changing designs, children took photos of their favourite part of the roller-coaster with the Educreations app on the class iPad. Using the features of this app, children circled various components in the photo and audio-recorded how they had constructed that component. The educator included this as part of her assessment.

REFLECTION

Consider Case study 10.4 and the following questions:

1. How does this case study demonstrate that loose parts lead to creativity and imagination?
2. What pedagogy did the educator employ as the children designed and developed their roller-coasters? Consider space, classroom layout and materials in your answer.

Using digital technology as a teaching tool or for children's learning

Digital technology – any technology controlled using digital instructions, including computer hardware and software. Computers, smartphones, digital cameras, printers and robots are all examples of digital technologies.

The role of **digital technology** has increased significantly in recent times in early childhood centres. In particular, many early childhood centres are using digital technologies to communicate with parents through private websites, blogs and other interactive multimedia sites. Photographs and records of children's learning/activity can be instantly forwarded to parents or uploaded to a secure site for later perusal and parent comment. Educators can provide children with extended understanding using immediate internet responses around children's queries. However, as indicated in Chapter 9, educators need to be careful of how and why they use digital resources.

A number of relatively inexpensive digital technologies can enhance children's learning. Apart from computers, small digital microscopes can be linked to a computer to increase a small image to computer size. As an animal is crawling across a small container, children can view in detail how the animal moves, what food it might stop to eat and how the different parts of its body are interconnected. Close observation, one of the science process skills, then becomes much easier for the children. The digital image can be frozen and saved onto the computer for children to use. The image can be used to allow a child to reconstruct their understanding of the animal in other ways (drawing, painting or construction). Similarly, iPads or digital cameras can be used in the classroom to record both still or moving images, which can be stored for future reference or use or can be incorporated into a further learning experience. An example of this is where children use the digital image and create a story about the object or image.

REPRESENTING SMALL ANIMALS

At a pre-school the educator provided the 4-year-old children with a digital hand-held micro-scope so that they could see the small animals they had just collected from the outside garden. The children were given the option of drawing or using plasticine to record their animal.

Rather than simply producing a fine piece of art, one child showed her detailed knowledge of spiders in making her plasticine spider. She knew that spiders have eight legs and two body parts and that the abdomen is generally bigger than the cephalothorax. She demonstrated that the legs are attached to only one part of the body, although she attached the legs to the abdomen rather than the cephalothorax. She also knew that a spider has eyes and often feelers or palps. Thus, the plasticine spider allowed this child to demonstrate six significant facts about spiders.

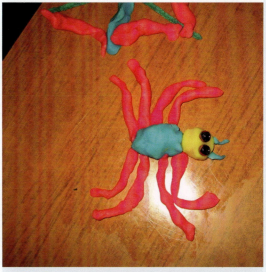

FIGURE 10.1   A plasticine spider made to record a child's understanding of the parts of a spider

Consider Case study 10.5 and the following questions:
1. Would you address the child's idea that a spider's legs are attached to its abdomen? Why or why not? If yes, how would you go about building her knowledge?
2. Suggest ways in which the child could extend her science knowledge to look at the spider's habitat, and finally to look at its place in an ecosystem.

The built environment

The **built environment** may include items such as play equipment along with structural elements such as taps, seating arrangements, walls, paths, buildings, fences and roads. The built environment provides children with opportunities to explore and develop scientific skills and understandings as well as technological skills and understandings. This may include experiencing the forces on the body of a swing or the effect of gravity when moving down a slide. While very young children are introduced slowly and are supported when using these items of equipment, older children quickly learn how to manipulate them to gain the best effect – for example, how to move their body in order to swing higher.

> **Built environment** – includes play equipment along with structural elements such as buildings, walls, taps, seating, paths, fences and roads.

FIGURE 10.2 Even young children can benefit from experience with a range of simple machines and the effect of gravity – using a slide also introduces children to other forces such as friction

Other aspects of the built environment can help children develop understanding of force as a 'push' or a 'pull'. Forces can make things move or stop, or hold things up or squeeze things. When children are pushed on a swing, they experience the force of the push, then the force of resistance created by the air pushing back as they move through the air. Children can feel the pull of gravity as the swing ascends, then a sense of weightlessness at the top of the travel of the swing, before gravity affects the movement of the child back towards the earth.

Conclusion

This chapter highlighted how educators can use the indoor learning environment to support science learning in play contexts. The features of space, layout and materials that enhance science learning in the indoor environment were described. Science learning opportunities were found to be more likely to occur where there was discourse between children and adults while interacting with materials. The characteristics and opportunities offered for science learning were described in relation to the use of digital technologies and the built environment.

Acknowledgement

The authors wish to thank the following early childhood educator for her story: Lynda Slavinskis for 'Chocolate potato cake'.

10 References

Chaille, C. & Britain, L. (2003). *The Young Child as Scientist: A Constructivist Approach to Early Childhood Science Education* (3rd edn), Boston: Allyn and Bacon.

Curtis, D. & Carter, M. (2003). *Designs for Living and Learning: Transforming Early Childhood Environments*, St Paul, MN: Redleaf Press.

—— (2008). *Learning Together with Young Children: A Curriculum Framework for Reflective Teachers*, St Paul, MN: Redleaf Press.

Department of Education, Employment and Workplace Relations (DEEWR). (2009). *Belonging, Being and Becoming: The Early Years Learning Framework for Australia*, Canberra: Commonwealth of Australia.

Fleer, M. (2000). Interactive technology: Can children construct their own design briefs? *Research in Science Education*, 30(2), 241–53.

—— (2009). Supporting scientific conceptual consciousness of learning in 'a roundabout way' in play-based contexts, *International Journal of Science Education*, 31(8), 1069–89.

Fraser, S. (2006). *Experiencing Reggio Emilia in the Classroom* (2nd edn), Toronto: Thomson.

Greenman, J. (2007). *Caring Spaces, Learning Places: Children's Environments that Work*, Redmond, WA: Exchange Press.

Harlan, J. & Rivkin, M. (2008). *Science Experiences for the Early Childhood Years: An Integrated Affective Approach* (9th edn), Columbus, OH: Pearson/Merrill Prentice Hall.

Nicholson, S. (1972). The theory of loose parts. An important principle for design methodology, *Studies in Design Education Craft and Technology*, 4(2), 5–14.

Robbins, J. & Jane, B. (2008). Developing young children's technological thinking through play with blocks, in H. Middleton & P. Pavlova (eds), *Exploring Technology Education Solutions to Issues in a Globalised World*, vol. 2, proceedings of the 5th Biennial International Conference on Technology Education Research, Griffith Institute for Educational Research, Queensland, 129–36.

Williams-Siegfredsen, J. (2012). *Understanding the Danish Forest School Approach: Early Years Education in Practice*, Abingdon: Routledge.

11 Learning science in informal contexts: the home and community

Jill Robbins

Science is everywhere, and learning about science may occur not only in formal school settings, but also in home and community contexts. Memories of some of the informal learning that occurred in years gone by, even when we were very young, can remain with us throughout our lives.

This chapter aims to highlight the importance of learning science outside formal spaces such as early childhood centres and schools. Families have substantial funds of knowledge that they can share with children through their everyday practices, such as cooking, gardening and tinkering in back sheds. These practices will draw on cultural knowledge from across generations and need to be taken account of respectfully by educators.

OBJECTIVES

At the end of this chapter, you will be able to:

- identify and acknowledge the significance of ways in which informal science processes and concepts are being developed within the everyday practices of families

- acknowledge the importance of science pedagogical content knowledge

- attempt to make conscious connections between the everyday concepts that children develop in informal settings, and scientific or academic concepts that are introduced in school or early childhood institutional settings

- draw on *Belonging, Being and Becoming: The Early Years Learning Framework for Australia* (DEEWR, 2009) and aspects of the Australian Curriculum: Science (ACARA, 2017) to inform your teaching of science.

The importance of early childhood recollections for science learning

Were there special people in your life, perhaps grandparents, aunts or elders, who taught you how to grow and harvest vegetables or herbs, or to cook cupcakes, told you traditional stories about the Sun, taught you to respect country, showed you how to knit, or how to fix a wobbly wheel on a cart?

> From birth children are connected to family, community, culture and place. Their earliest development and learning takes place through these relationships, particularly within families, who are children's first and most influential educators (DEEWR, 2009, p. 7).

When I think back to my childhood, I can remember so many wonderful experiences – especially building cubby houses. Sometimes this was done inside, with chairs and sheets and blankets, and at other times outside with pieces of wood, large pieces of material and strong cardboard (often discarded cardboard boxes which had originally contained some new household item). My dad occasionally allowed us to use some of his 'real', 'grown-up' tools – helping us at times when we couldn't hammer nails properly, or had trouble using a saw to cut through some thick hardwood. I remember, too, the fun I had stomping through puddles, getting my gumboots (Wellington boots) covered in mud and water. I also vividly recall making mud pies, and leaving them out in the sun to 'cook', while inside I would help Mum to make muffins or drop scones or prepare veggies for dinner.

> **Informal science** – learning about science may occur in home and community contexts.

What I didn't realise at the time was that, through these experiences, and so many more, I was engaging in **informal science**. For example, stomping through puddles and making mud pies, I was beginning to learn about the *properties of materials* (water is wet) and *physical change* (mud pies dry out and become hard in the sun, but can change back by soaking in water). In building cubby houses I was again learning about the properties of materials (wood is stronger for walls than sheets), while in making muffins I engaged with aspects of *chemical change* (when the ingredients are cooked they change and can't be changed back again).

FIGURE 11.1 Learning joining techniques with father

Practical task

MEMORIES FROM CHILDHOOD

1. Recall some memories from your childhood years, and then make a list of some of these recollections. Try to remember if some of these experiences occurred in the company of others. Who were these significant people?
2. Endeavour to note down two or three recollections, including how others might have supported your learning.
3. Next, using the 'Examples of simple science statements' in Appendix 2, attempt to identify the science concepts embedded in your examples.
4. Share these recollections, and the embedded science, with a colleague or friend or family member.

Everyday concepts – these are the understandings that children develop through their experiences in everyday events. They are generally not scientifically accurate, are context-based and are considered naïve.

It is important for teachers to understand how they might make connections between the **everyday concepts** that children develop in informal settings such as the home and their communities, and the abstract scientific or academic concepts they are introduced to in pre-school or school. Good science teaching requires us to do more than 'notice' where children are 'doing' science' (Larsson, 2013). It is essential that we have the appropriate content knowledge that we can introduce and make explicit in contextually and culturally appropriate ways. At the conclusion of this book you will find 'Examples of simple science statements or concepts', mentioned in Appendix 2, and on the companion website, you are provided with a range of additional resources, including websites that can be helpful for increasing teachers' own background knowledge. Add other resources to this list as you become aware of them.

Research on science in the home and community

Non-formal learning – learning that occurs outside a formal learning situation such as a school or educational institute. Museums may be considered places of non-formal learning as the material portrayed allows for learning, but it is not 'taught' through formal processes.

Citizen science – a method of research that brings together the community and scientists to gather scientific information for projects that often focus on environmental and sustainability issues.

Rennie (2007) wrote that science learning occurring outside formal school, early childhood or other educational settings has been described in a number of different ways, including 'informal learning; **non-formal learning**; informal education; free-choice learning, learning in out-of-school-contexts, settings or environments' (p. 126). Much of this research has focused on learning that occurs in museums, science centres, zoos, aquaria and botanical gardens (see, for example, Dierking & Falk, 1994; Watson et al., 2002; Cujas, Bartolli & Russo, 2014; Rönkkö, Aerila & Grönman, 2016). More recently, some attention has been paid to **citizen science**, a method of research that brings together the community and scientists to gather scientific information for projects that often focus on environmental and sustainability issues (Cohn, 2008; Bonney et al., 2009; Fitzpatrick, 2016). Through involving ordinary citizens, large amounts of data can be gained, not only to inform the scientific projects but also, simultaneously, to increase the public's understanding of these issues. Some citizen science projects involve schools in an attempt to connect science in schools to the wider community, or 'real world' (see, for example, Alexander & Russo, 2010; Paige et al., 2010). (See 'Additional resources' on the companion website for some examples of Australian citizen science projects.)

However, there is a dearth of research focusing on science learning that occurs in family settings, especially in relation to early childhood. In a seminal study, Fleer (1996) examined the links between children's science learning at home and in their child care centres, and the ways in which families can support children's exploration and learning of everyday and scientific concepts in family contexts. The study affirmed that there are benefits for both children and families when the boundaries can be fused between the learning that occurs in the home and in the early childhood centre. Cumming (2003), in her study of young children's understandings of the origin of foods, concluded that they learned more scientific information from families than their teachers might recognise. She suggested that bringing children's prior knowledge into science lessons can greatly enrich the science curriculum. Similarly, Mawson (2011) argued that children bring a wide range of technological knowledge and understanding with them when they enter early childhood settings – again, something that is not necessarily recognised or supported by their teachers. In addition, Mawson suggests that while it is important that educators are able to accurately identify children's real interests, it is also necessary for them to have sufficient personal content knowledge (as mentioned earlier) to be able to support those interests effectively.

In another study, Robbins and Jane (2006) examined some ways in which many grandparents support young children's learning in science through engagement in everyday activities, such as cooking, gardening, using playground equipment, fixing and using machines such as cars, trailers, lawn mowers and cameras, and visits to the park and beach. They found these experiences are strongly 'characterised by sustained concentration and **intrinsic motivation**' (DEEWR, 2009, p. 10), and are often rich in leisurely conversational exchanges between grandparents and grandchildren. Frequently, the grandparents shared their 'funds of knowledge' (Moll et al., 2001) – or their 'cultural and intellectual resources' (p. 132) – with their grandchildren.

> **Intrinsic motivation** – this arises from a child's own interest and governs their response to learning or task persistence.

Similarly, Riojas-Cortez and colleagues (2008) have described how Mexican-American parents and their pre-school children recognised science concepts and knowledge learned from everyday activities in their homes – such as gardening, cooking and using plants for home health remedies. More recently, Fleer, Adams, Gunstone and Hao (2016) have highlighted the not-insurmountable challenges that can exist in attempting to identify and support scientific knowledge in culturally and linguistically diverse families. They suggest 'role-playing with families could support the learning of science for not just the adults, but also the children' (Fleer et al., 2016, p. 137).

FIGURE 11.2 Grandfather shares his understanding of small water animals with his grandchildren

Implications for practice

Implications of these examples of research projects are for early childhood educators to recognise that 'children bring family and community ways of *being, belonging and becoming* to their early childhood settings' (DEEWR, 2009, p. 16). Consequently, it is crucial to work in partnership with families to build upon their funds of knowledge in meaningful and respectful ways (Upadhyay, 2006), and thus to contribute to successful transitions between home and early childhood settings. Following are narratives – first from a parent and then from a grandparent – providing examples of informal science concepts and processes that are being developed in community and home contexts. After both are some practical tasks for reflection and discussion on ways in which the children's learning could be supported and extended.

Case Study 11.1

ANNA'S STORY – LEARNING INFORMAL SCIENCE CONCEPTS AND PROCESSES AT THE BEACH

In the following case study, Anna, mother of Beth (5 years) and Davey (11 months), shares her experiences of a visit to the beach with her children's centre leader. This experience offered rich opportunities for the centre staff to make connections between the children's prior experiences and new learning, and to enhance explorations and discoveries in meaningful ways.

ANNA, BETH AND DAVEY

At the weekend we had a picnic on the beach. We love to do this. It was such a lovely day, and because the tide was out we went rock-pooling. Beth saw a little crab, and counted 10 legs. She was so excited, until it scampered away into a pool and hid in inside a large shell, 'Cos it was looking for a friend'. I explained to her that it was trying to keep out of danger. I held Davey in my arms while he kicked in the water. It was so warm and he loved it. He laughed and laughed! We looked at different kinds of seaweed piled high on the beach and Beth asked lots of questions about why all of it was brown and where it had come from and why some of it was slimy and some was hard. She loves to eat sushi, so I told her that we eat some kinds of seaweed – but not the sort that are piled up on the beach. Then we collected some shells on the beach, and sorted them into piles. There were all different shapes and colours. Beth said she could hear the sound of the sea in some of them, and we giggled at the smell. I had to stop Davey from putting them in his mouth, but he loved the sound they made when he held them in his hands and banged them together. Beth covered some of them with sand then helped him to find them again. She asked if we could take some of the shells home, but then said that maybe the crab might want to use them, 'Because crabs need the shells' – so we left them at the beach.

REFLECTION FOR BETH'S TEACHER

1. What does this narrative tell you about what Beth currently knows about the beach, and about relationships between living and non-living things?
2. How can you use this narrative to build on her current and future science learning?
3. What pedagogy do you think will best support her learning? You might find it useful to refer to *Belonging, Being and Becoming: The Early Years Learning Framework for Australia* (DEEWR, 2009).
4. How might you assist Beth to communicate her understandings to others in your centre's community?

REFLECTION FOR DAVEY'S TEACHER

1. Which scientific processes is Davey using here, and how might you support and extend on these in meaningful and relevant ways?
2. What specific language might be useful to support his learning?
3. What does this narrative tell you about Davey's sense of agency?

REFLECTION FOR CENTRE LEADER/MANAGER

1. How can you use *Belonging, Being and Becoming: The Early Years Learning Framework for Australia* (or other curriculum framework) to discuss with your staff the principles, practices and learning outcomes embedded in this narrative?
2. How might you use this narrative to encourage other families to share their family experiences with centre staff?
3. What ethical issues might exist with this sharing?

In Case study 11.1 there appears to be a very comfortable and relaxed relationship between Anna and the centre leader – encouraging Anna to share the family's experiences. In addition, for this family, going to the beach and exploring is obviously a familiar and culturally valued experience.

Children bring the culture and valued practices of their home into their early childhood settings, and learning is most effective when educators can make connections between science teaching and children's real-life situations (Upadhyay, 2006, Fleer et al., 2016). This, in turn, validates children's identities (DEEWR, 2009; Upadhyay, 2006). According to DEEWR (2009):

> [c]hildren learn about themselves and construct their own identity within the context of their families and communities ... When children have positive experiences they develop an understanding of themselves as significant and respected, and feel a sense of *belonging*. (p. 20)

Educators promote identity when they do such things as 'build on the culturally valued learning of individual children's communities' (DEEWR, 2009, p. 22), 'demonstrate deep understanding of each child, their family and community contexts in planning for children's learning' (p. 23), 'build on the knowledge, languages and understandings that children bring' (p. 23) and 'provide rich and diverse resources that reflect children's social worlds' (p. 23). However, in order to be able to plan *effectively* for children's learning, build on their knowledge and provide rich and diverse resources, it is important to understand the difference between everyday concepts and scientific concepts – and the value of both.

Everyday and scientific (or academic) concepts

Through their home and community experiences, children develop important dynamic 'everyday concepts' (Vygotsky, 1987) or 'intuitive tacit concepts embedded in everyday contexts' (Fleer, 2009, p. 282). Vygotsky (1987) argued that these concepts are important in their own right and form a dialectical relationship with what are known as 'academic or scientific concepts', or those concepts that are more formally taught in Western science education. While everyday concepts are contextually specific and generally cannot be transferred to other situations, scientific concepts exist within a hierarchical network of inter-related concepts and are able to be generalised, but may be disconnected from everyday life. Yet, both types of concepts, everyday and scientific, are important, and strengthen each other. An example of an everyday concept is Beth saying that crabs 'need' seashells and have 10 legs – ideas she has 'learned' through her direct experience during her visit to the beach.

However, these are intuitive concepts. Through learning scientific concepts related to crustaceans at school, she will come to understand about their anatomy, including that crabs have one pair of chelipeds (claws, pincers or nippers) and four pairs of walking legs (Museum Victoria, n.d.), their habitats, feeding, reproduction and so on. Learning *only* scientific concepts, though, may not automatically result in them being related to real-life experiences. Nor may they necessarily result in the curiosity and question-asking and engagement with the environment that Beth demonstrated – important processes in science. Nonetheless, both the scientific concepts and Beth's everyday concepts, in their own way, are examples of the science understanding that 'living things have basic needs' (ACARA, 2017) (see Table 11.1) – though at different developmental levels.

Hedegaard and Chaiklin (2005) suggested that learning is most effective when the educator consciously takes into account children's everyday concepts (such as Beth's belief that crabs have 10 legs) and, at the same time, the related scientific concepts (such as the crab's anatomy), and interlace the two. That is, if the educator consciously holds the scientific concept she can guide Beth to *explore and make observations by using the senses* (ACARA, 2017). Larsson (2013) refers to this as working to achieve contextual and conceptual intersubjectivity between children and teachers in children's play and learning.

Further, this is an example of intentional teaching (DEEWR, 2009), which 'involves educators being deliberate, purposeful and thoughtful in their decisions and action' (p. 15). Traditionally, early childhood educators as a group are not confident in teaching science (Akerson, 2004; Edwards & Loveridge, 2011). However, today many reputable websites, and books, exist that can help teachers to develop understanding of science concepts, and provide useful information to guide the day-to-day teaching and learning processes – some of which are listed at the end of this book. However, in order to gain deeper and more lasting understandings in science, it can be helpful for educators to seek **ongoing professional learning** or in-service opportunities.

> **Ongoing professional learning** – learning which is sustained over time through the use of strategies such as reflective practice or ongoing review.

Practical task

BEGINNING TO BUILD SCIENTIFIC CONCEPTS

Take some time to explore some of the websites listed at the end of the text to evaluate how useful some of these might be within your own context.

1. How easy or difficult do you find them to use and understand?
2. To what extent do they provide you with new information that you might find helpful in your teaching? How often do you find yourself saying 'I didn't know that?' as you read them?
3. Do you have any specific questions or things you want to find out about some area of science – natural science, engineering, space or physical science? Perhaps you could ask a question on one of the sites listed, such as How Stuff Works (science.howstuffworks .com).
4. Read through the Australian Curriculum: Science (www.australiancurriculum.edu.au/ f-10-curriculum/science) to become familiar with appropriate science content for the Foundation years. (See also Table 11.1 and Table 11.2.)
5. What professional learning or in-service opportunities exist within your region in relation to science education?
6. What topics or areas of interest would be of most use to you within your community?
7. If no professional learning opportunities currently exist, how might you go about organising for these to occur?
8. Are there any citizen science projects that you would be interested in becoming involved with? How might you also involve the children and families with whom you work?

Educators who actively work at attempting to increase their understandings in science are likely to gain more confidence in being able to support children's interests, and are therefore more able to 'actively promote children's learning through worthwhile and challenging experiences and interactions that foster high-level thinking skills' (DEEWR, 2009, p. 15).

Using the science curriculum to inform teaching

In the previous practical task it was suggested that you read through the Australian Curriculum: Science (ACARA, 2017). At the Foundation year level this document includes three inter-related strands: Science Understanding, Science Inquiry Skills and Science as a Human Endeavour (see Table 11.1). These strands should be taught in an integrated way, with the content organised into teaching and learning programs to be decided by the teacher (ACARA, 2017). This statement fits well with the sentiments of *Belonging, Being and Becoming* (DEEWR, 2009) – which also emphasises the integrated nature of learning – and educators, in collaboration with children and families, are urged to devise learning experiences relevant to the children in their local context.

TABLE 11.1 FOUNDATION YEAR CONTENT DESCRIPTIONS – THE AUSTRALIAN CURRICULUM: SCIENCE

Science Understanding	Science As a Human Endeavour	Science Inquiry Skills
Biological sciences Living things have basic needs, including food and water.	**Nature and development of science** Science involves observing, asking questions about, and describing changes in, objects and events.	**Questioning and predicting** Pose and respond to questions about familiar objects and events.
Chemical sciences Objects are made of materials that have observable properties.		**Planning and conducting** Participate in guided investigations and make observations using the senses.
Earth and space sciences Daily and seasonal changes in our environments affect everyday life.		**Processing and analysing data and information** Engage in discussions about observations and represent ideas.
Physical sciences The way objects move depends on a variety of factors, including their size and shape.		**Communicating** Share observations and ideas.

Source: ACARA, 2017.

While the Science Understanding strand can provide direction for curriculum decision-making for meaningful learning, the strand on Science Inquiry Skills matches aspects of the learning outcomes described in *Belonging, Being and Becoming* (DEEWR, 2009), some of which are presented in Table 11.2, and can be adapted according to the particular strengths, abilities and interests of children.

TABLE 11.2 SCIENCE INQUIRY SKILLS (ACARA, 2017) MATCHED WITH ASPECTS OF THE LEARNING OUTCOMES DESCRIBED IN *BELONGING, BEING AND BECOMING*

Science Inquiry Skills (ACARA, 2017)	Learning Outcomes (DEEWR, 2009)
Questioning and predicting Pose and respond to questions about familiar objects and events.	Use reflective thinking to consider why things happen and what can be learnt from these experiences (p. 35). Interact with others to explore ideas and concepts, clarify and challenge thinking, negotiate and share new understandings (p. 40).
Planning and conducting Participate in guided investigations and make observations using the senses.	Manipulate objects and experiment with cause and effect, trial and error, and motion (p. 35). Use their senses to explore natural and built environments (p. 37). Respond verbally and non-verbally to what they see, hear, touch, feel and taste (p. 40).
Processing and analysing data and information Engage in discussions about observations and represent ideas.	Explore ideas and theories using imagination, creativity and play (p. 37). Exchange ideas, feelings and understandings using language and representations in play (p. 40). Use the creative arts such as drawing, painting, sculpture, drama, dance, movement, music and storytelling to express ideas and make meaning (p. 42).
Communicating Share observations and ideas.	Engage with and co-construct learning (p. 36). Convey and construct messages with purpose and confidence, building on home/family and community literacies (p. 40). Contribute their ideas and experiences in play, small and large group discussions (p. 40).

Source: ACARA, 2017; DEEWR, 2009.

Practical task

USING *BELONGING, BEING AND BECOMING* (DEEWR, 2009) AND THE AUSTRALIAN CURRICULUM: SCIENCE (ACARA, 2017)

After reading Table 11.2, examine carefully the document *Belonging, Being and Becoming* (or other curriculum framework with which you work). What other learning outcomes can you find that correspond with aspects of Science Inquiry Skills?

1. Add also your own examples from your own particular context.
2. In what ways might your findings inform your curriculum decision-making?
3. How might you share your findings with others in your centre – both staff and families – to foreground the science learning that you are supporting in your children?

Case study 11.2 may provide an opportunity to explore some of these ideas further. While it provides examples of informal learning of science in the home, it demonstrates further how children do not come into our settings unskilled and unknowledgeable – especially in science. As you read through it, try to determine which science understandings and inquiry skills Grace and Ellie may be developing.

Case Study 11.2

NANNY G'S STORY – INFORMAL SCIENCE LEARNING AT HOME

It is a normal routine for Grace's (3 years) and Ellie's (20 months) grandmother (Nanny G) to have them for a sleepover one night a week, and for them to stay with her the next day. Nanny shares the following diary entries she has kept in relation to the experiences she has with her grandchildren.

NANNY G, GRACE AND ELLIE

We have a good vegetable garden with a plentiful supply of zucchini, squash and cherry tomatoes that I have been using in recent months to make two types of muffins that Grace and Ellie both like. They stand on chairs either side of me as we work together and take turns putting in the ingredients, stirring and putting into the tins for cooking. With practice, they have learned to prick each tomato with a small cocktail fork so that they don't burst during the cooking. When the mixture is ready, a dessertspoonful is put in each muffin pan, then a cherry tomato is put on top 'in the middle' before another spoon of mixture is put in to cover each tomato. While putting the mixture into each pan requires a lot of guidance (hand holding) on this occasion I noted that Ellie didn't try to put more than 'one tomato in the middle of each muffin'.

I had been telling Grace for some time that the corn she had helped me plant before Christmas had finished growing and we needed to pick what was left on the stalks, and that it was time for us to plant some bean seeds. They helped to identify and pick the two remaining cobs of corn. Grace had done this before so was more interested in smoothing out the ground with her garden fork. Ellie was delighted to be able to pick her first corn and carried it around for a long time trying to pull back the covering leaves to expose the corn that she indicated she expected to eat straight away. 'Ellie, the corn has to be cooked before you can eat it. Would you like me to cook it for you for lunch?' 'Mmm.' 'You can have one and Grace can have the other one. Let us put it down here while we plant the beans.' Her willingness to put the corn down indicated she understood the process.

A WEEK LATER

They helped to remove any stones and smooth out the row of soil for the beans. 'Now the dirt has to be watered so that it is ready for the seeds.' As I watered with the hose Grace said: 'You are making mud.' 'Oh, what makes mud?' 'Dirt and water.' 'Who likes mud?' 'Pigs.' Together we planted the seeds. As I made a hole in the ground with my finger they took turns to put one bean seed into each hole. Then we covered the seeds and gave the ground another watering.

AT LUNCH

Grace and Ellie helped get the two corn cobs ready to be put into the saucepan for cooking and were lifted up to view them boiling just prior to serving. 'I want the big one,' said Grace, who is always ready to have the advantage over her younger sister. 'I will give you both pieces of corn that are the same size,' I replied. As I handed out their bowls of corn, I said 'These are the two last pieces of corn from Nanny's garden.'

'Can we plant more corn seeds?', asked Grace. 'Not for a long time, Grace.' 'Why?' 'Because the weather is going to get too cold for the corn to grow so we have to wait until after the winter. I have got more corn in the freezer so we still have more pieces of corn to eat.'

REFLECTION

Earlier in this chapter it was contended that educators do not necessarily recognise the important learning that young children experience in their families (Cumming, 2003; Mawson, 2011). Reflect on the narrative in Case study 11.2 to address the following questions:

1. What is valued within this family context?
2. What have you learned in relation to Grace's and Ellie's science understandings? (Refer to Table 11.1.)
3. Which Science Inquiry Skills (ACARA, 2017) have they demonstrated here? (Refer to Table 11.2.)
4. Which learning outcomes (DEEWR, 2009) are evident?
5. Which pedagogies (practices that are intended to promote children's learning [DEEWR, 2009, p. 46]) has Grace's and Ellie's grandmother used?
6. What do you know about the experiences that children in your setting share with their grandparents or elders, and what they are learning?
7. How might you engage with Grace's and Ellie's family to ensure that the learning experiences you provide build on what they already know, and that it is contextually relevant and culturally meaningful?

Establishing relationships: working together to support learning in science

The DEEWR (2009) reminded us that '[c]hildren thrive when families and educators work together in partnership to support young children's learning' (p. 9). However, many teachers acknowledge that it is challenging to establish working partnerships with all families. At the heart of this is building relationships of 'belonging' within the centre – so that family members such as Anna, and Grace's and Ellie's grandmother, feel comfortable in sharing experiences, interests and stories with staff.

If possible complete the following task with colleagues – either fellow staff members, or with other students if you are currently enrolled in a course.

Practical task

WORKING AT ESTABLISHING RELATIONSHIPS TO SUPPORT CHILDREN'S LEARNING

Think about some of the ways that you can establish warm, respectful, reciprocal relationships with your families. How can you help families to feel they 'belong' in your centre or school?

Make sure you consider cultural issues.

Think also about what you might do to establish relationships with families that work long hours and do not have many opportunities to visit your centre or school.

1. What other constraints do you face in relation to developing reciprocal partnerships with families?
2. How might you attempt to overcome these constraints?

Once you have done this, try to think about ways in which you can support them to share with your school or centre staff some of the experiences their children have at home and in the community.

1. How can you demonstrate that you genuinely value their input and use their contributions?
2. How do/can you share with them how you could work together to support and extend children's interests, particularly in science?
3. To what extent do/can you plan for children's learning together?

Jacinta's story: one example of establishing relationships and building on learning that began at home

The following narrative provides an example of how one teacher, Jacinta, attempts to establish respectful relationships with families, and builds on children's learning outside the early childhood centre.

At the start of the year, Jacinta asks the parents and children to fill in jointly an 'interest form'. She believes this is an introduction to the way she intends to work with the children and families, and hopes that it gives them the sense that their ideas, skills, knowledge, interests and cultural traditions are welcome. She has a particular interest in technology and science, and provides materials and environments that promote discovery, creativity, improvisation and imagination. Jacinta frequently uses digital technologies with the children (as opposed to 'for' the children) to support and extend their learning. The discoveries and learning journeys (such as that in the 'Big Bang', described below) are regularly documented to be shared with the children, their families and the community. Through her teaching she tries to ensure children are confident and involved learners.

THE 'BIG BANG' – A LEARNING JOURNEY THAT BEGAN AT HOME

We had been assisting the children in the 4-year-old group to work like scientists for much of the year; for example, investigating their questions, observing and classifying objects and animals, and documenting children's theories and knowledge with learning stories and labelled drawings that we placed into portfolios to revisit and share with children, families and the community throughout the year.

One day Amelia, Elliott's mum, mentioned that Elliott had been asking questions at home about the 'Big Bang'. I supported his interest in astrophysics, and the growing interest of others, with activities such as:

1. Viewing and discussing interplanetary, interstellar and intergalactic photographs in a book called *Cosmos* by Giles Sparrow. The children loved these 'big' words – and the spiral shape of the Milky Way. We looked for spirals in other things in the environment, when the children remembered that the snails we had found earlier had spiral shells.

2. Reading the picture book *You are the First Kid on Mars* by Patrick O'Brien with the group over several sessions. The book raised so many questions. A new planet was discovered at the same time as we were reading this book, and so I took in a newspaper article about it, and several of the children (especially Elliott and Liam – who loves 'Ben 10: Alien' and wears his Heatblaster costume to kinder nearly every day) imagined that we were flying to the new planet. Of course, we needed space helmets as there was no oxygen for us to breathe!

3. Listening to Gustav Holst's *Planet Suite* streamed from the internet while sitting under a fabric-darkened table, followed by a documented appraisal of the music (for example, when describing *Mars, the Bringer of War*, a child said 'It sounds like in the movies, like a witch … or a mean person … or men breaking through the window').

4. Planning, making and appraising rockets with blocks. I also put out some shiny open-ended materials like silver duct tape tubes and fabrics, and the children used them to make rockets and space gear.

5. Gravity was talked about often and we pretended to fly to the Moon. I modelled taking slow, big leaps and walking like we were in low gravity. We sang 'Walking on the Moon' by The Police.

6. Visiting the NASA Kids website to investigate Zachary's question: 'What does zero gravity look like?' There is an option, too, to ask an expert on the website.

$\rightarrow$

→

7. Learning about Indigenous perspectives on the stars to begin to understand about multiple cultural ways of knowing about the world.

8. Going on an excursion to the planetarium at Scienceworks (Melbourne). I downloaded a lot of useful information before our visit to prepare for questions and concepts the children might ask and talk about after the visit.

During this time we had a visit from John – a grandparent attending our family participation program. When he told me he was a scientist (molecular biologist), I was very excited and shared his profession with a group of children as we ate our snack together. I suggested that the children might like to ask John some science questions while he was visiting. As we ate, we talked about how there are many different types of scientists. John explained that he worked with very small parts of things called molecules. Elliot said he knew what molecules were, they were like atoms, and then said he had a question to ask:

'If the universe was so small before the Big Bang, then how come it's so huge now?'

John said that he could not answer that question because nobody really knows the answer, although there are many scientists still trying to find out.

He then advised Elliott that if he wanted to become a scientist he should keep being curious and asking hard questions.

Here, Jacinta demonstrates how she is responsive to children's strengths, abilities and interests, and builds on these to ensure their motivation and engagement in learning. Though the topic is complex she is not making assumptions about the children's learning and setting lower expectations because of a bias against, or fear of, a challenging topic (DEEWR, 2009). She uses various resources (books, websites, family members) to help build her own understanding of science concepts, as well as those of the children, and thus, while working with everyday concepts, she holds the scientific concepts in mind also – an example of the 'double move' in teaching (Hedegaard & Chaiklin, 2005) (See, also, Larsson, 2013).

Practical task

SCIENCE AS A HUMAN ENDEAVOUR

After reading Jacinta's narrative, examine carefully the document *Belonging, Being and Becoming* (DEEWR, 2009), or other curriculum frameworks, to pinpoint what specific learning Jacinta is promoting. What is she conveying about Science as a Human Endeavour (ACARA, 2017)? (Refer to Table 11.1.)

Conclusion

In this chapter, learning in the home and community has been discussed. Some research on this topic was introduced, and stories from a mother, a grandparent and a teacher were presented as case studies. Reflective and practical tasks, focusing on the curriculum frameworks, were posed. Acknowledging the importance of families and educators working together in partnership to support young children's learning in science was highlighted.

Of particular importance is the need for early childhood educators to attempt to increase their content knowledge in science (or know where they can go to find answers), which in turn will develop confidence in teaching science. As stated, reputable websites and books can assist teachers in knowing how to address children's (and their own) questions and interests. Documents such as *Belonging, Being and Becoming: The Early Years Learning Framework for Australia* (DEEWR, 2009) and aspects of the Australian Curriculum: Science (ACARA, 2017) are also invaluable in informing teaching in science. However, in order to increase understandings at a deeper level, ongoing professional learning or in-service is suggested.

Acknowledgement

Sincere thanks to the families and teacher who contributed to this chapter: Grace's and Ellie's Nanny G., Anna (Beth's and Davey's mother), and pre-school teacher Jacinta Bartlett. Your input into this work has been invaluable, and I congratulate you on the wonderful things you are doing with your children or grandchildren.

11 References

Akerson, V. L. (2004). Designing a science methods course for early childhood preservice teachers, *Journal of Elementary Science Education*, 16(2), 19–32.

Alexander, A. & Russo, S. (2010). Let's start in our own backyard: Children's engagement with science through the natural environment, *Teaching Science*, 56(2), 47–54.

Australian Curriculum, Assessment and Reporting Authority (ACARA). (2017). The Australian Curriculum v8.3: Science, www.australiancurriculum.edu.au/science/curriculum/f-10, accessed 10 June 2017.

Bonney, R., Cooper, C. B., Dickinson, J., Kelling, S., Phillips, T., Rosenberg, K. V. & Shirk, J. (2009). Citizen science: A developing tool for expanding science knowledge and scientific literacy, *BioScience*, 59(11), 977–84.

Cohn, J. P. (2008). Citizen science: Can volunteers do real research? *BioScience*, 58(3), 192–7.

Cujas, M. L., Bartolli, P. & Russo, K. R. (2014). A preschool and a children's museum: Partners in promoting learning, *Teaching Young Children*, 7(3), 12–14.

Cumming, J. (2003). Do runner beans really make you run fast? Young children learning about science-related food concepts in informal settings, *Research in Science Education*, 33(4), 483–501.

Department of Education, Employment and Workplace Relations (DEEWR). (2009). *Belonging, Being and Becoming: The Early Years Learning Framework for Australia*. Canberra: Commonwealth of Australia, docs.education.gov.au/system/files/doc/other/belonging_being_and_becoming_the_early_years_learning_framework_for_australia.pdf, accessed 10 June 2017.

Dierking, L. & Falk, J. (1994). Family behaviour and learning in informal science settings: A review of the research, *Science Education*, 78, 57–72.

Edwards, K. & Loveridge, J. (2011). The inside story: Looking into early childhood teachers' support of children's scientific learning, *Australasian Journal of Early Childhood*, 36(2), 28–35.

Fitzpatrick, G. (2016). *Elster Creek Wildlife*, online video, www.youtube.com/watch?v=JPoQP3QirAs, accessed 11 June 2017.

Fleer, M. (1996). Fusing the boundaries between home and child care to support children's scientific learning, *Research in Science Education*, 26(2), 143–54.

—— (2009). Understanding the dialectical relations between everyday concepts and scientific concepts within play-based programs, *Research in Science Education*, 39, 281–306.

Fleer, M., Adams, M., Gunstone, R. & Hao, Y. (2016). Studying the landscape of families and children's emotional engagement in science across cultural contexts, *International Research in Early Childhood Education*, 7(1), 122–41.

Hedegaard, M. & Chaiklin, S. (2005). *Radical-Local Teaching and Learning: A Cultural-Historical Approach*, Aarhus, Denmark: Aarhus University Press.

Larsson, J. (2013). Contextual and conceptual intersubjectivity and opportunities for emergent science knowledge about sound, *International Journal of Early Childhood*, 45, 101–22.

Mawson, B. (2011). Technological funds of knowledge in children's play: Implication for early childhood educators, *Australasian Journal of Early Childhood*, 36(1), 30–5.

Moll, L., Amanti, C., Neff, D. & González, N. (2001). Funds of knowledge for teaching: Using a qualitative approach to connect homes and classrooms, *Theory Into Practice*, XXXI(2), 132–41.

Museum Victoria (n.d.). *Biology of Crabs*, museumvictoria.com.au/crust/crabbiol.html, accessed 3 May 2011.

Paige, K., Lawes, H., Matejcic, P., Taylor, C., Stewart, V., Lloyd, D., Zeegers, Y., Roetman, P. & Daniels, C. (2010). 'It felt like real science!': How Operation Magpie enriched my classroom, *Teaching Science*, 56(4), 25–33.

Rennie, L. (2007). Learning science outside of school, in S. K. Abell & N. G. Lederman (eds), *Handbook of Research on Science Teaching*, Mahwah, NJ: Lawrence Erlbaum Associates, 125–67.

Riojas-Cortez, M., Huerta, M. E., Flores, B., Perez, B. & Clark, E. R. (2008). Using cultural tools to develop scientific literacy of young Mexican American preschoolers, *Early Child Development and Care*, 178(5), 527–36.

Robbins, J. & Jane, B. (2006). 'Granddad, where does the sea go when the tide goes out?' Grandparents supporting young children's thinking in science and technology, *Journal of Australian Research in Early Childhood Education*, 13(2), 13–33.

Rogoff, B. (2003). *The Cultural Nature of Human Development*, Oxford: Oxford University Press.

Rönkkö, M-J., Aerila, J-A., & Grönman, S. (2016). Creative inspiration for preschoolers from museums, *International Journal of Early Childhood*, 48, 17–32.

Upadhyay, B. R. (2006). Using students' lived experiences in an urban science classroom: An elementary school teacher's thinking, *Science Education*, 90(1), 94–110.

Vygotsky, L. S. (1987). *The Collected Works of L.S. Vygotsky, Vol. 1: Problems of General Psychology*, R. W. Rieber & A. S. Carton (eds), N. Minick (trans.), New York: Plenum Press.

Watson, K., Aubusson, P., Steel, F. & Griffin, J. (2002). A culture of learning in the informal museum setting? *Australian Research in Early Childhood Education*, 9(1), 125–39.

Learning science in outdoor settings

Coral Campbell

Young children have a natural affinity for the outdoors and this can be enhanced to develop a sense of wonder for and delight in the outdoor environment. This chapter discusses a growing worldwide phenomenon where young children are taken into an outside environment (other than the school or early childhood centre) for play during formal learning time. Considering a range of outdoor settings, this chapter highlights the benefits of the outside environment for children's development and learning. Ways in which young children can be provided with meaningful outdoor experiences which enhance their science and environmental understandings are presented. Affordances for science learning through play which embrace 'bush' or 'beach' kindergarten time will be discussed. This chapter discusses how early years educators can enhance children's affinity with the environment through the appropriate use of play pedagogy.

OBJECTIVES

At the end of this chapter you will be able to:

- describe the benefits and importance of outdoor learning in early years education

- describe the relationship between science play and learning in outdoor settings

- describe the educator's role in promoting science learning in outdoor settings

- list the ways in which adults can scaffold children's science learning through play pedagogies in outdoor settings

- appreciate how science learning in outdoor settings is linked with environmental understandings.

Understanding 'outdoor settings'

Most children enjoy being outdoors, exploring their environment, getting dirty and following their own interests. Children's physical and cognitive development, along with their wellbeing, are enhanced through, with, and in the outside environment (Maxwell, Mitchell & Evans, 2008; Gill, 2014). While outdoor play areas are not a new phenomenon in Australia, the recognition of this environment as a means of enhancing children's learning is only recently emerging. There is a need to enhance the quality of outdoor play in early childhood education settings.

What does it mean to be 'outdoors'? The term 'outdoor settings' encompasses a number of different outside spaces, with variable opportunities for children's play. Within the idea of 'outdoors' are the following terms:

- outside – not within a building or defined inside space
- **outdoor setting** – any setting which is not indoors and includes both natural (e.g. parks, gardens, bush) and human-made settings which might incorporate structures (e.g. seats, climbing frames, play items)
- **natural environment** – an open-air environment which does not contain any human-made items or materials. (e.g. beach kindergarten)
- **bush setting** – a natural environment where trees and other plants (grasses) grow without human management; it may include creeks, bush, beaches or rocky mountainous areas.

Each of these settings provide different experiences and different opportunities for the young child.

Outdoor setting – any setting which is not indoors and includes both natural (parks, gardens, bush) and human-made settings which might incorporate structures (seats, climbing frames, play items).

Natural environment – an open-air environment which does not contain any human-made items or materials (e.g. beach kindergarten).

Bush setting – a natural environment where natural materials are not controlled by human management; this may include creeks, bush, beaches and rocky mountainous areas.

FIGURE 12.1   Outdoor setting – a normal centre enhanced with natural features

Case Study 12.1

CREATING IMPROVED 'OUTSIDE' SETTINGS

Research by Morrissey, Scott and Wishart (2015) found that redesigning the outdoor spaces of centres to include features such as different levels, slopes and additional green features, increased the level and variety of children's physical activity. The new features provided children with opportunity for different challenges. However, the variety of children's engagement was less than expected and it was suggested that educators' attitudes to new risks in the environment may have impacted on the children's free play opportunities.

REFLECTION

Consider Case Study 12.1 and the following questions:

1. What do you think the researchers meant when they talked about 'educators' attitudes to new risks'?

2. What other features could be included in the re-design of a kindergarten outdoor space and why would you include them?

FIGURE 12.2 Natural setting – beach kinder setting

In Australia, the general allocation for prescribed 'outdoor' time is currently a three-hour period within a 15-hour pre-school learning time. Overseas, this varies significantly from country to country, with some countries having all pre-school learning in outdoor settings. As indicated by Wells and Evans (2003), the greater the amount of exposure to playing and learning in the outdoors, the greater will be the benefits to the child. Buchan (2015) advocates that there is a big difference between short exposures (three hours/ week) and extended exposure (every day each week) to the outdoors. Children become familiar with the space and the greater the exposure the more 'ownership' they have, and the greater is their autonomy and connection to the space. There is a continuity of experience as children observe their nature space change over time and are involved in that experience.

The Early Years Learning Framework

The national Early Years Learning Framework (EYLF) recognises the importance of outdoor spaces for providing a range of opportunities for learning which are not available indoors. The framework comments on the open-endedness of these environments for inviting play which includes 'spontaneity, risk-taking, exploration, discovery and connection with nature' (DEEWR 2009, p. 15).

In terms of children's learning, the EYLF indicates that outdoor learning spaces are recognised for enhancing children's appreciation for the natural environment and for developing an awareness of the environment. It provides educators with a way to engage with environmental education.

Natural materials can be introduced to children to encourage exploration of new things. Opportunities exist for educators to link to the broader landscape and resources, highlighting the responsibilities of humans to care for the environment and for children to understand and develop a disposition of care for their natural world.

However, in the subsequent *Educators' Guide to the Early Years Learning Framework* (DEEWR, 2010, p. 31), questions were raised:

1. Is there an equal balance in the time and resourcing for play in the indoors and outdoors?
2. What potential does the outdoors hold that may not be fully realised?

The outdoor learning environments relate strongly to the outcomes in the EYLF. Interacting with outdoor settings, children are exposed to situations which require judgement, problem-solving, development of new skills and knowledge, and working with others. Within the EYLF, at the very least, children are developing the following outcomes:

Outcome 1 – children have a strong sense of identity
- children develop their emerging autonomy, inter-dependence, resilience and sense of agency
- children learn to interact in relation to others with care, empathy and respect.

Outcome 2 – children are connected with and contribute to their world
- children respond to diversity with respect
- children become socially responsible and show respect for the environment.

Outcome 3 – children have a strong sense of wellbeing
- children become strong in their social and emotional wellbeing
- children take increasing responsibility for their own health and physical wellbeing.

Outcome 4 – children are confident and involved learners

■ children develop dispositions for learning, such as curiosity, cooperation, confidence, creativity, commitment, enthusiasm, persistence, imagination and reflexivity

■ children develop a range of skills and processes, such as problem-solving, inquiry, experimentation, hypothesising, researching and investigating

■ children transfer and adapt what they have learnt from one context to another

■ children resource their own learning through connecting with people, place, technologies and natural and processed materials.

The importance of getting outdoors

There is an imperative for taking young children into outdoor spaces. A report commissioned by Planet Ark (2011), indicates that 10 per cent of Australian children only play outside once a week (or less). This statistic adds validity to the ideas of Louv (2005) and others who found that some young children are disconnected from nature and the natural world. Louv (2005, p. 34.) termed the phrase **nature deficit disorder**, describing children with diminished sensory use, attention difficulties and physical and emotional illnesses. Limited interaction with nature can result in children having limited empathy for and little understanding of the natural world.

> **Nature deficit disorder** – diminished sensory use, attention difficulties and physical and emotional illnesses.

Modern family life contributes to the erosion of children's involvement in the outdoors and the natural environment. Houses have small backyards which restrict children's play, playgrounds are designed with safety in mind and play can be directed around 'play furniture', a sedentary indoor lifestyle is promoted by both television and computer games, and parents restrict outside play due to a perception of 'stranger danger' and safety issues.

In addition, when considering outdoor play experiences, other significant factors which influence children's development were identified by Thomas and Thompson (2004, p. 3). These were:

■ equality of access to natural environments differed between children from rural and urban backgrounds

■ children use public outdoor space for play and personal development and this is influenced by their strong sense of the environment as a social space; without opportunity for outdoor play in natural spaces, this personal development is restricted

■ exploration of the natural environment develops children's understanding of environmental issues but this is constrained by restrictions to access of the outdoor environment.

All early childhood centres incorporate outdoor play into their programs, preferably in natural settings without specific play equipment. In most early childhood centres, there are ample spaces and places for free (and directed) play in natural spaces. Educators can use these spaces for introducing children to natural objects or for helping to set up children's own investigations. Within these natural spaces, children can play safely and can engage with the diversity of living things under the watchful eye of the educator.

The benefits of outdoor learning

With education in the outdoors, the environment is considered a site for learning. The ideas surrounding place and place-based education are articulated by many researchers (Mohammed et al., 2013; Kelly & White, 2013) as places which allow learning through participation in experiential phenomena, where the place provides children with a sense of safety and harmony.

The local community and environment can be used as starting points for children's learning around a range of ideas in language, arts, mathematics, social studies, science and other content areas (Sobel, 2004). The outdoors can provide a context for learning about sustainability and respect for the environment. Sobel (2004) indicates how children's experiences in the outdoors, where there is an emphasis on hands-on experiences with a real-world focus, can enhance children's understandings. Current research indicates that the most significant benefit of outdoor learning is that participation helps children to appreciate and care for their natural environment (Borradaile, 2006). One of the main purposes of education within the environment is to provide circumstances that allow children to increase their knowledge of their natural environment and develop an awareness of their roles in relation to the environment. For these reasons, the early childhood educator must provide opportunities for children to participate actively in the natural environment. 'Time spent in nature provides a diversity of sounds, sights, smells and textures, and a variety of plants, animals and landscapes that children can engage with' (Planet Ark, 2017).

The benefits of taking children to natural settings are multiple (Borradaile, 2006; Elliot, 2013). 'Children experience the natural world differently from adults and enter it more actively. Children want to touch, hold, dig, smell, taste, explore, and experiment' (Kos & Jerman, 2013, p. 190).

Children have the freedom to explore the settings with adult support, accepting challenges in situations which cannot be duplicated in a classroom or play area. Other benefits include children becoming more confident in risk-taking and becoming more independent in play. Children exhibit increased motivation and concentration, better language and communication skills, as well as improved motor skills, such as balance and coordination (Borradaile, 2006).

In the natural outdoor setting, children engage in free, unstructured play, using the resources of the setting. While some rules are applied for safety reasons, such as boundaries or care with animals, few resources are provided and intervention in children's play is minimal. Recent research into play in outdoor settings indicates that children become more imaginative and creative in their play (Campbell & Speldewinde, 2017, in press). When playing in groups, children will play with others to suit the circumstances of the outdoor resources. Often, in early childhood centres, the provided materials determine who plays with whom (educator interview, 2015). Educators have found that this enables children to mix socially in different ways and to enhance their relationships with other children.

Science play and learning in natural settings

Science play – children's play which allows children to experience science phenomena.

As a segue into introducing children to play in outdoor spaces, early childhood centres can help prepare children for play with natural objects through the use of loose parts incorporated into resources and a nature table. The table is usually a static display where children stop, look, touch, smell and sometimes taste material from the outdoor environment, such as leaves, rocks, feathers, etc. Children gain an appreciation of the attributes (size, weight, texture and shape) of an object through this interaction. This sensory play with natural material readily links with science learning. Another open-ended approach is to provide children with a range of natural materials which they can use in play outdoors. Children's imaginations allow them to see the material in different ways and for different purposes. Natural materials are re-purposed into imaginative play. For example, materials which can be used for imaginative play include seed pods, leaves, small branches or twigs, shells, sand, gravel/soil, clay and small rocks. Play with natural materials 'supports cultural inclusion', as the value of the items being played with is created by the play participants, rather than any predetermined contexts (Elliot, 2010, p. 64).

Case Study 12.2

A NATURE TABLE

In one kindergarten, educators had set up a nature table with a number of rocks of different sizes, shapes, colours and textures to enable children to develop an understanding of the different materials. In attending the centre, a visitor remarked to one child playing at the table, 'These are interesting rocks', in the expectation that he would off-handedly reply 'yes', as he was completely engrossed in his study of them. However, he quickly retorted, 'These are not just rocks, these are minerals!' He subsequently showed the visitor the mineral elements in some of the rocks.

REFLECTION

Consider the scaffolding that may have occurred in Case study 12.2.
1. How would you intentionally and purposefully scaffold the children's learning?
2. What other information about rocks would you provide?

Most people consider that science in natural settings is all about biology, ecosystems and the environment. However, play in natural environments leads to a greater understanding of other areas of science, including physics, chemistry and 'change-over time'. Playing in natural places creates greater challenges for children as these outside spaces are not ergonomically 'safe' environments. Overhanging branches need to be avoided, creating awareness of spacial relations (the body in space and what is around it). Kneeling on rocks requires care, leading to an awareness of natural surfaces. Even climbing low tree branches requires controlled use of motor skills, hand–eye coordination, an awareness of branch texture and branch strength. The outside natural environment requires greater concentration to move about freely. In addition to the physical movement in natural spaces, related to gravity, force, friction and resistance, children can interact with a vast range of living and non-living natural materials. They can smell the earth after a rain shower, or watch the way water pools in indentations in the landscape. Children observe that snails move about after rain or that ant activity increases before it rains. Natural surfaces may become more slippery and require greater care and concentration to navigate. Awareness of weather patterns becomes apparent as children dress for the outdoor environment and observe seasonal changes to the natural environment over time.

When children play in the natural environment, they can observe the small animals which are part of that environment. Holding snails, worms or slaters can fascinate children and provide them with empathetic approach in handling other living things. They can gain some understanding about habitats when observing where they find these small animals. With scaffolding, children can be guided to closer observation of the animal, noting physical characteristics and linking these with living requirements – for example, noting that a slater can roll up into a ball to protect itself from predators or harm. There are many opportunities for an educator to use these children's explorations for guided discovery and to scaffold children to a greater level of understanding, care and empathy for the natural world.

Creativity

Educators will often comment that children are more imaginative when playing in natural environments. Research by Campbell and Speldewinde (2017) highlights that this was a common belief of educators with whom they worked. Imagination and creativity are high-order cognitive skills which are used in many aspects of science exploration as children set out to investigate their world. **Creativity** involves children producing unique and novel solutions to problems. Recent research by Kim (2011) shows that creativity is in decline in all age groups, including young children. There was a suggestion that the learning environment suppresses opportunities to engage in creative thinking. Additional work by Cropley (2014) has found that creativity was enhanced when children were presented with:

> Creativity – producing unique and novel solutions to problems.

- open-ended tasks where a solution was not immediately apparent and multiple solutions were possible
- challenges which were authentic in their purpose – children really wanted to find the answer.

An outdoor setting, with many natural spaces, provides the opportunity for multiple solutions to challenging situations and enables children to develop their cognitive responses in terms of imagination and creativity.

The development of bush kinders and their affordances for science learning

The forest kindergarten movement of Europe, over the last 50 years, has translated into a number of outdoor approaches in early childhood settings in New Zealand and Australia. In New Zealand, 'The Ngahere Project' (Kelly & White, 2013) studied the multiple teaching and learning possibilities in nature settings in several early childhood settings. As engagement with the outdoors is considered a key element of life in New Zealand and is linked to its heritage, identity and culture, Kelly and White were interested in determining how nature-based learning was presented and what pedagogical aspects were evident. Their research found that:

- teachers use a combination of resources to inform their practice – not least their *Te Whāriki* (early childhood education curriculum)
- nature environments are powerful contexts for children's learning about that environment
- children, teachers and the environment are involved in 'place-responsive' relationship and the emergent curriculum of the natural environment.

In Australia, the forest kindergarten movement has translated to 'bush' or 'beach' kindergartens. Research in Australia around the benefits of a bush kinder approach (Elliot, 2013) has tended to focus on the overall positive aspects in terms of children's biophilia (appreciation and care for the natural environment), greater motivation and risk-taking behaviour. There has been little research into the specific science learning around biological/ecological systems, physical sciences and chemical sciences as children play in these bush or natural settings.

In 2015, Campbell and Speldewinde (2017) studied three bush kindergartens in Australia, specifically documenting the 'science through play' observed. As science educators, they recorded instances of children's science play and the interaction of the educators with the children in the natural settings. Educators discussed their perceptions of the science that was part of the children's play in the bush settings. Their study was focused around a number of questions:

- How is science learning and teaching being enacted across the bush kindergartens?
- What is available in the play environment that provided opportunities for exploration related to science?
- How do educators scaffold children's science learning?
- What was observed as 'science learning' in the bush setting?

The play environments differed across the three natural settings, which enabled different opportunities and experiences for the children's science learning. These are described in Table 12.1.

The off-site natural setting (Site 1) was an open, sparse, environment with small trees and flat terrain. The adjacent scrub (Site 2), by contrast, had lush grasses, multiple bushes and trees and a creek to explore. It was a richer environment in terms of the natural material available. The third setting (Site 3) was a small grassy paddock.

TABLE 12.1 DESCRIPTION OF THREE NATURAL SETTINGS IN RELATION TO RESOURCES AVAILABLE AND PLAY EXPERIENCES

	Characteristics		
	Site 1 **Offsite** – 5 kms from the normal kinder	**Site 2** **Adjacent scrub** – natural parkland just outside the back gate of the kinder.	**Site 3** **Adjacent scrub** – grassy paddock
Resources	Trees to climb Loose material Natural scrub grasses Small animals Birds Mud puddles Pathways/bush tracks Waterway	Trees to climb Loose material Natural green grasses Small animals Birds Mud puddles Waterway Housing fence line	Plenty of trees to climb Loose material (had to be provided) Semi-mown grass Small animals Mud puddles Housing fence line Additional equipment such as magnifying lenses, drawing requisites.
Play experiences	Unstructured + structured (30 minutes planned)	Totally unstructured	Unstructured + structured (30 minutes planned)

The discussions with educators indicated that they had expectations that the natural bush settings would be productive spaces for learning about the environment – biological, ecological concepts and an ethos of caring. Often educators highlighted a biological concept or process to draw children's attention to science-related ideas in the physical environment, where the natural phenomenon was the catalyst for children's play.

It was observed that the physical phenomena children are closest to, such as manipulating objects and/or exploring the physicality of their own bodies, was generally related to physical sciences, e.g. balancing, manipulations of force and energy. The researchers' observations of the science confirmed that physical sciences were strongly represented in the children's play. There were instances of children learning how to balance their bodies on rocks or branches and how they would persist at this task until they conquered it. Children were able to advise their peers on how to do it, using concepts of balance, weight distribution and body positioning. Biological experiences observed (but not limited) included children finding and carefully holding small animals (snails, worms, slaters, millipedes), studying leaf colours, investigating bark texture and thickness and observing changes in plant growth over time.

Across time, environmental and biological understandings were supported most strongly by educators in the play experiences of the children. Physics experiences were less well supported, although discussions did occur around 'slipperiness' of wet surfaces, and balance, often related to safety. The texture of surfaces was also part of this conversation, with changes to surfaces observed over time.

1. Consider the categories of outdoor settings provided earlier in this chapter. Where would you place 'bush kinders', based on the descriptions given above?
2. Given the breadth of science observed in the bush setting, how do you think this compares with a normal kindergarten setting? In what ways is it similar or different?

The educator's role in promoting science learning in outdoor settings

Young children are continually trying to make sense of the world. Educators who become co-investigators with children, or encourage further exploration, provide them with opportunities to extend their own investigations (Campbell & Jobling, 2010). Van Hoorn et al. (2014) indicate that potential science learning opportunities for children can occur when the science is recognised by the educators. While it may be easy to recognise the science in biological and ecological activities, it is more difficult for the physical sciences.

Within children's play, there are a number of recognised aspects which can involve the educator in enhancing children's science learning:

Play-based learning – children learning through their play.

Child-centred interests – children's own interests lead their play.

Educator scaffolds – intentional teaching – purposeful, deliberate and thoughtful actions and decisions.

Integrated learning experiences – holistic learning where no discipline boundaries exist.

Directed teaching – educators specifically introduce some learning experiences.

- **play-based learning** – children have free choice of what they do and where they do it, within safety considerations (e.g. a child may decide to climb trees, experiencing aspects of gravity, friction, weight distribution and space)
- **child-centred interests** – children's own interests lead their play (e.g. a child may be interested in space, so uses the outdoor material to construct a space station)
- **educator scaffolds** – intentional teaching – purposeful, deliberate and thoughtful actions and decisions, the educator sees an opportunity to assist children, it is not intrusive or managerial (e.g. when children construct a nest from sticks and leaves, the educator may ask them to consider what else a bird might need in the nest)
- **integrated learning experiences** – educators may provide additional material to offer children the opportunity to integrate their play experiences (e.g. if children are collecting small animals, the educator might provide them with containers or magnifying lenses to see the small animal more clearly)
- **directed teaching** – occurs occasionally, this might include pointing out specific changes to the environment, or highlighting how the natural environment connects with some interest that has been raised by the child previously (in some instances outside experts, for example, a marine biologist, might visit to respond to children's interests).

Educators need to be flexible in their approach to responding to children's science learning. There is a time to approach children at play and a time to let children explore on their own.

The educator's experience and knowledge of the children and their play habits will help to determine what approach is used. Experienced educators may recognise the science in spontaneous events and can make use of these to develop children's deeper understandings (Campbell, 2012).

One way for an educator to scaffold children's play is to help children link their current play experiences with their prior knowledge (constructivist theory – see page 58). Effective questioning (see page 82) focuses children's thinking and helps them construct new understandings. Consider the question stems of 'what', 'where', 'how', 'why' and construct questions around this:

- What do you use this for?
- Where does this live?
- How does this work?
- Why does it move like that?
- What else could it be?

Enhancing science understandings in outdoors settings

In the Australian Curriculum (ACARA, 2017), the areas of science include Science Understanding (biological sciences, physical sciences, chemical sciences, Earth and space sciences), Science as a Human Endeavour (nature and development of science, use and influence of science) and Science Inquiry Skills (questioning and predicting, planning and conducting, processing and analysing data and information, evaluating and communicating). All these strands and substrands have been discussed in Chapter 3. But how do these apply in outdoor settings where the resources are determined by the place and space? How can an educator enhance children's understandings, with minimal additional resources?

What is required is for the educator to recognise the science in the 'everyday'. Just as children develop 'everyday' concepts of science because they are actually experiencing the science as phenomena which affects them, so can educators start to train themselves to recognise the science involved in children's play. One way to do this is to listen to the language associated with children's play. If you find yourself saying, 'That child is balancing on the rock', the word 'balance' relates to the child experiencing gravity, and probably friction. Similarly, in the statement, 'You have a good grip on your shoes', the word 'grip' relates to friction. See the list of possible words associated with science understandings:

- **physical sciences** – most physical science words relate to children's movement of their bodies
  - force, gravity, friction – moving, stopping, spinning, rotating, rolling, pulling, pushing, braking, accelerating, falling, throwing, bouncing, glowing, reflecting, shading, sound, floating, sinking, flying
  - heat, energy, light, sound, magnets
- **chemical sciences** – think about children making potions and mixtures from soil, sand and water.

Physical science – involves the non-living world and the study of materials, force and energy.

Chemical science – the study of the substances of matter, their properties and interactions.

– mixing, dissolving, separating, gluing, sticking, wetting, absorbing, dyeing, melting, freezing, evaporating, boiling, condensing, rusting

■ **biological sciences** – observing or handling living and non-living things in the environment

– natural materials, caring, animal home, environment, growing, changing, food chains, similar/different

■ **Earth science** – observing the nature of the Earth and the factors that influence the pattern of the day

– weather, seasons, rain, sun, hail, land, sand, soil, water, day and night

■ **Science Inquiry Skills** (see page 40 where these are discussed in detail)

– these words are related to children exploring and investigating their world

– observing, measuring, asking questions, classifying, problem-solving, analysing, using science words.

Biological sciences – the study of living things.

Earth science – observing the nature of the Earth, its materials and the factors that influence the pattern of the day.

Science Inquiry Skills – asking questions, exploring to gather or collect information.

(Some of the phenomenon words were developed by Sofie Areljung, Umeå University, Sweden.)

Common activities in outdoor spaces which relate to science include:

■ investigating natural materials such as bark on trees, leaves or rocks

■ using the senses to smell plants, feel texture, describe colour

■ mixing soil and other materials to make a 'cake' or magic potion

■ using materials in different ways – a tree branch becomes a horse or a train and can take on passengers

■ balancing on tree branches or rocks

■ swinging from tree branches

FIGURE 12.3   A child's rock collection from the beach – the child was interested in colour and size difference

- informally measuring body lengths against trees or branches
- classifying natural materials by making collections of rocks, bark, leaves or flowers
- making miniature 'gardens' or 'fairy gardens'
- collecting or holding small animals.

Connecting science and environmental education

Earlier in the chapter, the connection between science learning and children's development of understanding of their natural environment was mentioned in relation to 'sustainability and respect for the environment'. Littledyke (1997, p. 641) comments;

> There is a need for an understanding of the relationship between science and environmental education which draws on science to support knowledge of the causes of environmental problems, as well as the complexity of ecological systems.

In outdoor settings, particularly natural environments, there are much greater opportunities for enhancing children's 'wonder' with science and the natural world. If science is described as a way of defining the world through investigation, the gathering of evidence and socially negotiated explanation, how does this generalised understanding relate to education in, about and for the environment? Environmental education encourages environmentally responsible behaviour where children can and do make informed decisions about the environment.

At the level of a young child, there is a natural weaving of science and environmental understandings which develop when in outdoor settings. In fact, a knowledge of science can increase children's sensitivity, understanding and appreciation of the interconnectedness of all living and non-living things. This sensitivity then plays out in an environmental awareness, which can be linked successfully to environmental sustainability through further education of the social, political and cultural aspects of a situation.

An environmental education approach in pre-schools or schools should build children's understandings *about* the environment, through play *in* the natural environment and possible educator-instigated explorations. As children develop an ethic of care *for* the environment, they become considerate in their decisions relating *to* the environment. McKenzie & Blenkinsop (2006) provide theoretical perspectives on the development of caring (or ethic of care), indicating that children start with a care of self and those close to them, but develop caring for more distant things, including nature. As children start to understand the science of biology and the understanding of how living things are inter-related, they develop the background to make judgements about the environment within the environment.

Environmental education should foster 'wonderment' about the environment. For example, snails should not be seen as pests that eat the plants in the garden, but as exquisite living creatures that have a life cycle that children are able to observe. Worms should not be seen as wriggly, cold wet things, but animals that have a positive influence on our soil and gardens, and which also have an interesting life cycle. Through the use of the environment, children's empathy and respect for the environment can be developed, along with their confidence to make a difference.

FIGURE 12.4 A child displaying an 'ethic of care' when handling a snail

A review of the literature reveals that there is much research in the area of young children's environmental understandings. Almost none are specifically linked with science. However, there have been some studies undertaken in primary schools with 8–9-year-old children (Birdsall, 2007; Lindemann-Matthies, 2002). For example, Lindmann-Matthies (2002) found that children undertaking environmental education where they participated in the environment through field trips of outside activities demonstrated enhanced understanding of both biodiversity and environmental issues. Research by Campbell and Speldewinde (2017) in bush kinders found that most educators in these settings were making the connections between science and environmental understandings for the children, although the children themselves seemed to be unable to make the links.

Case Study 12.3 LINKING SCIENCE AND ENVIRONMENTAL UNDERSTANDINGS

Birdsall (2007) studied a primary class of 8-year-olds to investigate the children's understandings of environmental sustainability concepts over many weeks. Interviews were conducted to determine the children's initial understanding of biological science concepts. Using a local park, Birdsall set up explorations for the children to help them to develop the relevant science understandings in an environmental setting. She also provided extended opportunities, through discussion and role play, for the children to develop understandings of needs of the living things (plants and animals), knowledge of language and environmental sustainability, both at the park and back in the classroom. After their visits to the local park, classroom follow-up consisted of further investigation and discussion of children's science and environmental questions. In addition, children were involved in writing a submission to the local council to ensure the safety of the trees in the park in light of a local development which may have impacted on the number of trees available. At the end of the unit of learning, Birdsall conducted a post-interview with the children. Her findings indicated that children demonstrated increased complexity in understandings:

1. In their descriptions, initially, children had exhibited simple understanding ' … if they (trees) all die, we won't have so much fresh air and we need fresh air'. At the end of the unit, children's understandings were more complex ' … putting the rocks to stop avalanching … so fish can breathe and find their food … having some native trees … to make lots of oxygen and for native birds to be around.'

2. In their submission to the local council:

   ' ... how important it is to have shady banks. For the macroinvertebrates as well as the importance of protecting breeding sites (for native birds). We think that this needs to be taken into account when considering lakeside developments ... '

Birdsall (2007) concluded that it is important for children to have a strong understanding of the environment and environmental issues and that science can provide deeper understanding of issues when taught in conjunction with environmental understandings. Environmental education can provide a 'real life' situation or vehicle through which to explore science understanding.

REFLECTION

1. How do you think you could enhance children's environmental understandings, as they were developing greater understanding of the biology and ecosystems of the outside environment?
2. How does this 'fit' with your professional philosophy of working in outdoor settings with children?

Practical task

Visit a local park or natural setting. List all the material at the site which you think children might play with. Chose one of the materials and consider how you might build children's science understandings. Photograph the material and prepare a learning story outline (see Chapter 15, page 247 for details) – ready to include a child's play with the material.

Conclusion

This chapter discussed the importance of outdoor settings for enhancing children's science understandings. The chapter highlighted that the term 'outdoor settings' can describe a variety of settings from outside a building to completely natural environments. The benefits, implications and purpose of science learning through play in outdoor environments are described for the more natural settings. The chapter highlights the nature of science and play learning, showing that it is much broader than just a biological focus. In light of the unstructured play, opportunities in natural spaces, children's imagination and creativity are enhanced. Pedagogical approaches to the way young children play are featured along with other suggestions for educators to recognise children's learning of science through their play in natural environments. One such approach uses everyday language attached to the play phenomena. Finally, the chapter links science and environmental education together to assist in developing children's empathy for living things, knowledge of ecosystems, and an understanding of the inter-relationships between elements of the environment.

Areljung, S. (2016) Science verbs as a tool for investigating scientific phenomena – a pedagogical idea emerging from practitioner–researcher collaboration. *NORDINA*, 12(2), 235–45.

Australian Curriculum, Assessment and Reporting Authority (ACARA). (2017). *Australian Curriculum, 'Science – Content Structure'*, www.acara.edu.au/curriculum/learning-areas-subjects/science, accessed October 2017.

Birdsall, S. (2007). Linking science with environmental studies, paper presented at the Australasian Science Education Research Association Conference, June 2007.

Borradaile, L. (2006). Forest School Scotland: An evaluation, Research or Forestry Commission Scotland and Forest Education Initiative.

Buchan, N. (2015). *Children in Wild Nature: A Practical Guide to Nature-based Practice*, Australia: Teaching Solutions.

Campbell, C. (2012). *Teaching approaches*, in C. Campbell & W. Jobling (eds), *Science in Early Childhood*, Melbourne: Cambridge University Press, 54–67.

Campbell, C. & Jobling, W. (2010). A snapshot of science education in kindergarten settings, *International Research in Early Childhood Education Journal*, July 2010.

Campbell, C. & Speldewinde, C. (2017). Bush kinder in Australia: A new learning 'place' and its effect on local policy. *Policy Futures in Education Special Issue*, accepted February 2017.

Cropley, D. (2014). Fighting the slump: A multi-faceted exercise for fostering creativity in children, *The International Journal of Creativity and Problem-solving*, 24(2), 7–22.

Department of Education, Employment and Workplace Relations (DEEWR). (2009). *Belonging, Being and Becoming: The Early Years Learning Framework for Australia*, Canberra: Commonwealth of Australia.

—— (2010). *Educators' Guide to the Early Years Learning Framework for Australia*, DEEWR for the Council of Australian Governments, Canberra: Commonwealth of Australia.

Educator interview (2015). Interview with Coral Campbell, undertaken as part of the project 'Bush Kinder in Early Childhood'.

Elliot, S. (2010). Children in the natural world, in J. Davis (ed.), *Young Children and the Environment, Early Education for Sustainability*, Melbourne: Cambridge University Press.

—— (2013). Play in nature: Bush kinder in Australia, in S. Knight (ed.), *International Perspectives on Forest School: Natural Spaces to Play and Learn*, London: Sage Publishing.

Gill, T. (2014). The benefits of children's engagement with nature: A systematic literature review, *Children, Youth and Environments*, 24(2), 10–34.

Kelly, J. & White, E. J. (2013). *The Ngahere Project: Teaching and learning possibilities in nature settings*. New Zealand: Wilf Institute of Educational Research, Waikato University.

Kim, K. H. (2011). The creativity crisis: The decrease in creative thinking scores on the Torrance Tests of Creative Thinking, *Creativity Research Journal*, 23(4), 285–95.

Kos, M. & Jerman, J. (2013). Provisions for outdoor play and learning in Slovene preschools, *Journal of Adventure Education and Outdoor Learning*, 13(3), 189–205.

Lindemann-Matthies, P. (2002). The influence of an educational program on children's perception of biodiversity, *Journal of Environmental Education*, 33(2), 22–31.

Littledyke, M. (1997). Science education for environmental education? Primary teacher perspectives and practices, *British Educational Research Journal*, 23(5), 641–59.

Louv, R. (2005). *Last child in the Woods: Saving our children from nature-deficit disorder*. New York: Workman Publishing Company.

Maxwell, L., Mitchell, M. & Evans, G. (2008). Effects of play equipment and loose parts on children's outdoor play behavior: An observational study and design intervention, *Children, Youth and Environments*, 18(2), 36–63.

McKenzie, M. & Blenkinsop, S. (2006). An ethic of care and educational practice, *Journal of Adventure Education and Outdoor Learning*, 6(2), 91–105.

Mohammad, N. M. N., Saruwono, M., Said, S. Y., Hariri, W. A. H. W. (2013). A sense of place within the landscape in cultural settings, *Procedia – Social and Behavioural Sciences*, 105, 506–12.

Morrissey, A. M., Scott, C. & Wishart, L. (2015). Infant and toddler responses to a redesign of their childhood outdoor play space, *Children, Youth and Environments*, 25(1), 29–56.

Planet Ark (2011) Climbing trees: Getting Aussie kids back outside, Research summary, Tree Day. planetark.org/documents/doc-535-climbing-trees-media-summary-2011-06-17-final.pdf, accessed 6 April 2017.

—— (2017). Grow more – just add nature, treeday.planetark.org/about/health-benefits.cfm, accessed 6 April 2017.

Sobel, D. (2004). *Placed-based education: Connecting classrooms and communities*, USA: The Orion Society.

Thomas, G. & Thompson, G. (2004). *A child's place: Why environment matters to children*, UK: Green Alliance/DEMOS.

Van Hoorn, J., Monighan, P., Scales, B. & Alward, K. R. (2014). *Play at the center of the curriculum* (6th edn), NJ: Pearson.

Wells, N. & Evans, G. (2003). Nearby nature: A buffer of life stress among rural children, *Environment and Behavior*, 35(3), 311–30.

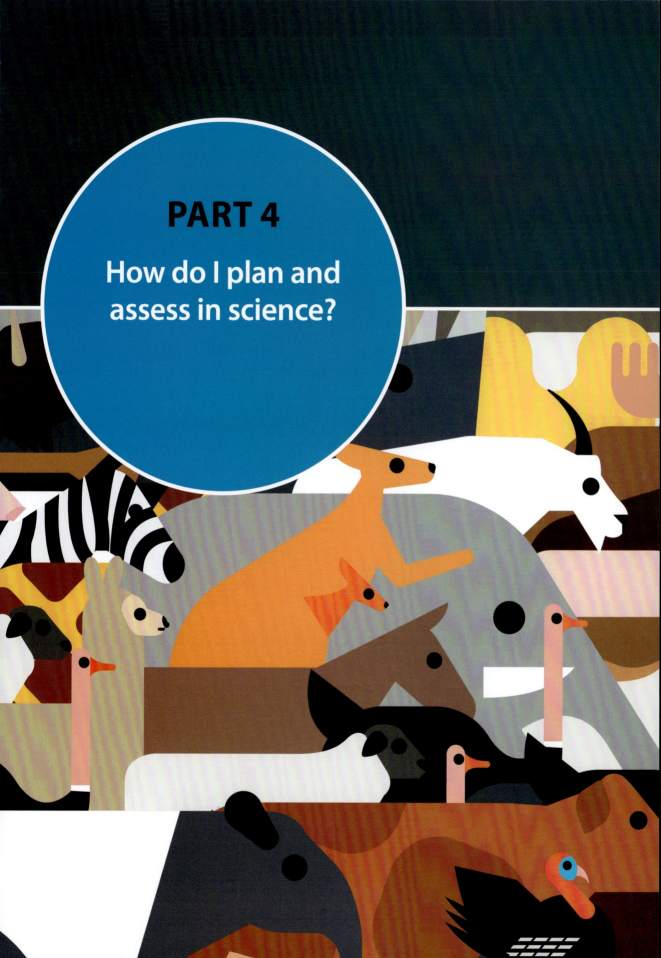

PART 4

How do I plan and assess in science?

Planning for teaching science in the early years

Christine Howitt

In delivering science to young children, early childhood educators perform many functions: co-constructing knowledge with young children; being a source of expertise, skills and knowledge; encouraging children to ask questions; asking appropriate questions of children; modelling scientific skills and attributes, such as curiosity, cooperation, persistence and resilience; providing children with time to explore, discover, learn skills and develop understanding; and planning, observing and documenting or assessing children's learning (Brunton & Thornton, 2010; Howitt, Morris & Colvill, 2007). While planning is mentioned towards the end of this list, it is fundamental to all science teaching and learning. Effective planning ensures that children are engaged in appropriate science learning experiences that follow a logical and coherent sequence, and have relevant documentation or assessment. Planning considers not only what to teach but how to teach.

Just as teaching is a complex task, so is the planning for science teaching and learning. Effective planning requires time, consideration, creativity and logic (Preston & Van Rooy, 2007). Planning documents are official documents and should be professionally presented for principals, team leaders or relief staff. Planning can be done on various levels: whole-school or centre, term planning, and individual lesson planning. The first two are described in this chapter, while the latter is covered in Chapter 14.

OBJECTIVES

By the end of this chapter you will be able to:

- describe the important place of planning in teaching and learning science
- distinguish between whole-school and term planning of science education
- describe the components of the 5E teaching and learning model
- develop a science program using the 5E teaching and learning model.

Whole-school or centre planning

Planning – the development of a logical and coherent sequence of science learning and teaching experiences that are supported with relevant documentation and assessment.

Whole-school plan – an overview of the school's approach to teaching science along with a scope and sequence for science topics across all year levels.

Some schools use a whole-school approach to **planning**. A **whole-school plan** presents an overview of the school's approach to teaching science along with a scope and sequence for science topics across all year levels. This approach to science planning caters for schoolwide interests while ensuring a systematic and logical development of science concepts over time. An example of a scope and sequence, taken from the national Primary Connections program, can be found in Table 13.1. A whole-school approach to planning provides children with the opportunity to build on what they have learnt in previous years rather than repeating the same content. For educators, advantages of this approach include knowing ahead what topics will be taught, knowing what and when children have been taught topics, and recognising how individual topics within each year level fit into the school science plan. The whole-school approach also ensures that the four sub-strands of biological sciences, chemical sciences, Earth and space sciences, and physical sciences are covered every year.

TABLE 13.1 EXAMPLE FROM THE PRIMARY CONNECTIONS PROGRAM OF A WHOLE-SCHOOL SCIENCE SCOPE AND SEQUENCE, FOUNDATION TO YEAR 6

Year level	Biological sciences	Chemical sciences	Earth and space sciences	Physical sciences
F	**Staying alive** or **Growing well**	**What's it made of?**	**Weather in my world**	**On the move**
1	**Schoolyard safari** or **Dinosaurs and more**	**Spot the difference** or **Bend it! Stretch it!**	**Up, down and all around**	**Look! Listen!**
2	**Watch it grow**	**All mixed up**	**Water works**	**Push–pull**
3	**Feathers, fur or leaves?**	**Melting moments**	**Night and day**	**Heating up**
4	**Friends or foes?** or **Among the gum trees**	**Material world** or **Package it better**	**Beneath our feet**	**Smooth moves** or **Magnetic moves**
5	**Desert survivors**	**What's the matter?**	**Earth's place in space**	**Light shows**
6	**Marvellous micro-organisms** or **Rising salt**	**Change detectives**	**Earthquake explorers** or **Creators and destroyers**	**Essential energy** or **Circuits and switches**

Source: © Primary Connections, Australian Academy of Science 2018.

The content of the whole-school plan may include an introduction, aims and rationale, scope and sequence, outcomes and assessment (Preston & Van Rooy, 2007). The introduction should describe the context of science teaching within the school, and may include information on how science is taught, whether science is taught by the classroom educator or a science specialist, and what specialist science facilities or resources are available. The aims and rationale should relate to the Australian Curriculum: Science but take into account the specific school context. The scope and sequence will show all the science topics taught across all the year levels (see Table 13.1). To demonstrate the outcomes of the whole-school program, a mapping exercise may be done to align with the requirements of the Australian Curriculum: Science. An overview of assessment procedures should also be included.

Planning for early learning centres should follow a procedure similar to the one outlined above. However, major differences will occur in the content covered as this should relate more directly to the children's interests. Table 13.2 provides a summary of science topics that could be taught in early learning centres. Alternatively, topics may arise from children bringing in a special item, such as a shell or a tooth. Topics will run for shorter periods of time (sometimes only a few weeks) when compared to the full term in a school. Outcomes should relate directly to the Early Years Learning Framework (EYLF). Rather than assessment, sources of documentation that highlight children's ongoing development should be incorporated.

TABLE 13.2 POSSIBLE SCIENCE TOPICS FOR USE IN EARLY LEARNING CENTRES, BASED AROUND THE FOUR SUB-STRANDS OF THE AUSTRALIAN CURRICULUM: SCIENCE

Biological sciences	Chemical sciences	Earth and space sciences	Physical sciences
I am special	Classifying a range of natural and processed objects	Exploring rocks	Water play
The five senses	Exploring mixtures	What is the weather doing?	Floating and sinking
How do animals move?	Cooking	Water	How can we move this heavy object?
Caterpillars and butterflies	Let's be engineers	A night stalk	Ice play
Growing a herb garden	What can you do with a box?	Mud	Magnets
Why are trees important?	Bubbles	Night and day	Basic pulleys
Exploring seeds and seed pods	Recycling	What can you do with sand?	Exploring light, colour and shadows
Exploring leaves and flowers	Potions	By the sea	How noisy and quiet can we be?

Educator school-term planning

While there is no set structure for writing a **term planning** document, it generally consists of an overview followed by a plan for the specific unit of work. Units of work can be between five and 10 weeks in duration, generally depending on the length of the school term. Children in early childhood should have at least one hour of science a week. It is important

Term planning – an overview followed by a plan for the term science unit of work.

to note that once developed, a term plan is not set in stone but can be modified as the children respond to various learning experiences. In this sense, a program is a working document.

Integrated or separate science subject

Science at school can be taught as an integrated subject or as a separate subject. Some schools have specialist science educators who teach science as a separate subject. When taught in an integrated manner science can readily integrate with the English, mathematics and technology areas of the curriculum, and can address the cross-curriculum priority area of sustainability. Different approaches to curriculum integration include rich tasks, problem-based learning, technology-based projects, a thematic approach, a cross-curricular approach or being involved in local community projects (Venville, 2004). An integrated approach to science can provide children with more meaningful connections to the real world. Further, an integrated approach may provide children with the opportunity to receive more hours of science a week.

The planning process

Planning process – involves developing sequential lessons that will logically progress children's knowledge and understanding of science content, skills, values and attitudes over a period of time.

The **planning process** involves developing sequential lessons that will logically progress children's knowledge and understanding of content, skills, values and attitudes over a period of time. Thus, the sequence of activities should be carefully considered (what children will learn and how they will learn) along with appropriate resources and ongoing assessment.

There are many resources that educators can draw on in the planning process. These include the Australian Curriculum or EYLF documents and supporting materials; textbooks or resource books, such as those published for the Primary Connections program (see www.primaryconnections.org.au) or *Planting the Seeds of Science* (Howitt & Blake, 2010); audiovisual media, such as movies, television documentaries, the internet, iPad apps or YouTube; sites for possible excursions; organisations that provide incursions; professional science teachers' associations; government and non-government organisations; scientists; family connections, including grandparents or a family member with a specific hobby or interest in the topic being studied; previous programs; and educators' brain-storming.

Some educators choose to follow closely the sequence of lessons in the Primary Connections curriculum programs, while others modify them based on their children's needs and interests. Still other teachers will plan their science programs around a significant local event. Such events could include shark attacks, habitat destruction or extreme weather events (e.g. flooding or bushfires).

A further component of the planning process relates to the educator extending their content knowledge on the particular topic being taught. The resources mentioned above can assist educators to improve their knowledge, along with many selective websites.

Components of a science program

A science program must contain enough detail so it is clear what children will learn, how they will learn and how the educator will know what the children have learnt. This detail is also required for relief staff. A term science program should have a clear purpose, and provide detailed information for each lesson on learning outcomes, learning experiences, classroom management, resources and assessment, or some similar combination of these aspects. Learning outcomes provide a summary of the objectives for the lesson. Learning experiences describe the activities children will be doing during the lesson. Classroom management identifies whether the children will be doing individual, group or class work, or some other form of work. Resources list all the resources required for the given lesson. Assessment provides a means to check children's understanding.

Constructivist approach to science planning

A constructivist approach to science planning involves three basic tasks (Garbett, 2013):

- determine children's prior understanding
- engage children in thoughtfully considered activities that challenge them to add to, clarify or re-think their understandings
- evaluate how successfully children have moved their understandings towards the accepted scientific understanding.

This approach places emphasis on finding out what children already know and uses this as a starting point. It acknowledges the importance of using topics that can be directly explored and that are drawn from the children's immediate environment. Thus, topics are engaging for both the children and the educator. The constructivist approach allows children to explore concepts from multiple perspectives, in depth and over time. Activities are selected that challenge children's ideas and assist them to further develop their ideas. Finally, this approach encourages children to reflect on their ideas and learning.

Planning with the 5E model

The 5E teaching and learning model (Bybee, 1997) is based on the constructivist approach to planning. The model consists of five distinct yet interconnected phases: Engage, Explore, Explain, Elaborate and Evaluate. Each of these phases has an associated form of assessment – diagnostic, formative or summative. A summary of the **5E model** is presented in Table 13.3.

The Engage phase involves setting the context and engaging the children in the phenomenon under investigation, determining children's prior knowledge and raising questions for inquiry. This phase is associated with diagnostic assessment. In the Explore phase children are provided with a range of hands-on experiences of the phenomenon. They have an opportunity to test their ideas and try to answer their own questions. The common experiences provided in this phase assist in the next phase. The Explain phase is where the children attempt to come up with an explanation of the science behind the phenomenon.

> **5E model** – consists of five distinct yet interconnected phases: Engage, Explore, Explain, Elaborate and Evaluate.

TABLE 13.3 THE 5E MODEL		
5E	**Description**	**Assessment**
Engage	Engage students and determine their prior knowledge.	Diagnostic assessment
Explore	Provide hands-on experiences of the phenomenon.	
Explain	Develop science explanations for experiences and representations of developing conceptual understanding.	Formative assessment
Elaborate	Extend understandings to a new context or make connections to additional concepts through a student-planned investigation.	Summative assessment of the investigating outcome
Evaluate	Students re-represent understandings and reflect on their learning journey and teachers collect evidence about achievement of outcomes.	Summative assessment of the conceptual outcomes

Source: Primary Connections, 2014a.

Case Study 13.1

DEVELOPING A TOY PROGRAM

Lesley knew that her Year 2 children were very interested in toys, as they had been a favourite topic in their daily news. She also knew from the school science plan that next term she had to teach physical sciences (ACSSU033: a push or a pull affects how an object moves or changes). After looking through various resources Lesley decided that the final outcome of her program would be a class toy museum, with parents invited to come and purchase the toys the children had made. From here she developed a science program based around the 5E model (see Table 13.4). Lesley recognised that the toy museum theme allowed for integration across science (investigating how toys move), literacy (writing descriptions of toys, convincing others to buy toys), mathematics (drawing plans of the classroom and using symbols), technology (designing, making and appraising a range of toys) and humanities and the social sciences (exploring the history of modern toys). Lesley decided to use some of the lessons provided in the Primary Connections module 'Push–Pull', but to develop her own lessons to fit the theme. Working with a school that had class sets of iPads, Lesley also wanted to utilise these in various lessons.

REFLECTION

1. Look over Table 13.4 and check that you can recognise each of the Es in the 5E model.
2. Select one of the Es from Table 13.4 and think of an alternative way it could have been delivered and assessed.
3. A balanced science program should address science content and inquiry and assist the children in developing more positive attitudes towards science. Explain how the toy museum program is a balanced science program.
4. An effective science program should maximise children's engagement; cater for individual differences; monitor student understanding through diagnostic, formative and summative assessment; encourage open-ended questioning and discussion; link science with the children's everyday lives and interests; use a range of learning technologies; and provide links with the local community. Which of these components does the toy museum program address?

TABLE 13.4 LESLEY'S SCIENCE TOY MUSEUM PROGRAM BASED ON THE 5E MODEL

Lesson	Learning outcome	Learning experiences	Classroom management	Resources	Assessment
Engage **Lesson 1**	Children share their prior knowledge of how toys move.	Discuss knowledge of *Toy Story*. Explore and play with different moving toys. Draw and explain how a toy works.	Whole-class discussion. Small group exploration of toys. Individual drawings.	*Toy Story* book, range of toys, colouring pencils, paper.	Children's drawings and explanations.
Explore **Lessons 2–3**	Children describe how toys move. Children move like the toys	Classify and group toys based on how they move (push, pull or both). Use the eBook Magic app to develop a short book that describes the classification and common features of the toys. Perform push, pull, bounce, slide, roll and spin actions using movement and gesture of the body.	Small group classifications. Pairs for eBook Magic. Whole-class body movements.	Range of moving toys at different stations. Station signs. Class set of iPads.	Developed book. Checklist of children's movements.
Explain **Lessons 4–5**	Children explain the terms push, pull, bounce, roll, slide and spin. Children develop a comic strip of how toys move using correct language.	Explain terms using words and body movement. Develop storyboard for a comic strip of up to six images to demonstrate two of the terms. Use ComicBook app to take photographs of toys and captions from the storyboard. Share comic strips with the class.	Whole-class explanation. Pairs to develop and make comic strips. Whole-class sharing.	Toys from Lesson 2. Paper and pencils for storyboards. Class set of iPads.	Comic strip to check children's understandings of the science concepts and new terms. Children's language used during sharing.
Elaborate **Lessons 6–7**	Children plan and conduct an investigation to test how far different-sized toy cars travel, with guidance from teacher.	Post questions about the investigation. Predict potential outcome of the investigation. Identify materials for the investigation. Conduct the investigation using informal measurement. Record data in provided sheet. Discuss the procedure. Draw and describe what they did and what they found.	Whole-class investigation. Individual drawing and description of investigation.	Four different-sized and weighted toy cars, ramp, paddle pop sticks for measuring, recording sheets.	Checklist of children's ability to predict and conduct the investigation. Questioning students. Drawings and written description of investigation.
A range of history and mathematics lessons would sit here, with the children discussing museums and their purpose, and then designing a layout for the class toy museum. Children would also look at the history of toys.					
A range of design technology and literacy lessons would sit here, with the children designing and constructing their own toys, and then writing short descriptions of their toys to convince someone to buy them.					
Evaluate **Lessons 8–9**	Children represent their knowledge about how their toy moves.	Prepare a two-minute talk about their toy. Practise the talk with a friend. Video each other with an iPad. Describe what they liked most about the toy program.	Individual, to prepare the talk. Pairs, to practise and video the talks. Individual reflection.	Access to the toys they have made. Class set of iPads.	Video of talk to check children's understandings of the science concepts. Children's reflection.

The educator will then provide the correct explanation and scientific terms that can be used in interpreting evidence and explaining the phenomenon. These correct explanations and terms are then applied to the common experiences the children had in the previous phase. It is important to note that an explanation of the correct science only comes *after* the children have had various experiences with the phenomenon and have tried to provide their own explanation. Formative assessment is associated with the Explore phase – it is used to check on the children's understanding of the scientific concepts. The emphasis of the Elaborate phase is to apply the concepts that have been learned in the previous phase through a child-planned investigation. Summative assessment of the investigating outcome is carried out in this phase. The final phase is Evaluate. In this phase the children re-represent their understanding of the phenomenon and reflect on their learning. Summative assessment of the science concepts is carried out in this phase.

While the 5E model is appropriate for children from Foundation onwards, some educators consider it too prescriptive for children in earlier years. These educators would choose to modify the model for their young children and specific context and may only use the first three Es. If an investigation is to be done, it is usually highly scaffolded by the educator and done as a class or in small groups.

Early learning centre topic planning

When planning for children in an early learning centre it is important to start with the children and their interests or questions, and take into account their developing understandings. Planning around the child, their family and their community makes the learning more meaningful, and allows the connection to be made between everyday concepts and science concepts. An educator's passions and interests can also provide a starting point for planning.

Along with connecting to the children's world, planning should include play-based experiences (both intentional and free play) that provide adequate time and space for children to explore. Through repeating actions in new play situations children can 'consolidate their knowledge, practise new skills and better understand science concepts' (Aitken et al., 2013, p. 25). It is also important for educators to model a sense of wonder and curiosity and share in the excitement of children's discoveries. Alongside this, 'actively listening to children's ideas, providing guidance rather than answers, initiating and stimulating talk, and modelling how to think things through in a logical sequence' result in quality pedagogy for children's learning (Blake & Howitt, 2012, p. 297).

As highlighted in Chapter 10, science-rich environments should be used to support young children's scientific learning. This includes:

- giving consideration to the indoor learning environment in terms of colour, light, sound and materials
- creating starting points for scientific learning through the use of intentional resources, such as treasure baskets, sand, water, clay, collections or construction materials

- providing resources that invite children to engage with them, such as a range of natural materials, open-ended materials or recycled materials

- using real and quality tools and equipment, such as magnifying glasses, plastic tubing and pipettes, magnets of varying size and shape, collectors' trays, child-sized gardening tools, large mirrors or overhead projectors

- determining how the outdoor area might be available for exploration and investigation – for example, whether it has a garden, sandpit, building den, rocks and soil, or plants for exploring insects (Brunton & Thornton, 2010; Curtis & Carter, 2003).

Including these aspects into the science learning environment respects children's agency and provides children with opportunities to demonstrate their understandings.

Case Study 13.2

'LISTEN! IT'S THE SEA!'

Four-year-old Emma could not wait to show her friends the large shell she had found on the beach during her holidays. She held the shell up to Trent's ear and said 'Listen! Listen! It's the sea!' Trent listened and looked inside the shell curiously. Emma then held the shell up to Cara's ear and repeated her statement: 'Listen! It's the sea!' Cara's eyes widened as she listened intently.

The three friends talked about the sea all day, sharing their experiences from the holidays. As they played outside in the sandpit they pretended they were at the sea. Over the day the other children in the room listened to Emma's special shell and started talking about the sea. The educators agreed that this should be the next topic to be covered and set about planning around the theme of the sea. They decided that the book *There's a Sea in My Bedroom* (Wild & Tanner, 1984) would be the perfect place to start.

REFLECTION

1. Brain-storm a range of ideas that you could use in your teaching and learning that relate to the sea.
2. How do your ideas compare to the mind map presented in Figure 13.1?
3. Did you consider seaweed or the use of real fish in your planning? If not, why not?
4. Think about how your ideas, or those presented in the mind map, could address the five points for developing science-rich environments?

Practical task

DEVELOPING A SEQUENCE OF LESSONS

Use the mind map in Figure 13.1 to develop a sequence of science activities to cover a two-week period. The photographs in Figure 13.2 and Figure 13.3 may give you some more ideas. Compare your ideas to those suggested in the 'Activity plan' for Chapter 13 that is presented in Appendix 1.

→

FIGURE 13.1 Mind map of possible ideas using the sea as a theme

FIGURE 13.2 A treasure box being used to collect 'favourite' shells

FIGURE 13.3   Children playing at the 'fish market'

Chapter 14, 'Intentional teaching of science', extends the planning process presented in this chapter and describes intentional teaching and its purpose. It also includes detailed information on lesson planning. Case study 13.2 is extended in Chapter 14.

Conclusion

Planning for teaching is a complex, dynamic and creative process that requires decisions on the choice and timing of activities along with appropriate teaching strategies in order to best support children's learning. In this chapter whole-school or whole-centre planning and term planning were described, with case studies presented to demonstrate major points. The 5E teaching and learning model was introduced to illustrate a constructivist approach to developing science programs at school. In this model children's prior knowledge is determined first, followed by activities to challenge children's understanding, with various forms of assessment used to determine learning. In early learning centres, the emphasis should be on the child, their family and their community to make the learning more meaningful. Science planning in this setting should include play-based experiences that provide adequate time and space for children to explore.

Acknowledgement

I wish to thank Laure Wilson for sharing her inspirational toy program in Table 13.4. I also wish to thank the pre-service teachers Ellie Dwyer, Tom Pinder and Claire Powelson for sharing their ideas and learning centres for the sea theme (covered in Case study 13.2).

13 References

Aitken, J., Hunt, J., Roy, E. & Sajfar, B. (2013). *A Sense of Wonder: Science in Early Childhood Education*, Albert Park, Victoria: Teaching Solutions.

Blake, E. & Howitt, C. (2012). Science in early learning centres: Satisfying curiosity, guided play or lost opportunities, in K.W.D. Tan & M. Kim (eds), *Issues and Challenges in Science Education Research: Moving Forward*, Dordrecht: Springer, 281–99.

Brunton, P. & Thornton, L. (2010). *Science in the Early Years: Building Firm Foundations from Birth to Five*, London: Sage.

Bybee, R. (1997). *Achieving Scientific Literacy: From Purpose to Practices*, Portsmouth, NH: Heinemann.

Curtis, D. & Carter, M. (2003). *Designs for Living and Learning*, St Paul, MN: Redleaf.

Garbett, D. (2013). Making science work in the primary classroom, in A. Fitzgerald (ed.), *Learning and Teaching Primary Science*, Melbourne: Cambridge University Press, 247–59.

Howitt, C. & Blake, E. (eds) (2010). *Planting the Seeds of Science: A Flexible, Integrated and Engaging Resource for Teachers of 3 to 8 Year Olds*, Perth: Curtin University and Australian Learning and Teaching Council.

Howitt, C., Morris, M. & Colvill, M. (2007). Science teaching and learning in the early childhood years, in V. Dawson & G. Venville (eds), *The Art of Teaching Primary Science*, Sydney: Allen & Unwin, 233–47.

Preston, C. & Van Rooy, W. (2007). *Planning to teach primary science*, in V. Dawson & G. Venville (eds), *The Art of Teaching Primary Science*, Sydney: Allen & Unwin, 87–107.

Primary Connections (2014). An Elaboration of the PrimaryConnections 5Es Teaching and Learning Model, www.primaryconnections.org.au/about/teaching, accessed 1 October 2014.

Venville, G. (2004). Integration of science with other learning areas, in G. Venville & V. Dawson (eds), *The Art of Teaching Science*, Sydney: Allen & Unwin, 146–61.

Wild, M. & Tanner, J. (1984). *There's a Sea in My Bedroom*, Camberwell: Penguin Books Australia.

14 Intentional teaching of science

Christine Howitt

Intentional teaching involves educators being deliberate about their actions in order to develop children's skills, concepts, understandings and dispositions. It is an important component of the teaching and learning process. This chapter describes intentional teaching and its purpose. It outlines the relationship between intentional teaching, guided play and child-directed play. The place of scaffolding in intentional teaching is described, with a range of verbal scaffolding strategies to extend children's science skills, knowledge and understanding presented. The components of a lesson plan are then introduced and illustrated to demonstrate how to plan for intentional teaching in science.

OBJECTIVES

At the end of this chapter you will be able to:

- describe intentional teaching and its purpose

- outline the relationship between intentional teaching and play

- describe the use of science verbal scaffolding strategies as part of intentional teaching

- describe the components of a lesson plan

- plan for intentional teaching in science using a lesson plan.

What is intentional teaching?

The Early Years Learning Framework (EYLF) defines **intentional teaching** as 'educators being deliberate, purposeful and thoughtful in their decisions and actions' (DEEWR, 2009, p. 15). Intentional teaching is a process where educators deliberately plan and instruct learning activities and experiences in order to develop children's skills, concepts, understandings and dispositions. It can be argued that, to some extent, all teaching is 'intentional' as educators are continually making decisions about the learning environment, daily program, resources to be made available to the children, and teaching strategies to be used.

> **Intentional teaching** – educators being deliberate, purposeful and thoughtful in their decisions and actions.

The process of developing intentional teaching is involved and thoughtful. Learning experiences should be meaningful and challenging to children. A range of teaching strategies should be incorporated to help extend children's thinking and learning. These could include modelling, guided practice, demonstrating, questioning, brain-storming, wondering, explaining, sustained shared thinking, or problem solving. In intentional teaching, educators demonstrate an awareness of when to lead children, when to interact with children and when to let children lead. Intentional teaching can occur with individual, small group or whole class activities. Intentional teaching can also happen incidentally when educators take advantage of 'teachable moments' throughout the day.

Children continually explore their world. Thus, intentional teaching can be incorporated in science learning experiences to expose children to scientific inquiry and involve them in scientific processes. Epstein (2011, p. 43) noted that children 'depend on us [educators] to give them the rich environment for inquiry and to develop their child-guided discoveries into a growing understanding of how science works.'

As summarised by Aitken et al. (2012), educators can use intentional teaching to assist children learn to science by:

- acknowledging that children are highly capable and competent learners who display curiosity, creativity and imagination
- accepting that children possess a range of prior knowledge and understandings to help them make sense of their world
- developing learning experiences with specific science learning goals
- providing rich science learning environments with opportunities for creative science inquiry
- providing stimulating open-ended materials to support science learning
- using a wide range of teaching strategies to support science learning
- asking a range of relevant questions to support science learning
- providing time and encouraging children to explore science experiences
- modelling scientific thinking and problem solving (without solving the problems) for the children
- modelling enthusiasm, curiosity and wonder of science.

These points highlight the many varied ways in which educators can support intentional teaching in science.

The importance of intentional teaching

As highlighted in the EYLF, educators should have high expectations of all children from birth to 5 years. In order for children to achieve these expectations, educators must be purposeful in all decision-making processes in relation to teaching and learning. Research findings over the last 20 years have highlighted the importance of the 'more learned other' in assisting children to develop their skills and understanding. The best science learning opportunities have been found to occur when children and adults are in meaningful conversations while interacting with materials (Fleer, 2009). When educators engage in intentional teaching, children's learning is supported.

Educators have 'expert' knowledge and understanding of young children along with an awareness of the holistic needs of each child. This is brought to bear in planning and setting goals for each child. Through their purposeful, intentional teaching; use of resources such as the environment, equipment and materials; and their positive interactions with children, educators are in a unique position to assist in the development of young children.

Practical task

WHAT INTENTIONAL TEACHING HAVE YOU SEEN?

Think back to a science learning experience you saw on your practicum. Consider just how 'intentional' this was. In what ways did the educator plan and instruct the learning experiences? Consider the learning environment, activities, resources and teaching strategies used. Were there specific science learning goals for this science learning experience?

DRAWING A SEEDLING – INTENTIONAL TEACHING

This case study is adapted from Preston (2016). Young children have been found to draw what they know rather than what they see. Use of intentional teaching of drawing techniques can guide children to draw what they see, assisting them to make more accurate scientific observations.

The 5-year-old children were doing a unit of work on living things. The children had germinated seeds in a ziplock bag stuck to a window so that they could observe the process of germination. The seedlings were then transferred to small pots so the children could continue observing them grow. The goal of this particular lesson was for the children to accurately draw and label a seedling. The simplified steps of the lesson are presented below. For more detail and examples of drawings, see Preston (2016).

1. Show the children a photograph of a simple plant seedling (which will only have a few leaves and no flowers).

2. Model how to draw the seedling by drawing two incorrect seedlings first and then the correct one. For example, the first drawing could have a flower and the second could have many leaves. Ask the children if the drawing looks like the actual plant seedling. Enhance

the children's observation by asking how the drawing is different to the actual seedling. Think aloud the mistakes you have made in the drawing. For example, 'I don't draw a flower if my plant doesn't have a flower' and 'I don't draw many leaves if my plant only has a few leaves.' Describe in detail the actual seedling and then draw it.

3. Ask the children if the drawing looks like the photograph of the plant seedling.

4. Show the children another plant that they have to draw. As a class describe the features of the plant. How many leaves are there? Where are the roots, and what do they look like? What colour is the stem? Label the parts of the plant with the children's help.

5. Children now draw and label their own plant.

Consider Case study 14.1 and the following questions:

1. How many of the 10 dot points presented earlier in the chapter (based on Aitken et al., 2012) on how educators can use intentional teaching to assist children learn science can you recognise in Case study 14.1?

2. Describe the range of teaching strategies used within this lesson. Why has the educator incorporated failed attempts at drawing as part of her pedagogy? Would you use this as one of your teaching strategies? Explain your answer.

REFLECTION

Intentional teaching and play

Intentional teaching, guided play and child-directed play can be viewed as complementary teaching approaches, with all three belonging in a balanced early years learning program. In all three approaches the educator is central to providing significant teaching and learning opportunities and supporting and extending children's learning (Dockett & Fleer, 2002). More explicitly, all three involve the educator considering the specific needs of the children, providing appropriate teaching strategies, creating an appropriate learning environment, and providing appropriate resources for the children.

Guided play is the purposeful use of co-constructed play where educators and children work together to achieve explicit learning outcomes. In guided play the educator manages the environment, resources and classroom interaction with the purpose of achieving the specific outcomes. Common with intentional teaching, guided play activities can be used to develop skills, concepts, understandings and dispositions through a range of shared learning activities and experiences. Within guided play activities there is a continuum of educator assistance and support that varies from brief, in the moment of shared interactions, to sustained intervention with scaffolding. The educator actively participates in the play context, sometimes leading, co-constructing, guiding, listening and responding as the play activity unfolds (Rice & Rohl, 2011).

> **Guided play** – co-constructed play where educators and children work together to achieve explicit learning outcomes.

In **child-directed play**, the educator creates an environment that offers opportunities for discovery and challenge, with the aim of encouraging children to actively construct their own learning experiences. Children may choose how, when, with what and with whom to engage and interact.

> **Child-directed play** – play where children choose how, when, with what and with whom to engage and interact.

FIGURE 14.1   Mase demontrates his concentration when free drawing

Case Study 14.2

GUIDED PLAY WITH SEED PODS AND INTENTIONAL TEACHING

This case study is adapted from Blake and Howitt (2012). Sydney and Bryce (both 3 years old) were standing around the nature table with an educator. They were looking at the assortment of natural objects placed on the table: a range of different sized seed pods, leaves, bark and a bird's nest. However, they were not touching any of them. The educator started talking about the different seed pods on the table, describing some to the children by highlighting similarities and differences. She then asked the two children to use their senses to find the differences between a gum nut and a pine cone. Both children participated, but showed little interest. The educator then suggested that the children sort the seed pods into two groups – big seed pods and small seed pods. After the seed pods had been sorted according to the children's definition of 'big' and 'small', they were asked to reclassify one of their groups using the same criteria: big and small. The two children were then left to make their own classification. Sydney sorted the pine cones from all the other seed pods, while Bryce placed all the pods with 'sharp' edges together. Both children remained at the table for another 10 minutes, eagerly playing with the materials and sharing their ideas with each other and the educator.

In this example of guided play, intentional teaching can be seen through the educator providing a wide range of resources, developing conversations with the children, providing guidance rather than answers, modelling actions and how to think, questioning to extend the children's thinking, and providing time for the children to explore the resources and their ideas. The guided play activity led to the development of the children's scientific skills of observation, classification, problem solving and creativity (Blake & Howitt, 2012).

REFLECTION

Consider Case study 14.2 and the following questions:

1. Describe how the educator's assistance and support varied throughout Case study 14.2. Can you identify the different roles the educator took: leading, co-constructing, guiding, listening and responding?
2. Take the opportunity to observe an experienced educator in a guided play situation and actively notice the different roles they take. How have each of these roles assisted the children's learning?

The educator is present in the play context, and is responsive to the focus and direction of children's play. In child-directed play children select and direct their own learning of skills, concepts, understandings and dispositions by participating in a range of learning activities and experiences (Rice & Rohl, 2011).

Scaffolding

Scaffolding is a strategy to enhance and extend children's skills, knowledge and understanding that can be readily used in play situations. Jerome Bruner first used the term scaffolding to highlight the importance of social interaction in children's learning and development (Nolan & Raban, 2015). Effective scaffolding involves breaking down a task into manageable steps in order to achieve a specific learning goal, while maintaining a responsive and sensitive interaction with children (Dockett & Fleer, 2002). As children are active participants in the scaffolding process, their responses should guide the level of involvement from the educator as well as the nature of that involvement. Scaffolding strategies used should be viewed in the context of the given task or experience.

A range of **verbal scaffolding strategies** to extend children's skills, knowledge and understanding are presented in Table 14.1. These strategies include direct guidance, explanation, cues and questions, demonstration and modelling, goals and problem identification, planning, mindfulness, and evaluating actions. There is similarity between these questions and those presented in Chapter 5 (p. 82) in the section titled 'Effective questioning as part of the scaffolding practice'.

Incidental teaching

Incidental teaching is where teachers take advantage of 'teachable moments' to enhance children's learning. Taking advantage of teachable moments requires intentionality on the part of the educator, along with the use of a range of professional knowledge, to identify and implement the next learning experience.

Scaffolding – a strategy to enhance and extend children's skills, knowledge and understanding that can be readily used in play situations.

Verbal scaffolding strategies – scaffolding strategies that include direct guidance, explanation, cues and questions, demonstration and modelling, goals and problem identification, planning, mindfulness and evaluating actions.

Incidental teaching – unplanned teaching that occurs when educators take advantage of 'teachable moments'.

TABLE 14.1 VERBAL SCAFFOLDING STRATEGIES WITH SCIENCE EXAMPLES		
Strategy	**Explanation**	**Science examples**
Direct guidance	Explaining what is to be done.	I wonder what would happen if we put the leaf on the water? Will it float or sink?
Explanation	Helping children interpret information and actions.	How does … ? Why do you think that happened?
Cues and questions	Encouraging reflection on thoughts and actions with the aim of clarifying thinking.	What can you see, hear, smell, feel? How are these similar or different? I wonder why that happened?
Demonstration and modelling	Highlighting appropriate strategies.	Let me show you how to … Let's start by …
Goals and problem identification	Working out what is required and how it might be achieved.	What do you want to find out? How can you make … ? Can you find a way to … ?
Planning	Determining the order of actions, may involve breaking the task into smaller steps.	How can we do this? What should we do first? What do we need to make this? Where can we find what we need?
Mindfulness	Keeping on track or on task.	What are you thinking? What are you making/building?
Evaluating actions	Reviewing the process.	How can you show this to others so they can understand? Please share with me how this works. What are you doing in this photograph?

Source: adapted from Dockett and Fleer, 2002, p. 194.

Case Study 14.3

INCIDENTAL TEACHING DURING CHILD-DIRECTED PLAY

It had been raining on and off all morning. Three-year old Peta was holding an umbrella over her head and standing underneath a dripping gutter. An educator quietly asked, 'What can you hear?' Peta listened, turned with a smile and exclaimed, 'Drip, drop, drip, drop!'

The 4-year-old class had read *Wombat Stew*. Kaleb and Marc were outside talking. They hurried up to the educator and proudly announced that they had decided to make their own stew. The educator replied enthusiastically, 'What a good idea. What will you do first?' The children replied that they were going to collect some 'leaves and gum nuts and feathers and mud'. The teacher asked, 'They are interesting objects to collect. What will you put them in as you collect them?' The two boys looked at each other and ran off excitedly to find an appropriate container.

Year 1 children Jeremy, Anya and Francois had built an elaborate 'city' from a range of blocks, ramps and toys. They had worked on the construction over a period of three days. The children had been given an iPad to take photographs of their city. The educator was sitting with the three children looking at these photographs. She asked, 'That is an interesting tower you have made there (pointing). How did you get it to balance like that?'

Consider Case study 14.3 and the following questions:

1. All three examples in Case study 14.3 highlight incidental teaching with appropriate verbal scaffolding. Can you recognise which verbal scaffolding strategies were used? The educator used a question to focus Peta's attention on one specific aspect – the sound of the rain on the umbrella. Planning was used for Kaleb and Marc to direct them to the first step of finding a suitable container in which to place the stew ingredients. Evaluating was used in the final example with the educator asking the children to explain how they had constructed their tower.

2. In all three examples the educator asked questions without providing answers. This approach allows for children's creativity and open-endedness. Explain how creativity and open-endedness could be captured in these three examples.

Lesson planning for intentional teaching

Lesson planning is an essential component of teaching as it provides the sequence and the timing of activities during a given lesson. For pre-service teachers, lesson planning is even more important as the plans produced provide the structure and guidance for each lesson. This, in turn, gives pre-service teachers the confidence to deliver lessons. Prior preparation is extremely important in teaching. Detailed lesson plans assist in being fully prepared for each lesson taught.

Lesson planning – lesson plans provide the sequence and the timing of activities during a given lesson.

Practical task

PREPARE A LESSON ON THE SEA

This practical task is an extension of Case study 13.2 'Listen! It's the sea!' As a student on practicum with 4-year-old children you have been asked to prepare a lesson on the sea. The children had been talking about their sea experiences while on holiday. The educator had previously read the book *There's a Sea in My Bedroom*. You have been told the room is to be turned into a beach, and that your lesson is to start this process with the topic of waves. What do you teach? How do you plan to teach this?

Preston and Van Rooy (2007) summarised various starting points for planning lessons, depending on the given teaching situation: a lesson that is part of a particular topic, a lesson that seeks to develop specific (skills and/or content) outcomes, a lesson that is built around an activity, or a lesson that fosters the development of children's understanding of a concept. Each approach leads to different content within the lesson plan.

Lesson plans consist of various components: lesson objectives; connections with the Australian Curriculum or the EYLF; children's prior knowledge; resources; the lesson itself, which consists of an introduction, body and a conclusion; timing of the lesson; classroom management during the lesson; and assessment/documentation. Table 14.2 presents a detailed lesson plan for introducing the subject of waves to 4-year-old children. Various points from this lesson plan will be discussed below.

Good lesson plans will show a clear connection between objectives, the lesson body and assessment/documentation – as all three of these will be targeting the same concept covered in the lesson. Objectives state what children should achieve by the end of the lesson. Only two to four objectives are required. Objectives should be specific, measureable, attainable, realistic and time-targeted. An acronym to remember this is SMART. Objectives should always start with a verb that describes what the children will be doing. In Table 14.2 the objectives start with 'express', 'describe' and 'relate'.

TABLE 14.2 DETAILED LESSON PLAN FOR EXPLORING WAVES

Group: 4-year-olds	Topic: The sea
Date, time: 25 minutes	Lesson 2: 'Exploring waves'

Specific lesson learning objectives (What will the children learn in this particular lesson?)

At the conclusion of this lesson each child should be able to:

- express interest and curiosity about turning their room into a beach
- describe what waves look like, sound like and (might) feel like
- relate the waves in the YouTube clip to the blue sheet in the room.

Links to the EYLF

Outcome 4: Children are confident and involved learners:

- children develop dispositions for learning such as curiosity, cooperation, confidence, creativity, commitment, enthusiasm, persistence, imagination and reflexivity
- children transfer and adapt what they have learnt from one context to another.

Outcome 5: Children are effective communicators:

- children express ideas and make meaning using a range of media.

Children's prior knowledge

- children have read the book *There's a Sea in My Bedroom*.

Preparation (classroom layout, resources, grouping)

Have ready access to:

- a mat area with whiteboard and pens to record children's ideas
- the book *There's a Sea in My Bedroom*
- a YouTube clip showing waves (or own short video of waves)
- blue sheets to represent the waves
- a prepared Y-chart (what does the sea look like, sound like and feel like?)
- a camera.

Time	Lesson progression (Include: introduction, lesson steps, activities, focus questions and conclusion)
5 min	*Introduction* (whole group on mat) 1. Show the cover of the book *There's a Sea in My Bedroom*. Ask who remembers this book from the other day. Can they remember what the story was about? 2. Re-read the book with an emphasis on the pictures, highlighting all the things that represent the sea.
15 min	*Body* (whole group on mat, moving to groups of six) 3. Tell the children we will be turning their room into a beach over the next two weeks. 4. Ask: 'Let's think of some things that were in the story that we could have in our room?' Record ideas on whiteboard. 5. Tell the children that today we are going to add waves to our room. 6. Ask: 'What do you know about waves?' 7. Record ideas on the whiteboard. 8. Show a YouTube clip of waves on a beach. 9. Add children's ideas to the Y-chart on what waves look like, sound like and (might) feel like. 10. Introduce the blue sheet as waves. 'Do you think we could pretend these big blue sheets are the waves?' 'How can we get the sheets to move like the wave in the YouTube clip?' 11. Allocate six children to a sheet (three at each end). Let them try all their ideas to make waves with the sheets. Practise small waves and big waves. All children have a turn. Take photographs of the children. Record language being used by the children. 12. Place sheets on ground. 'Who would like to pretend to swim in the sea?'
5 min	*Conclusion* (whole group on mat) 13. What have we found out about waves today? How did we make big waves? How did we make small waves? 14. Leave sheets out for children to play 'waves' during the day.

Assessment/documentation for children's learning

What will you assess/document?	**How** will you assess/document? What evidence will you collect?
• express interest and curiosity about turning their room into a beach • describe what waves look like, sound like and (might) feel like • relate the waves in the YouTube clip to the blue sheet in the room.	Develop a 1–2 page summary of what the children did to show parents based on: • the Y-chart • photos of the children with the sheet and their associated language.

All lesson plans should have connections to appropriate documents such as the Australian Curriculum or the EYLF. The activities presented in a lesson must align with these documents, and in particular the appropriate year level within the Australian Curriculum. Be aware of the prior knowledge the children bring to a lesson as each science lesson should be sequential from the previous lesson. Being fully prepared for teaching means making a list of all resources required during a lesson. Table 14.2 illustrates each of these three components.

The teaching in the lesson consists of three parts: an introduction, a body and a conclusion. The introduction should set the context for the lesson and should engage the children so they are motivated about learning. It may connect directly with a previous lesson (as in the example in Table 14.2) or it may determine children's prior knowledge. The body of the lesson involves a range of activities that develop the concept to be covered. Here it is important to consider what activities are to be offered and how many, how the class is to be organised (are children working individually, in pairs, small groups or as a whole class), the timing and the location of the activities. A range of focus questions to encourage discussion should also be included. Focus questions in the 'Exploring waves' lesson are: 'What do you know about water?' and 'How can we get the sheets to move like a wave in the YouTube clip?' Additionally, a lesson should include teaching strategies to support children's learning. The conclusion of the lesson provides a recap of what has been covered in the lesson and the opportunity to highlight major concepts. It also tells the children the lesson has finished.

The final component of a lesson plan is assessment/documentation. This component provides assessment of the children's learning. What is assessed relates directly to the objectives of the lesson. How the objectives are assessed is based on the various forms of evidence of the children's learning that can be collected during the lesson. A detailed discussion of assessment/documentation is presented in Chapter 15.

Science activities and materials

Prior preparation is essential when conducting science activities. To ensure that the lesson will go smoothly, it is important to be familiar with the actual activity and to have all necessary materials at hand.

When choosing science activities to use, always check the materials required and the steps involved in the process. Never assume an activity will work just because you read it in a book. Always 'rehearse' the activity before doing it with children. This will help you to identify the adequacy of the materials and the appropriateness of the steps, and gain confidence in yourself. If necessary, find alternative materials or use simpler steps, depending on the capability of your children.

Science tends to use a wide range of materials. Many of these can be purchased from the supermarket or a hardware store. Experienced educators tend to have favourite science suppliers from whom they purchase more specialised equipment (for example, magnifying glasses). Recycling depots are also excellent places to pick up a wide range of materials that can be used for teaching across all areas. Additional information on materials is presented in Chapter 10 on the science learning environment.

Practical task

A THIRD LESSON ON THE SEA

What might be a third sequential lesson on the sea for these children? Write a lesson plan incorporating the various components that have been described: lesson objectives; connections with the EYLF; children's prior knowledge; resources; a lesson with an introduction, body and a conclusion; timing of the lesson; classroom management during the lesson; and assessment/documentation.

Practical task

DEVELOP A LESSON PLAN FOR 'DRAWING A SEEDLING'

Develop a detailed lesson plan from Case study 14.1 around assisting the children to draw accurate representations of a seedling. Remember to incorporate the various components that have been described: lesson objectives; connections with the EYLF; children's prior knowledge; resources; a lesson with an introduction, body and a conclusion; timing of the lesson; classroom management during the lesson; and assessment/documentation.

Conclusion

This chapter described intentional teaching and why it is an important part of teaching and learning. Intentional teaching is an involved and thoughtful process where educators deliberately plan and instruct learning activities and experiences in order to develop children's skills, concepts, understandings and dispositions. The relationship between intentional teaching, guided play and child-directed play was presented and illustrated. A range of verbal scaffolding strategies to extend children's science skills, knowledge and understanding were also presented. Lesson planning was described and illustrated as a means to develop intentional teaching, as it provides the sequence and the timing of activities during a given lesson.

14 References

Aitken, J., Hunt, J., Roy, E. & Sajfar, B. (2012). *A Sense of Wonder: Science in Early Childhood Education*, Melbourne: Teaching Solutions.

Blake, E. & Howitt, C. (2012). Science in early learning centres: Satisfying curiosity, guided play or lost opportunities, in K.C.D. Tan & M. Kim (eds), *Issues and Challenges in Science Education Research: Moving Forward*, Dordrecht: Springer, 281–99.

Department of Education, Employment and Workplace Relations (DEEWR). (2009). *Belonging, Being & Becoming: The Early Years Learning Framework for Australia*. Canberra: Commonwealth of Australia.

Dockett, S. & Fleer, M. (2002). *Play and Pedagogy in Early Childhood: Bending the Rules*, Melbourne: Thomson.

Epstein, A. (2011). *The Intentional Teacher: Choosing the Best Strategies for Young Children's Learning*, Washington, DC: National Association for the Education of Young Children.

Fleer, M. (2009). Supporting scientific conceptual consciousness of learning in 'a roundabout way' in play-based contexts, *International Journal of Science Education*, 31(8), 1069–89.

Nolan, A. & Raban, B. (2015). *Theories into Practice: Understanding and Rethinking our Work with Young Children and the EYLF*, Melbourne: Teaching Solutions.

Preston, C. (2016). Try this: Drawing like a scientist, *Teaching Science*, 62(4), 4–8.

Preston, C. & Van Rooy, W. (2007). Planning to teach primary science, in V. Dawson & G. Venville (eds), *The Art of Teaching Primary Science*, Sydney: Allen & Unwin, 87–107.

Rice, J. & Rohl, M. (2011). *Defining and Clarifying Intentional Teaching, Guided Play and Child-directed Play and Learning*, Perth: Western Australian Primary Principals' Association.

Observing, assessing and documenting science learning

Coral Campbell

Educators are required to determine what children know and understand so that they can effectively enhance children's learning opportunities. Evidence of learning may be based on how children explore and interact within their environment or through specific competency tests. Data relating to science learning is usually obtained through a process of observation, anecdotal note-taking, journal entries, checklists and folios of children's work. However, this data needs to be analysed by considering the full picture – who the child was playing with, what they were doing, what science underpinned the play activities and the children's dispositions at the time. The determination of children's science knowledge and understanding and of children's development may be easier said than done. This chapter describes and provides examples of children's learning in science with reference to the EYLF (DEEWR, 2009a) and the Australian Curriculum: Science (ACARA, 2015), which together provide a comprehensive framework for decision-making about children's learning as well as enhancing educators' planning for future learning.

OBJECTIVES

At the end of this chapter you will be able to:

- ■ describe and document children's learning in science with reference to the Early Years Learning Framework (EYLF) and the Australian Curriculum: Science
- ■ describe ways in which children's explorations can demonstrate and enhance their understanding
- ■ describe different strategies for observing, monitoring and documenting science understanding.

Children's learning

The EYLF (DEEWR, 2009a) advocates that children learn through play and that play-based learning is 'a context for learning through which children organise and make sense of their social worlds, as they engage actively with people, objects and representations' (p. 3). Within play-based learning, the role of the educator is crucial for developing children's understandings of the world around them and the science within it.

The EYLF proposes that educators can enhance children's learning by:

Holistic approaches – recognise the connectedness of mind, body and spirit, as well as the connectedness of knowledge.

Intentional teaching – educators being deliberate, purposeful and thoughtful in their teaching.

- adopting **holistic approaches**
- being responsive to children's questions
- planning and implementing learning through play
- providing **intentional teaching**
- creating environments that have a positive impact on learning
- valuing the social and cultural contexts of children and families
- facilitating continuity of experiences and enabling success
- assessing and monitoring children's learning. (Adapted from DEEWR, 2009a, p. 14)

Chapter 13, 'Planning for teaching science in the early years', discussed how educators can plan for learning through play, both intentional and focused. In considering this planning, we need to reflect on what questions educators should ask themselves as part of the planning process. These questions are focused on children's prior knowledge, motivation, what children want or need to learn and what the best approach to take is with each of these. When planning learning experiences, the educator is also making decisions about the learning expectations, and how to assess the children's learning.

The Australian Curriculum: Science (ACARA, 2015) for Foundation to Year 2 (which caters for children aged 5–8 years) has as its focus 'awareness of self and the local world'. As described in Chapter 3, 'Science in the Australian Curriculum', children's learning in these early years of school should be centred on their exploratory and purposeful play in their immediate environment. As part of the assessment, monitoring and reporting process in schools, educators should focus on the set ideas indicated in the Australian Curriculum: Science. They may access sample programs from resources such as the Primary Connections units of work (discussed in Chapter 13), which are integrated across other curriculum areas and provide examples of possible assessment.

Background research on children's learning

With the introduction of the EYLF (DEEWR, 2009a), the focus in early childhood centres shifted from incidental learning through play to delivering a planned curriculum, with play as the vehicle to achieve this. This intentional, discipline-based teaching has changed the **pedagogical focus** of early childhood educators. Educators have to re-think what constitutes a 'learning experience' and also reflect on practices they can implement to support the new approach. Goodfellow (2009) indicated that 'the goal is to enrich children's learning

Pedagogical focus – deals with the theory and practice of teaching and learning.

experiences through purposeful actions by educators in collaboration with children and families' (p. 2). Providing an attractive and interesting environment is not sufficient to stimulate deep learning and sustained engagement (DEEWR 2009b). Furthermore, Arthur (2010) supported the idea of strong guidance by the educator when she stated that 'intentional teaching reflects a socio-cultural approach to learning which emphasises the value of an experienced educator building a scaffold so that the child moves to higher levels of understanding' (p. 10). An example might be thinking about a child exploring a plant growing. Using an incidental approach only, the educator might move towards the child's play and ask questions related to what the child is doing. Using a more 'intentional' approach, the educator might try to relate what the child is doing to other things she knows about the child (i.e. build links to prior learning), or bring other children into the experience to promote the learning further (i.e. socially embed the learning).

However, some early childhood educators are not comfortable with engaging in 'guided learning' or in educator-led practices, or intentionally planning for discipline-based learning outcomes to occur through children's autonomous actions during play (Campbell & Jobling, 2009; Edwards & Loveridge, 2011). According to the EYLF, 'Curriculum decision making is informed by the context, setting and cultural diversity of the families and the community' (DEEWR, 2009a, p. 45). The quality of the child's experience is enhanced when early childhood educators know about the concepts and look for opportunities during play to foster understanding in children (Cullen, 2007). Siraj-Blatchford (2004) also commented that 'Effective pedagogy is both "teaching" and the provision of instructive learning and play environments and routines' (p. 6).

Educators at all levels employ a range of verbal scaffolding strategies that aim to effectively help children to extend their knowledge, understanding and skills (Dockett & Fleer, 2002). These include direct guidance, explanation, cues and questions, demonstration and modelling, goal and problem identification, planning, keeping on track and evaluating actions.

Observing science learning

Much of an educator's time is spent observing the children in his/her care. This observation forms the basis of their judgements about behaviours, **dispositions** and learning. However, for this observation to be used as a means of analysing a child's knowledge or understanding in science, the educator needs to be aware of the context of learning. Fleer (2009, p. 287) highlighted that to understand a child's science knowledge, the educator needs to be aware of 'the social contexts which permit authentic understanding of young children's thinking in science'. There is recognition that, particularly for children, learning is strongly contextualised and that to fully understand young children's thinking we need to understand the context which enabled the learning. Tytler, Peterson and Prain (2007) found that young children's understandings fluctuated depending on the context they found themselves in.

> **Disposition** – a child's attitude, in the absence of coercion, exhibited as a pattern of behaviour.

The implications for the educator are that observations of children's learning should be accompanied by a description of context. As context differs, the children's understandings might flex and be impermanent. An observation, analysed against an understanding of the key science ideas, can be recorded as children learning. However, for an educator to have faith in the academic judgement of learning, repeated observations of the same understanding in different contexts should to be made to be certain of the science learning.

Observation of learning is related to finding out what children do know and what they can do. It is not about what they cannot do. In observing children, an educator should be focusing on children's strengths and taking in the entire learning experience.

Practical task

SEEING THE SCIENCE IN AN EVERYDAY ACTIVITY

Observe what children are doing in the photograph in Figure 15.1 and describe the context as fully as possible.

FIGURE 15.1   Observe the children in this photograph

Having now described the context, can you indicate what science is involved in this 'snapshot' of the activity? Are you able to differentiate the possible learning between the children? What does the child at the bottom know? What does the child at the top know?

Observations may help educators in their decision-making about curriculum and instruction, as well as helping to determine how much progress children are making. Observations may be informal or formal. Informal observations include the educator noticing how children respond to a task or questions and may include their gestures, such as a puzzled look, hand-raising or lack thereof. Formal observations are usually linked with a specific learning outcome and recording strategy.

However, the other element of observation is that of a child, who through play, is experiencing a 'science phenomenon'. The experience is recorded in the child's mental schema and revisited when the phenomenon is experienced again. Repeated success may lead the child to developing some understanding which may be observed by the educator. However, an intentional educator will provide further opportunities for the child to experience and clarify the understanding. Hence, observation is usually linked with educator involvement in the learning.

To be able to accurately determine science learning as it is happening through the observed experiences of children's play, the educator needs to have a reasonable understanding of the science. One way to do this is through the observation of common activities in early childhood centres or schools which have science implicit within them. Table 15.1 provides examples of various phenomena and the science associated with them.

TABLE 15.1 THE SCIENCE AND LANGUAGE OF VARIOUS SCIENCE PHENOMENA

Type of activity or phenomenon observed	Possible language link	Area of science
Child balancing on a rock	Balance	Physics – force
Child rolling down a hill	Roll	Physics – force
Children mixing 'potions'	Mixing	Chemistry – physical change
Child playing with water	Floating	Physics – force
Child watering plants	Plant drinking	Biology – requirements of living things

Documenting and assessing

Accurate observations and comprehensive documentation allow educators to monitor and assess children's learning in a range of experiences. According to the EYLF (DEEWR, 2009a), educators, through adopting a range of approaches for observing, gathering and documenting children's learning, are able to:

- use evidence to inform future planning
- reflect on the effectiveness of teaching
- make judgements about a child's developing capabilities and respond in appropriate ways

■ reflect on and evaluate their planning program and pedagogical practices.

While using the learning outcomes of the EYLF, educators can monitor children's progress and provide effective measures for enhancing children's learning. The EYLF advocates that educators should engage children as active participants in recording and reflecting on their own learning. The sharing of this information with parents and caregivers supports children's learning beyond the early childhood centre.

> Assessment for children's learning refers to the process of gathering and analysing information as evidence about what children know, can do and understand. It is part of an ongoing cycle that includes planning, documenting and evaluating children's learning. (EYLF, p. 17)

Documenting science learning: what do we do?

Earlier chapters have discussed how children learn science and the importance of science in children's lives. It is equally important that an educator plans for science experiences (as described in Chapter 13) and is able to monitor children's understanding and progress. Of course, there are many questions an educator can ask, such as:

1. What do we monitor or assess?
   - ■ scientific conceptual growth – children's developing understandings
   - ■ inquiry skills (process knowledge)
   - ■ skill development
   - ■ scientific attitudes and responsibility
   - ■ scientific communication.

2. How often do we monitor or assess?
   - ■ before, during and after an experience.

3. Why do we assess?
   - ■ to improve children's learning by informing our teaching
   - ■ to improve the content and delivery of our teaching
   - ■ to inform children and parents
   - ■ to meet the accountability requirements of the various governing bodies.

Monitoring – observing and checking progress over time.

Documenting – collecting and recording information.

Assessing – analysing and making meaning of information about children's learning.

Both informal and formal **monitoring**, **documenting** and **assessing** require three different approaches. Diagnostic assessment (probing for prior understanding) helps determine what a child already knows. Formative assessment, occurring while children are undertaking a science exploration, provides information about children's growing understandings, which assists the educator in the development of further learning experiences. Finally, summative assessment relates to progression of learning and is the final reporting of achievement.

Chittendon and Jones (1998) commented:

> Interest in science assessments brings the opportunity to explore methods that require a central role for early childhood science teachers ... For teachers, recognizing the science in children's behaviour may well be more problematic than observing children's

development as readers and writers, in part because of the teachers' own limitations of content knowledge. In addition, the boundaries of the child's development as a 'scientist' are less clear. Children's ways of figuring out how the world works are not constrained by science lessons but cut across the curriculum areas. (p. 1)

These points argue for greater involvement of educators in the documentation and analysis of children's science learning, both for professional development of the educator and for the design of appropriate assessments.

When we consider monitoring, documenting and assessing, it is important to use a range of different strategies that relate to children's learning requirements. During any activity or learning experiences, the educator needs to share the learning goals with the children and provide effective feedback to the children during their explorations. The monitoring, documenting or assessment should identify a child's current level of learning achievement, the next level up and any gap. It should also provide feedback about how to close the gap and engage the learner in using the feedback to close the gap.

There are a large number of ways to gain information about a child's learning: oral presentations, posters, or models; self/peer assessment; **portfolios**; concept mapping; interviews/questioning; observations; rubrics; representational challenges; writing; performance assessment and problem-solving; and practical assessment. Three of these approaches are described below.

> **Portfolio** – a collection of children's work that highlights their learning.

Monitoring, documenting and assessing using interviews

With young children, the term 'interview' is loosely employed to describe any concentrated opportunity the educator uses to ask a number of well-focused questions about a conceptually related science idea. This can occur when children are playing or exploring, or through a specific experience devised by the educator. The main purpose of the questioning is to elicit children's understandings so that the educator can more purposefully inform their own teaching. Educators can identify children's alternative concepts, gaps in understanding or areas that need additional clarification. They can observe how children apply their knowledge to the questions asked of them. When children are playing with objects, the educator can document the skills employed by the children and the content-specific procedures they use.

Practical task

USING INTERVIEWS ABOUT LIVING THINGS

This task allows educators to determine children's understanding about living things. Children are provided with a range of photographs of living things (such as those below) and are asked questions about how they would categorise the photographs and why they made their choice.

→

FIGURE 15.2 A range of photos for using interviews about living things .

Possible questions to ask include:

1. How would you group these living things?
2. Why do they belong together (assuming children have placed all the dogs together or the monkeys together)?
3. How are the groups different?

Depending on the age of the children or on their level of conceptual development, the educator may introduce the idea of 'humans as animals' or species (similar characteristics, capable of breeding).

Monitoring, documenting and assessing using observations

As indicated earlier in this chapter, and in previous ones, it is now accepted that children learn through the construction of their understanding or meaning, usually through social situations. Therefore, as educators observe children in science play and explorations, they should consider all factors as contributing to the learning. For example, while watching children playing with small insects from a garden, educators should be aware of the children's interactions with each other, as well as their interactions with the animals and the way they behave individually. Educators would not only be watching what the children do, but also listening to what they say to each other. They should also be aware of the need to come into the discussion with a focusing question or some other form of scaffolding to assist children's learning. The observation of children learning needs to take all these factors into consideration. As indicated by Fleer and Robbins (2004), such observations are:

> vibrant, reflective and complex. The focus shifts from what the individual in isolation can or cannot do, to the dynamic interplay of pairs or groups of children, or children and adults, noting the scaffolding, supporting, extending, leading and following ... Without this, we may run the risk of not only missing vital aspects that are helpful in understanding how both individuals and groups of children are learning and developing, but we might possibly 'get it wrong' in our interpretations. (p. 25)

The EYLF (DEEWR, 2009a) places emphasis on holistic learning, taking into account children's identity, wellbeing, confidence as learners, communication skills and connectedness to their world. Effective observation of the children and their circumstances will lead to effective planning and further support of a child's individual learning pathway. The educator needs to form sensitive and attached relationships with children to ensure that observation is carried out on multi-sensory levels. This is particularly relevant for young children. Gandini and Golhaber (2001) observed that the educator's role is 'to construct a shared understanding of children's ways of interacting with the environment, of entering into relationships with other adults and other children and of constructing their knowledge' (p. 125). Formal observations, which tend to include a recording of children's understanding, are usually planned and include a number of recognised strategies:

- discussions – these can provide information about children's understanding, identifying children's process skills and thought patterns
- anecdotal records – these are usually written records of children's behaviour/learning (e.g. children's understandings, questions and possible misunderstandings)
- checklists – these may be used to evaluate knowledge, skills or attitudes (benefits of using checklists include that they are time-saving and can focus on individual children; as documented evidence of a child's progress, checklists are useful for discussions with children and parents).

In school settings, the science learning may be more structured in approach, but will still contain elements of scaffolding, even through the assessment process. Scaffolding can include, but is not limited to, underlining key words in instructions to a child; providing pictures, diagrams or story maps; clarifying what should be included in a child's response; indicating what materials may be used; providing some background information;

reminding children of prevous discussions; giving hints; asking a child to focus on certain things; or providing the children with a checklist they can use to check their work. Scaffolding becomes part of the task and should be provided to all students.

Set learning outcomes are determined at the point of planning, so the educator has pre-planned aspects of assessment that need to be monitored. In the EYLF these are very broad when applied to science. In the Australian Curriculum they are more defined (see Chapter 2 and Chapter 3). Observation, anecdotal notes and the successful completion of specific tasks can be tools used by the educator to monitor children's learning.

Observation is one of the primary means of collecting information or evidence of children's learning. For an educator, busy with 20 or more children, how can observations remain in their mind? How can the recording of this learning consider all factors and be kept for future reference? This is the single most difficult aspect of monitoring children's learning. There are a number of possibilities of recording. The educator could, at that time and instant, write up comprehensive anecdotal notes of what has happened to indicate learning. The educator could take a digital image of the learning and later in the day write notes to accompany the image, using the image to stimulate recall. Finally, the educator could write up brief key words for use as memory stimulants of the learning experience for further elaboration at a later time.

Case Study 15.1

A SIMPLE RECORDING TOOL

Rebecca, working in a small rural pre-school, came up with a recording strategy that worked for her. With 20 lively 4–5-year-old children, she was aware that her time for recording was limited. Rebecca developed a simple grid of blank squares (4 × 5) on one A4 sheet of paper. In each grid, she typed a child's name in the top left-hand corner, leaving space in the rest of the grid square for her comments to be inserted. She copied enough single grid sheets for each week of the term and placed them in an open binder on her desk. When she observed learning she would record it in brief points in that child's grid and in the others' if it was shared learning. At the end of each week, during her planning time, Rebecca wrote out more comprehensive notes on each of the learning incidents and placed these in the child's portfolio. Sometimes she took photographs as well. At the end of each week, Rebecca was aware of which children had demonstrated learning that she had been able to 'capture' and those children she had missed. She then made a concerted effort to observe the other children in the following week and to determine whether she needed to spend more time with them, scaffolding their learning.

Monitoring, documenting and assessing using rubrics

Rubric – a brief, written description of different levels of a child's performance.

A scoring **rubric** is a brief, written description of different levels of a child's performance. All rubrics contain the level of performance expected and the rating that should be allowed for different levels of performance. One really useful aspect of using a rubric is that it allows a child to view their work relative to a desired standard or achievement. There are two basic types of rubric: one measuring the overall quality of the work rather than specific details, and the other assigning points for virtually every aspect of a child's performance.

Rubric criteria may include understanding of concepts, use of higher-order thinking ability, level of creativity, presentation, or level of collaboration. Table 15.2 presents an example of a science rubric based on Foundation level biological science in the Australian Curriculum: Science. The table also presents information relevant to the strands Science as a Human Endeavour and **(Science) Inquiry Skills**, and to the use of scientific language.

(Science) Inquiry Skills – skills involved in a process of active exploration as children engage in questions of interest to them

TABLE 15.2 SCIENCE RUBRIC FOR THE FOUNDATION LEVEL OF BIOLOGICAL SCIENCE ('LIVING THINGS HAVE BASIC NEEDS, INCLUDING FOOD AND WATER')

	Level of understanding of science content	Use of scientific language	Science as a Human Endeavour	Science Inquiry Skills
	Living things have basic needs, including food and water.		Science involves exploring and observing the world using the senses.	Planning and conducting. Processing and analysing data and information. Exploring and making observations by using the senses. Communicating.
4	There is evidence that the child has a full and complete understanding.	Excellent use of scientific language, demonstrating understanding of the terms.	The response reflects a complete synthesis of information.	The child displays excellent science inquiry skills.
3	There is evidence that the child has a good understanding.	Good use of scientific language, demonstrating understanding of the terms.	The response reflects some synthesis of information.	The child displays good science inquiry skills.
2	There is evidence that the child has a basic understanding.	Occasional use of scientific language, demonstrating some understanding of the terms.	The response provides little or no synthesis of information.	The child displays science inquiry skills.
1	There is evidence that the child has some understanding.	Little use of scientific language.	The response addresses the question.	Some science inquiry skills evident.

Documentation of science learning

The documentation of learning in an early childhood setting should include what children do and say, as well as the interactions between children. It should also include the context in terms of the tools or artefacts the children are using at the time and how they are using them. As part of the documentation process, the educator might involve parents to gain some background to children's prior understandings. Recording parents' comments, as well as the educator's comments, can provide a more comprehensive account of children's learning. The documentation should be in-time and accurate, as indicated in the discussion below. **Anecdotal note-taking** is a term used in a range of contexts but essentially means the notes that educators record about a specific instance of children's learning. To be of value, the notes should be recorded as soon as possible after the observation and should contain a number of specific elements. These were noted previously, but include the context of the learning, what the child says or does and with what, and how other children interact, and any interaction with the educator. Anecdotal notes are subjective, based largely on observations, but also on how well the educator knows the children. It is for this reason that other documentation or evidence is collected. This could be in the form of photographs, children's work or children's words (recorded).

Anecdotal note-taking – educator notes taken during activities which are used to record specific observations of individual children.

In Figure 15.3, the child depicts her awareness of body parts – hair, eyes, pupils, mouth, head, arms and legs. She is also starting to form letters and recognise her name. Six months later (see Figure 15.4), the child has already advanced in her depiction of body parts, indicating an increased awareness of her whole body. She now draws the trunk, belly button (umbilicus), fingers and feet in addition to what was included previously. By collecting this

FIGURE 15.3 Learning about the body – a child's drawing at 42 months of age

artwork at the time, educators were able to see the changing understandings of this child. This example demonstrates Outcome 4 of the EYLF: 'Children are confident and involved learners, who create and use representation to organise, record and communicate … ideas and concepts' (DEEWR, 2009a, p. 35). This child is using representation to organise, record and communicate science ideas and concepts.

FIGURE 15.4   Evidence of developing understanding of body in the same child, six months later

Documenting using a learning story

One current strategy for observing and documenting a child's learning and progress is through the use of a **learning story** (Arthur et al., 2005). A learning story was first described by Podmore and Carr (1999) as a narrative or storied approach to assessment that describes a child's learning process, and is one way of documenting that learning. Goodsir and Rowell (2010) indicated that the elements of a good learning story include the child's interests and achieve-

Learning story – a narrative approach to assessment where educators record children's learning context, assess learning and suggest ways forward.

ments; their strengths, knowledge and feelings; their interactions with peers and adults; and the influence of their family, heritage, culture and community. A learning story generally starts with the child's initiative or with how they have responded to a learning opportunity offered. The educator takes a photograph of what is happening and adds a comment after discussion with the child. The learning story can take place at one time (see 'Josie's Drip' at earlylearningstories.info) or can cover a longer period as a child comes back to further explore an activity or task. More photographs can be added as well as a narrative of descriptive details. Towards the end, the educator analyses the learning through a 'What does it mean?' approach, describing why these events are significant. The educator would then add a page indicating what adults can do to assist this learning further. Often, parents are also given a page where they can add any significant historical, cultural or contextual elements or perspectives.

EXAMPLE OF A LEARNING STORY

Daniella was playing quietly in the corner of the garden on a path. We noticed a small group of children were starting to form around her, so we went to investigate. We found that they were watching Daniella drip water onto the path. We photographed the incident. As Daniella dripped water, using a small cup and bucket, she was watching which way it went. 'See,' she said to the others, 'it always goes that way.'

One of the others wanted to try, so Daniella handed over her water. 'I can do it too,' the boy exclaimed proudly, before handing the water back to Daniella. Daniella wanted to know why the water always went the same way. Rather than respond to the question, I asked her whether she had tried other parts of the path. She had not, but was eager to investigate. She moved further along the path, about two metres. This time when she dripped the water, it did not go in quite the same direction; it seemed to go more sideways. This fascinated her and she proceeded to try other parts of the path, still with a small group following her and watching what happened. Several more photographs were taken. After a while, she appeared to give up. I approached Daniella and asked her why she had stopped. She smiled at me and said: 'I know what happens. The water is always going downhill.' With that she wandered off to try other adventures in the garden.

WHAT DOES THIS MEAN?

Daniella was able to undertake an investigation of her own interest. With scaffolding, she persisted with her investigation. She was prepared to share her knowledge with others and was generous in allowing another child to try things for himself. After multiple observations, Daniella was able to come up with a scientific reason for her observations. She demonstrated good problem-solving skills as well as persistence and motivation.

FURTHER LEARNING

As Daniella has demonstrated an ability to persist in her own investigations, we will ensure that we provide her with other challenges of a similar nature and help her achieve some success as she learns to solve problems and draw conclusions from evidence.

Documenting using portfolios

A portfolio is a collection of children's work that highlights their learning. It contains work samples, records of systematic observation, anecdotal notes, photographs (annotated), learning stories, video snippets, checklists, journal entries and parents' contributions. A child's portfolio can be in a hard copy and it can be kept in an accessible place so that it can be easily retrieved, due to the philosophy that portfolios are for the children and parents as well. However, many early childhood centres now adopt digital portfolios, and can upload photographs or notes almost instantly. Parents have ready access to these. One advantage of a hard copy portfolio is that children's learning can be enhanced if the child has the opportunity to extract a piece of work or a learning story and offer further elaboration. Children delight in sharing their portfolios with each other and illustrating their learning to others.

A portfolio must have an explicit purpose to guide the decisions about what to include as part of the portfolio. As such, a portfolio should contain a statement indicating its purpose. The portfolio should make sense of children's work and learning artefacts, and how this work relates to the broader context of the children's progressive learning. Material in the portfolio should be ordered chronologically and by category (discipline area) as well as category of development. Portfolios are widely used in pre-school and school settings. For examples of portfolio entries in the early school years, see the annotated work sample portfolios provided on the Australian Curriculum, Assessment and Reporting Authority's (ACARA) website (www.acara.edu.au/curriculum/worksamples/Foundation_Year_Science_Portfolio_Satisfactory.pdf).

Case Study 15.3

EXAMPLE OF A PORTFOLIO ENTRY

David, aged 4, drew two caterpillars on the same sheet of paper (Figure 15.5). One drawing had the segments of the body and multiple legs. The other showed a caterpillar with hairs on the body and different dots. Both drawings indicated that there was a head end (the direction in which each caterpillar was moving). In terms of science understandings, the educator could determine that David had observed the insects closely and noted differences between them. He had noticed that one had a clearly defined segmented body and both had multiple legs, with the legs starting after the defined head.

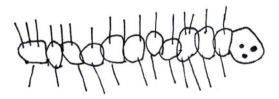

FIGURE 15.5 Evidence of David's developing understanding of caterpillars through his drawings

Another example for a portfolio might be a systematic observation of a child at play outside. Systematic observations should be objective, stating only what is actually seen or heard and should not include the educator's opinion. They should be unobtrusive, in that the educator does not enter into the play or learning scenario. Finally, systematic observation should be carefully recorded to include all details. For example, an educator may set up a discovery table with a range of rocks of different origins and with different features, and then may sit at a distance recording how children interact with the display. This systematic recorded observation can then provide the educator with information about the content of intentional teaching relating to rocks.

Documenting using floorbooks or children's own records of learning

Floorbooks – books that are developed with children to document and record their ideas and learning.

In pre-schools, some educators have been using **floorbooks** – books that are developed with children to document and record their ideas and learning. Sometimes referred to as 'Big Book Planners' or 'Talking and Thinking Books' they were developed to involve children in thinking through and talking about their learning. The books record children's ideas, without the educator reinterpreting what the children say. They are used to record children's questions for discussion and to record any subsequent reflections. Floorbooks can promote higher-order thinking, depth of learning and collaborative learning.

Similarly, in the early schooling years, educators will often provide children with a book to create a 'science journal'. Children can note their own observations as they undertake an exploration and record their own questions for group discussions. The book has blank spaces to allow for drawing or writing, or for children to stick in pictures from magazines or their own photographs. Employed appropriately, a science journal can accurately record what children know about a topic and what they still need to learn. Using the journal allows children to return to the exploration time and time again. They can add additional information or just re-read what they wrote/drew previously. An educator can use the journal as a means of gaining knowledge of children's understanding.

Analysing children's understanding in science

While observation and documentation are important, it is the analysis undertaken by the educator that adds meaning to the observation. What learning are children demonstrating? For accurate measurement of children's learning, the educator must have a good understanding of science or be prepared to find this out. This is problematic as many educators

Case Study 15.4

A WHOLE-GROUP APPROACH

As a means of keeping parents informed of children's learning opportunities, many early childhood centres keep a 'big book' where the educator documents what planned activities the children have been involved in as well as any child-led learning initiated across the week.

The photograph in Figure 15.6 below presents an activity that all children participated in. Using hydrophilic beads, children observed the beads before and after the addition of water. They made predictions of what they thought the water would do to the beads, and after observing the result in subsequent days, detailed their descriptions of what happened. Some children were able to offer an explanation. All children's comments were recorded by the educators involved.

Photograph 1, Tim: 'They will float and then blow up'.

Photograph 2, Tim: 'They are soft like melting snowmen'.

Photograph 3, Lexi told her family how a sponge absorbs water.

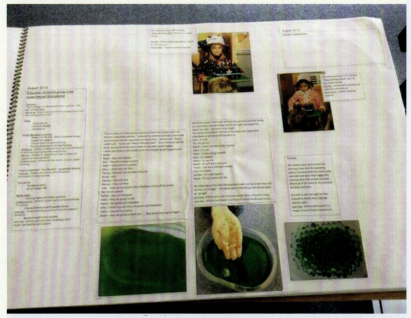

FIGURE 15.6 Hydrophilic beads activity

have come through schooling with little emphasis on science in general (Campbell & Jobling, 2009). There are a number of ways to consider children's learning. As mentioned previously, educators are assessing and analysing children's science understandings (conceptual), inquiry skills (how to undertake an investigation), skill development (such as observation, measurement or reasoning), scientific attitudes (dispositions) and communication.

In any given observation of children's learning, educators should actively look for the science so that the science learning is not missed due to a concentration on, for example, social learning. When children jump in a puddle, they are investigating what will happen. They are undertaking science. When children pile blocks higher and higher, they are investigating what will happen. Often they will repeat the investigation again and again, just to make sure that their information is correct. They have just learnt to undertake multiple tests to confirm findings.

With a focus on the basics of science, an educator can quickly learn the important concepts relevant to young children's understanding. For content knowledge, educators can focus on general broad statements of knowledge, such as 'Jenna understands about the living things in her environment', or at the level of specific information, such as 'Jenna knows that snails have shells and that these shells have distinct patterns'. Of these two statements, the second is much clearer about what Jenna knows and it allows the educator to build on Jenna's understanding in the future. In science, these statements of specific information are called 'concepts'. For science, there are many such statements or concepts that help educators articulate children's understanding at a defined level. Examples of these include:

- sight, sound, touch, taste and smell are very important senses we use to interpret our world
- objects float if the upthrust force from the water can balance their weight
- our ears are used to detect and hear sound
- light travels in straight lines.

See Appendix 2 at the end of this book, 'Examples of simple science statements or concepts', for many science concepts related to areas of science knowledge and understanding.

Inquiry skills are demonstrated when a child follows a process of active exploration, using critical and problem-solving thinking, to engage in questions of interest to them. They seek solutions to their own questions through exploration. Consider Case study 15.2, where Daniella was interested in finding out why the dripping water moved in a particular way. She devised a series of experiments to firstly confirm her original observation, then she changed one of the parameters (variables), to finally arrive at a conclusion. In this inquiry, she demonstrated a number of other science skills, including observation, investigating, fair testing (changing only one variable), reasoning, communicating (collaborating with other children) and problem-solving. When it comes to the demonstration of skills, educators need to consider what the appropriate skills are that young children are able to demonstrate. Many of these skills were more fully described in Chapter 5, 'Approaches to enhance science learning'. The first step in an inquiry approach in science requires the engagement of children in the learning process. Children's engagement and motivation are important aspects of learning. Campbell and Tytler (2007) note that children's motivations includes their values, interests, goal orientation and how they rate the importance of the science tasks. Children need to believe that they have some control and are capable of doing the science, with a likelihood of achievement. The context, the chosen task and the effectiveness of the teaching are all contributing factors. If children do not become sufficiently involved in the learning task, then the best result is likely to be surface learning.

Children's dispositions in science learning are important to ensure that children are actively involved in their own learning. Katz (1993) defines dispositions as 'a pattern of behaviour exhibited frequently ... in the absence of coercion ... constituting a habit of mind' (p. 16). She comments that dispositions are under some level of conscious control and that they are influenced by interaction with others (weakened or strengthened). The EYLF (DEEWR, 2009a) identifies a range of positive dispositions for learning within Outcome 4 – that children are confident and involved learners. These include curiosity, cooperation, confidence, creativity, commitment, enthusiasm, persistence, imagination and reflexivity (p. 34). Nearly all of these dispositions are involved in science explorations. Consider, for example, children building a tall tower from blocks. They exhibit confidence in the belief that they are capable of completing the task. They collaborate creatively as they work together to build the tower. They persist (usually) if the tower falls down. They problem-solve to work out how to replace fallen blocks. They demonstrate enthusiasm and commitment to the task. When finished, one outcome might be that they reflect on the finished product and decide to build it in a different way.

Ensuring that the learning environment promotes positive dispositions is key to being able to observe these dispositions in children. Arthur (2010) comments that 'active, play-based, hands-on experiences promote enthusiasm and engagement for learning. Collaborative problem-based play environments encourage cooperation, persistence and reflexivity, as well as deep learning and high-order thinking' (p. 13). Documentation of learning can be through the use of portfolios, learning stories or floorbooks. The involvement of children in documenting their own learning is a powerful tool for improving their dispositions for learning.

Case Study 15.5

EXAMPLE OF INTENTIONAL TEACHING IN SCIENCE AND THE SCIENCE ASSESSMENT

LESSON TOPIC: 'PLANTS'

The concept discussed in this class of 4–5-year-olds was that plants are living organisms needing water and energy to grow and develop. The following conversation demonstrates the prior knowledge of the children.

Child 1: The plants are alive just like me and you, all of us. And one day is gonna be the day that we die. Just like the old trees at my house did.

Child 2: They're living because they need water and energy and breathe and move a little bit.

Child 3: They need the Sun but need a rest from it and a big drink, otherwise they can die.

Child 4: Yeah, well the plants can't run around with us in the Sun, but they are alive. They don't move, ya know. Only if the wind is strong.

Child 5: Because they always drink water and get wet in the rain. That's the same for a tree and for the kids playing.

From this conversation we can make some judgements about what the children already know about living objects. Child 1 has developed a definition for 'alive' and can provide examples of 'dead' things. Child 2 can expand the definition by incorporating some of the characteristics of living things: water, energy, respiration and movement. Child 3 indicates that the Sun provides something for the plant but can extend that thought to the consequences of too much Sun and not enough water. Child 4 picks up on the inconsistency in the characteristics of living things – that plants are living things even though they cannot move freely. Child 5 cannot add a great deal in terms of content but is using his reasoning skills in determining that some features of living things are common for plants and children. These children already know much about what makes a plant a living thing.

The children were subsequently given the opportunity to explore the diversity of living things in the outside environment. They were supplied with a digital camera and the educator followed them around to guide their learning and help them confirm the characteristics of living and non-living things. She also discussed categorising and differentiating between living things such as plants and animals.

→

LEARNING THAT CHILDREN ACQUIRED

The children learnt about science concepts as they explored their own environment. They scaffolded each other's learning and at times deeply discussed whether certain things were living, or whether to photograph certain things. They generally had these discussions as they observed items such as wood chips and cut flowers. Subjects of the children's photographs included:

- a wide variety of trees, bushes, flowers and plants
- other caregivers
- children from the other group
- sticks, bark chips, dirt and mulch
- a bird.

Child 1: Of course Catherine [educator] and the children are living things.

Child 2: I know that this tree is alive but I don't know why it can't move from one place to another if it is a living thing. All other living things like people and animals can move from walking or crawling and sliding and stuff like that. The tree never changes spot.

Child 3: This [photograph] is the best one of living things because it has many [living things] in one picture. There's a bird, tree, grass and people at the bottom.

Child 4: We don't need a photo of the bark and leaves because it doesn't need water or Sun anymore. When it was with the tree it needed that but now it's dead.

FINAL LESSON'S LEARNING

The children confirmed their previous understandings of living things. Again, one child could not resolve the issue of the lack of movement of the tree when he was convinced that it was a characteristic of other living things. Perhaps this was a time when the educator could have stepped in with a few focusing questions so that the child may have realised that there is movement in plants, but it occurs in one spot. Child 3 recognised the diversity of living things while Child 4 was able to identify non-living things in the environment.

Children require time and multiple opportunities to grasp a single topic or concept. They need to make sense of the world through practice and experience. Taking photographs enabled the children in the above case study to raise questions and to make decisions about living things. To further this activity, the children could display their photographs for others to see, or the photographs could be annotated and included in their portfolios. The educator could facilitate the key concepts that a plant is a living organism by writing up some of the text from the discussion. Displaying the plant in the classroom allows the children to look at it throughout the day and subconsciously encourages them to think about the science of plants.

Conclusion

Children play, explore, make friends and have fun the entire time they are learning. The role of the educator is to monitor that learning, to make sense of children's investigations and to plan for extended opportunities for further learning. This chapter discussed how the educator can monitor and assess the learning, using a range of strategies for recording the developing understandings of children in science. It considered how the educator can use child-instigated learning experiences or educator-led explorations. The chapter's case studies demonstrated the multiple opportunities educators have for observing, assessing or documenting science learning in the pre-school setting and in the early years of school.

Acknowledgement

I would like to thank Megan Beer, early childhood educator, for her story on the intentional teaching of plants.

Arthur, L. (2010). *The Early Years Learning Framework: Building Confident Learners, Research in Practice Series*, Canberra: Early Childhood Australia.

Arthur, L., Beecher, B., Death, E., Dockett, S. & Farmer, S. (2005). *Programming and Planning in Early Childhood Settings*, Melbourne: Thomson.

Australian Curriculum, Assessment and Reporting Authority (ACARA). (2015). The Australian Curriculum: Science F-10, www.australiancurriculum.edu.au/f-10-curriculum/science/.

Campbell, C. & Jobling, W. (2009). Science professional development for early childhood educators – some identified issues, paper presented to the 11th New Zealand Early Childhood Research Conference, Wellington.

Campbell, C. & Tytler, R. (2007). Views of student learning, in G. Venville & V. Dawson (eds), *The Art of Teaching Primary Science*, Sydney: Allen & Unwin, 23–42.

Chittendon, E. & Jones, J. (1998). Science assessment in early childhood programs, paper presented at the Forum on Early Childhood Science, Mathematics and Technology Education, First Experiences in Science, Mathematics, and Technology, The American Association for the Advancement of Science.

Cullen, J. (2007). Literacy debate in the early years: The New Zealand context, in R. Openshaw & J. Soler (eds), *Reading Across International Boundaries: History, Policy and Contexts*, Charlotte, NC: Information Age Publishing, 111–28.

Department of Education, Employment & Workplace Relations (DEEWR). (2009a). *Belonging, Being and Becoming: The Early Years Learning Framework for Australia*, Canberra: Commonwealth of Australia.

—— (2009b). *Towards a National Quality Framework for Early Childhood Education and Care, report of the Expert Advisory Panel on Quality Early Childhood Education and Care*, Canberra: Commonwealth of Australia.

Dockett, S. & Fleer, M. (2002). *Play and Pedagogy in Early Childhood: Bending the Rules*, Melbourne: Thomson.

Edwards, K. & Loveridge, J. (2011). The inside story: Looking into early childhood teachers' support of children's scientific learning, *Australasian Journal of Early Childhood*, 36(2), 28–35.

Fleer, M. (2009) Understanding the dialectical relations between everyday concepts and scientific concepts within play-based programs, *Research in Science Education*, 39, 281–306.

Fleer, M. & Robbins, J. R. (2004). Beyond ticking the boxes: From individual developmental domains to a sociocultural framework for observing young children, *New Zealand Research in Early Childhood Education*, 7, 23–39.

Gandini, L. & Goldhaber, J. (2001). Two reflections about documentation, in L. Gandini & C. P. Edwards (eds), *Bambini: The Italian approach to infant/toddler care*, New York: Teachers College Press, 124–45.

Goodfellow, J. (2009). *The Early Years Framework: Getting Started*, Research in Practice Series, Canberra: Early Childhood Australia.

Goodsir, K. & Rowell, P. (2010). Learning stories – narratives of the complex way that children learn, *Putting Children First, Magazine of the National Childcare Accreditation Council*, 5, 12–13.

Katz, L. G. (1993). *Dispositions: Definitions and Implications for Early Childhood Practices*, Catalog no. 211, Perspective from ERIC/ EECE Monograph Series no. 4, ecap.crc.illinois.edu/eecearchive/books/disposit.html.

Podmore, V. & Carr, M. (1999). *Learning and Teaching Stories: New Approaches to Assessment and Evaluation*, www.aare.edu.au/99pap/pod99298.htm, accessed 1 May 2010.

Siraj-Blatchford, I. (2004). Educational disadvantage in the early years: How do we overcome it? Some lessons from research, *European Early Childhood Education Research Journal*, 12 (2), 5–20.

Tytler, R., Peterson, S. & Prain, V. (2007). Representational issues in students learning about evaporation, *Research in Science. Education*, 37(3), 313–31.

16 Science education professional learning through reflective practice

Christine Howitt and Coral Campbell

Reflection is a major part of the teaching–learning process, and an essential part of professional learning, as it assists educators in examining and reviewing their own teaching and their children's learning. This chapter introduces reflective practice and critical reflection. A range of strategies to assist in reflective practice are presented. The term science education pedagogical content knowledge (PCK) is introduced and the components of PCK are described. The importance of PCK to science education learning and teaching is highlighted.

OBJECTIVES

At the end of this chapter you will be able to:

- describe various forms of science education professional learning

- describe the place of reflective practice in science education professional learning

- differentiate between reflective practice and critical reflection

- describe a range of strategies for reflective practice

- describe science education pedagogical content knowledge (PCK) and its components, and reflect on its importance for effective science education teaching and learning.

Science education professional learning

Maintaining **science education professional knowledge** requires a commitment to ongoing learning and reflection. Science education professional learning can take a range of forms: informal collegial interactions about science education teaching and learning; reading science articles of interest from newspapers, journals, websites or blogs; joining and contributing to an online science teacher community; accessing science educational resources through organisations, websites (such as Pinterest) or blogs; trying new science education activities and ideas; joining local science education associations; attending science education conferences; presenting at science education conferences; becoming involved in research projects related to science education teaching and learning; or enrolling in postgraduate studies relating to science education. Excellent teachers of science education are committed to improving their own knowledge and understanding of science education, how students learn science, and how science can best be taught. They are also committed to reflecting on their own science education learning and practice

> **Science education professional knowledge** – a commitment to ongoing learning and reflection in order to became a better teacher of science.

Reflective practice and critical reflection

Teaching is a complex process that involves making decisions about yourself as an educator, the approaches to be used in your teaching, and about the children you are teaching. Such decisions include choices of curriculum content, strategies for learning and teaching, methods of assessment and reporting, techniques for differentiation, and approaches to classroom management (Duchesne & McMaugh, 2016). **Reflective practice** can assist educators in this process. Research into how young children learn highlights new perspectives and approaches. To ensure that their work with children is current, relevant and effective, educators need to question their accepted practices and the 'taken for granted' strategies which may have worked in the past, and consider the place of new approaches.

> **Reflective practice** – focuses on the ways in which educators think about their experiences and formulate responses as they happen (thinking in action) as well as after they happen (thinking on action).

Incorporated into the EYLF is a requirement that educators undertake ongoing reflective practice to ensure that all children in early childhood settings receive quality teaching and learning. Within this document, reflective practice is defined as:

> a form of ongoing learning that involves engaging with questions of philosophy, ethics and practice. Its intention is to gather information and gain insights that support, inform and enrich decision-making about children's learning. (DEEWR, 2009, p. 13)

Reflective practice focuses on the ways in which educators think about their experiences and formulate responses as they happen (thinking in action) as well as after they happen (thinking on action). Reflective educators draw on metacognitive (thinking about thinking) knowledge as they plan, monitor and evaluate their teaching and their children's learning. Further, the process of reflective practice allows educators to make links between theory and their practice.

> **Critical reflection** – analysing your own and others' thinking and beliefs by questioning existing knowledge, assumptions, perspectives, interpretations, expectations and values.

Critical reflection is the deepest type of reflection. It involves analysing your own and others' thinking and beliefs by questioning existing knowledge, assumptions, perspectives, interpretations, expectations and values (Duchesne & McMaugh, 2016). It includes making links between your beliefs, experiences and knowledge and how these have shaped your practice (Nolan, 2008). The process then brings all this knowledge together to 're-imagine and ultimately improve future experiences' (Ryan & Ryan, 2015, p. 16). Critical reflection involves high levels of self-awareness – thinking and questioning about why you and your colleagues behave the way they do. The EYLF further defines critical reflection as 'closely examining all aspects of events and experiences from different perspectives' (DEEWR, 2009, p. 13). The critical reflection process encourages the creation of new ideas and perspectives to develop quality practices, drawing on everyday experiences and understandings, while linking to contemporary early childhood theory (Cartmel, Macfarlane & Casley, 2012).

Practical task

REFLECTION ON A CRITICAL INCIDENT IN YOUR LIFE

Reflect on a critical incident that has impacted on your life. This could be something related to your choice of career, or some other incident in your life that made you stop and take stock. What was it about the incident that made it significant? What other factors were involved?

REFLECTION ON A SPECIFIC ASPECT OF YOUR PRACTICE

Think about a chapter that you have read in this book and relate its content to your current practice of teaching science. Write a 'good practice' list based on what the authors have shared in the chapter. Based on this list, what could you do to improve your science teaching and learning? Share this information with a colleague. What additional suggestions did the colleague add? Reflect on what you would do, or change, to improve your science teaching and learning.

Strategies for reflective practice

A range of strategies can be used to support reflective practice, including reflective journals and portfolios, observation, consulting with mentors and developing a community of practice. All of these strategies can be used to evaluate current practice in order to identify assumptions which underpin practice, assist in determining future professional learning at the level of individual need, and map out an educator's professional learning journey.

A reflective journal is a written record of your experience, with the entries being examined and evaluated. Specific questions can be used to help frame the reflective process in a reflective journal (as illustrated in Case study 16.1). Portfolios extend the idea of the reflective journal by including a collection of materials and resources which highlight the educator's journey over time. Portfolios may include work samples, lesson plans, comments about a child, or a reflective account of an incident (Duchesne &

McMaugh, 2016). Most importantly, reflective commentary should accompany the collection. Often a professional portfolio is geared towards professional standards of practice and may be organised in such a way as to include evidence of competence against those standards.

Observation includes others observing your teaching along with you observing others' teaching. Alternatively, you can audio or video record yourself. If doing any recording, make sure to gain the consent of the children and to clearly inform them about the purpose of the recording. When others observe you, or you observe yourself in a recording, specific aspects (such as listening skills or explanations) can be targeted and reflected on. When observing other educators, also target specific aspects and reflect on how these may apply in your situation.

Mentors are defined as 'expert practitioners who take on a responsibility to share their skills and expertise with a novice to help them to develop professional expertise' (Duchesne & McMaugh, 2016, p. 9). Mentors can assist by providing guidance on reflective practice, directing towards sources of information, suggesting alternative teaching strategies, or critically appraising practice in a constructive and collaborative manner. Mentors should have good levels of communication; be reflective; be someone you can trust; be experienced; match your philosophy of teaching and learning; and have time to listen, talk and watch you teach (Duchesne & McMaugh, 2016). Different mentors can perform different roles – from those who provide you with emotional support through to senior colleagues who offer advice.

A 'community of practice' approach, taken from the work of Wenger (1998), is where educators attempt to articulate to their colleagues the way they think about aspects of their profession, why they work in different ways, and the reasons behind their decision-making. There are three elements within a community of practice that can contribute to enhanced reflection: educators talking and thinking about their daily practice; educators looking beyond practice to reflect on theories, curriculum and pedagogy; and educators exploring their values and beliefs which underpin their ideas (Nolan & Raban, 2015). Educator reflection within a community of practice can lead to 'an ongoing cycle of review through which current practices are examined, outcomes reviewed and new ideas generated' (DEEWR, 2009, p. 13).

Reflective practice, and in particular critical reflection, is not easy. Most people are not socialised to be reflective thinkers and can find the process challenging. Personal commitment and dedication to reflection are essential, along with finding time to enable the reflective process to occur (Maloney & Campbell-Evans, 2002). Where immediate recording of information is not possible, mechanisms such as the use of photography for the stimulated recall of an event, or writing points on a sticky note and temporarily placing it into a notebook, can be used. Reflections on these events can then be written later, with the photograph or note becoming the reminder. Fear of the unknown, along with the fear of judgement by peers, can also limit the reflective process (Richert, 1990). Honest, trusted and supportive mentors can allay such fears. All early childhood educators should establish effective ongoing reflective practice for their own professional learning, the appropriate development of all key elements of the learning environment, and for long term planning of children's development.

Case Study 16.1

SANDPIT REFLECTIVE JOURNAL ENTRY

Using before/after questions (as provided in Cartmel, Macfarlane & Casley, 2012, p. 6), educator Cassie developed the following written science education reflection of a sandpit learning experience with a group of eight 3 and 4-year-old children.

BEFORE

Q: **What are my thoughts and feelings before commencing the day's session?**

A: I am looking forward to letting the children explore the sandpit. I feel prepared. I am expecting the children to be very excited and ask many questions. I realise that I may not be able to answer all these questions, so I plan to write down those I am not sure about.

Q: **Describe some of the plans or purposes or intentions I have before commencing today's session.**

A: We have been reading books on dinosaurs. I plan to bury some plastic and 'clean' real bones in the sandpit and let the children find them, so they can role play being archeologists. I will then ask the children what type of dinosaur and which part of the dinosaur the bone might have come from. My goal is to encourage the children to use their imagination and their knowledge of dinosaurs in answering these questions.

AFTER

Q: **What are my thoughts now?**

A: This learning experience went in a very different direction to what I had planned.

Q: **How do I understand the experience that occurred during the session? What was influencing my understanding/practice?**

A: The children were very excited about digging up the bones. Each child found at least one bone. When I asked about the type of dinosaur, I received a range of answers depending on which dinosaur was the children's favourite. When I asked about which part of the dinosaur the bone may have come from, the children had great difficulty. They were unsure of the names of the parts of their own bodies – which made it hard to name the parts of a dinosaur body. I had not adequately assessed their prior knowledge before doing this learning experience.

Instead, the children found a range of objects and started burying these in the sandpit. They went inside their classroom and brought out plastic and wooden dinosaurs to bury. Some of the other educators appeared to be angry with this, stating that 'inside toys should stay inside'.

Q: **Did I have any internal thoughts, feelings or reactions during the session that I did not share with my colleagues or with the children? What were they?**

A: I felt embarrassed that I had not assessed the children's prior knowledge. It showed that I need to get to know these children more.

I was disappointed that my colleagues would set certain boundaries with toys – when burying the toys in the sandpit and digging them up again made perfect sense to the children. This told me that learning experiences need to be shared with all educators so that there is a whole-centre awareness and approach.

Q: **How did I come to know about those ideas?**

A: It was only when the learning experience shifted direction, a result of the children following their own interests, that I realised my well-prepared intentional teaching was perhaps too difficult and too structured. And it was only through the children playing with the dinosaurs in a manner that was meaningful to them that I came to realise that communication at the centre was not as good as it should be.

Q: **What would I have liked to have seen happen?**

A: I would have liked to see more open-minded educators joining in with the children as they collected objects to bury. Just think – we could have had a giant buried treasure experience! That would have been awesome!

The before/after questions in Case study 16.1 provided a clear structure to write a reflection.

1. How critical was Cassie in this reflection? Can you identify where she challenged her own thinking and ideas?

2. Think about how you could use the same questions while reflecting on different science learning experiences.

REFLECTION

FIGURE 16.1 Linc enjoys his time digging in the soil pit

The 5R framework for reflection

The **5R framework for reflection** was developed by Bain and colleagues (2002). This framework provides a systematic approach to develop deep and purposeful thinking about teaching and learning experiences. The 5Rs of reflection are 'reporting,' 'responding', 'relating', 'reasoning' and

> **5R framework for reflection** – a systematic approach to develop deep and purposeful thinking about teaching and learning experiences that consists of 'reporting','responding','relating', 'reasoning' and 'reconstructing'.

'reconstructing'. These five levels 'increase in complexity and move from description of, and personal response to, an issue or situation; to the use of theory and experience to explain, interrogate, and ultimately transform practice' (Ryan & Ryan, 2015, p. 16). A description of each of these levels is presented in Table 16.1.

TABLE 16.1   THE 5R FRAMEWORK FOR REFLECTION

The 5Rs	Description	Question
Reporting	Describe the situation/issue.	What happened? What was the situation/issue involved?
Responding	React to the situation/issue.	What did you think or feel about the situation/idea? What makes you feel/react that way?
Relating	Report on personal and/or theoretical understandings relevant to the situation/issue.	What connections are there between the situation/issue and your experience, skills, knowledge and understanding?
Reasoning	Explore and explain the situation/issue.	What theoretical ideas help make sense of the situation/issue?
Reconstructing	Draw a conclusion and develop a future action plan.	How will the situation/issue impact on your practice? How has the situation/issue impacted your viewpoint?

Source: adapted from Bain et al., 2002.

Case Study 16.2

QUESTIONING MY OWN QUESTIONING

The following 5R reflection was developed by Dan after an introductory lesson on the topic of 'What makes us alive?' to a class of 20 4-year-old children.

REPORTING

I showed the class some photographs of living and non-living things. As a class, the children enthusiastically classified the photographs into living and non-living, based on their prior knowledge. There was much discussion about what makes us living. To ensure that all the children had an opportunity to contribute, I had a few set questions to ask each child.

RESPONDING

The children made some interesting comments that could have been explored further in order to obtain a more comprehensive understanding of their ideas of living things. I realised that there was more I could have done to extend the conversation meaningfully. I was disappointed with my single-mindedness to have every child contribute and therefore my restricted questioning.

RELATING

My questioning related to asking the children whether an object in the photograph was alive, followed by an open-ended question on how the child knew this. Based on the children's responses, there were many opportunities to probe that I had not taken. Placing them in the living pile, Louise commented that bees can sting and spiders can bite. This would have been a good opportunity to ask her why bees sting and spiders bite, to find out if she ascribed purpose to this action. Phillipe noted that plants have to drink water, and classified them as living. A small group of children agreed. This was another opportunity lost. I could have asked the children what would happen if plants do not have water, to see if they understood the importance of water to living things. I could have also asked if bees and spiders need water to live.

REASONING

In early childhood contexts, sustained shared conversations are central to the development of children's thinking. Learning occurs through engaging in deep, authentic conversations, which educators can facilitate by means of open-ended questioning. Effective questioning can reveal children's existing knowledge, as well as promoting their thinking and reasoning. Through the use of sustained shared conversations, I could have gained more evidence of the sophisticated nature of the children's ideas about living things.

RECONSTRUCTING

Children's prior knowledge is an essential component of science instruction, as their pre-existing ideas form the basis for the development of subsequent scientific understandings. In order to gain an authentic and comprehensive understanding of children's existing knowledge, the quality of my conversations with them needs to improve. I must practise listening to children's answers and engaging with these responses.

Consider the following related to Case study 16.2:

1. Note how the 5R structure increases in complexity, starting with a description of the issue in 'reporting' and finishing with a forward looking statement in 'reconstructing'. Can you identify the theoretical concept (sustained shared conversations and the effective use of questioning) within 'reasoning'?

2. How important is critical reflection in the process of developing the 5R reflection?

REFLECTION

Science education pedagogical content knowledge

Early childhood educators are required to be familiar with the content and pedagogy related to many curriculum areas. Due to the nature of many early childhood centres, children's explorations are privileged through child-instigated pedagogy. Consequently, children's explorations around key science ideas are a significant part of young children's learning experiences. Early childhood educators therefore require professional understanding of science content and science education pedagogy.

Experienced science educators have strong **science education pedagogical content knowledge** (PCK). PCK is 'content knowledge transformed by the teacher into a form that makes it understandable to students' (Appleton, 2006, p. 31); it is knowing what to teach and how to teach. Science education PCK is

> the knowledge a teacher uses to construct and implement a science learning experience or series of science learning experiences. It is a dynamic form of knowing that is constantly expanding and being transformed

Science education pedagogical content knowledge – knowing what to teach and how to teach in science.

from other forms of teacher knowledge, and through the experiences of planning, implementing, and evaluating science teaching and learning. (Appleton, 2006, p. 35)

Science education PCK consists of many types of teacher knowledge including content knowledge, educator confidence, context, educator's orientation to learning and teaching, and knowledge of students. The following description of these types of teacher knowledge is adapted from Appleton (2006).

Content knowledge

Content knowledge – knowledge of the subject matter or the content to be taught.

Educators should have knowledge of the subject matter or the content to be taught. While early childhood educators may say they have limited formal science **content knowledge**, they frequently have informal everyday science knowledge arising from their own hobbies, interests and experiences. This is an example of practical knowledge centered on everyday events. For example, the hobbies of gardening, cooking, along with many sports, are all based on scientific concepts. To improve content knowledge, educators may use descriptions of successful teaching and learning experiences or specific science curriculum resources that include appropriate descriptions of scientific concepts. There are a wide range of science websites that provide science curriculum resources. They may also undergo professional development sessions such as attending conferences to improve their science education content knowledge.

Educator confidence

Educator confidence– educator perceptions of their ability to teach science, the adequacy of their own science knowledge, and their ability to learn science for themselves.

Many early childhood educators tend to lack **confidence** in their own ability to teach science, in the adequacy of their own science knowledge, and in their ability to learn science for themselves (Campbell & Jobling, 2010). This lack of confidence tends to be due to their limited science content knowledge. Educators with very low levels of confidence may avoid teaching science altogether, thus developing little or no science PCK. To improve confidence, educators may use detailed descriptions of experiences that work and detailed science curriculum resources, be mentored or co-teach science with an experienced educator, seek out conversations with other educators to exchange science experiences that have worked or other aspects of science education PCK, or observe an experienced educator teach science.

Context

Context refers to a broad group of other forms of teacher knowledge: classroom management, assessment, curriculum, environment and resources. The role played by each of these depends on the situation – with the educator rejecting or modifying science activities accordingly. Some questions that educators ask in relation to context include: 'Will the teaching and learning experience be done in groups, individually or modelled to the whole class?', 'How will the experience be assessed?', 'Which part of the science curriculum does the experience address?', 'Is the classroom physical environment adequate for the experience?', 'Are there adequate resources for the experience?'

Science can be resource-intensive requiring print resources, electronic resources or manipulative equipment. Many early childhood teaching and learning experiences use everyday equipment (such as boxes or plastic containers) that can be recycled from homes, while other equipment can be purchased from supermarkets or hardware stores. Being a member of a recycling organisation is also useful for obtaining appropriate resources. Some science experiences require prior preparation. Being organised and prepared is the key to working with various science resources.

Educator's orientation to learning and teaching

An **educator's orientation** (or view and belief) of how learning occurs has a critical influence on the development of their science PCK. As described in Chapter 5, there are different approaches to science teaching and learning: process skills approach, guided discovery approach, inquiry learning approach, problem-based learning approach, and project approach. The approach (or orientation) chosen can influence the choice of learning goals, learning experiences and teaching strategies. For example, an educator who takes a guided discovery learning approach would provide a range of play experiences for the children to discover a particular science phenomenon, but also recognise the importance of scaffolding by an experienced adult who can act as a co-investigator and/or ask questions to encourage further investigation. An educator who takes an inquiry learning orientation would allow children's questions to lead to explorations, support the development of children's ideas, ask focused questions, encourage children–children and children–teacher interactions and even argumentation, suggest alternative ways of thinking, and assist children in developing responses. While both approaches could be used for the same teaching and learning experience, they can result in the educator using different types of science PCK.

> **Educator's orientation –** educator's view and belief of how learning occurs.

Knowledge of children

Knowledge of children plays an important role in the teaching and learning of science. This knowledge can relate to children's abilities, learning strategies, age/developmental levels, attitudes/motivation, and prior knowledge. Many educators use knowledge of their children's interests and their ability to work in groups to decide whether to use a particular activity or not, and what pedagogy to use when implementing that activity. A key consideration here is if the activity will engage the children. In a constructivist orientation, knowledge of children's pre-conceptions or prior knowledge is considered the initial step in a teaching sequence. Within this orientation, learning experiences will focus on ascertaining and challenging children's ideas, and the sequencing of those experiences to enhance understanding. Knowledge of children can influence many aspects of teaching science, from selecting activities to use, developing pedagogical sequences for a unit of work, using particular lesson teaching strategies, through to deciding which children to choose to answer a question.

Practical task

REFLECTION ON YOUR SCIENCE EDUCATION PCK

Consider the elements of science education PCK that were presented above: content knowledge, educator confidence, context, educator's orientation to learning and teaching, and knowledge of students. For each component, honestly rank yourself on a scale of 1 to 5, where 1 is very low, 3 is average and 5 is very high. For any components ranked 3 or less, list some methods of how you might improve in order to increase your overall science education PCK.

Case Study 16.3

DIGESTING PEAS

Kaye was on a practicum with a group of 20 4-year-old children who enjoy their art. Her mentor teacher had mentioned that the children had an interest in food and their bodies, and asked Kaye if she could deliver some learning experiences to introduce the children to digestion. Kaye had done human biology in Years 11 and 12, so was reasonably comfortable with the content, although it was a while ago. She was unsure how she could teach this topic to 4-year-old children so they could understand it.

Kaye, and the mentor teacher, supported a constructivist-inquiry approach to learning and teaching. Using online materials and books from the school library, Kaye initially read about digestion to remind herself of the process. She then selected some of the books to use in class, along with finding appropriate short YouTube clips. Kaye found a need to be quite critical in choosing the YouTube clips, so that the images and comments were appropriate for the age of the children. Kaye's mentor also had four children's digestion aprons that consisted of the different parts of the digestion system (mouth, oesophagus, stomach, small intestines, large intestines, rectum) that could be velcroed on to the apron. Kaye also checked the internet, in particular Pinterest, and emailed her university science education lecturer, to find a range of suitable activities.

Kaye developed the following sequence of activities:

Session 1: Find out what the children know about digestion. Start with a class discussion on 'What happens to our food once we put it in our mouth?' Any key words will be placed onto a word wall. (Note to self: Check with the mentor if the word 'poo' is okay to use in class.)

Session 2: Trace around the body of each child onto butcher paper. Each child is to then draw what they think happens to their food on these life-size tracings. Children will be encouraged to label the parts of the body they know. Children describe their understanding of the process of digestion, with educators annotating onto the tracing. (Note to self: may take a few sessions – work around other daily activities.)

Session 3: Ask the children again, 'What happens to our food once we put it in our mouth?' Introduce and play child-friendly animated YouTube clip. Class discussion of the parts of the digestion system. Laminated parts of digestion system placed onto whiteboard as discussed. Parts labelled, with short explanation of part given. Mouth = eat, chew. (Note to self: children fascinated with this. Look at finding a real video rather than animated. Check with mentor.)

Session 4: Play child-friendly animated YouTube clip again and remind children about parts in the digestion system. Take eight children. Split them into groups of two and give them the aprons. One child to wear the apron, the other to place the parts onto the apron and state the right name and what that part does. Swap around. Repeat later in the day with rest of the class.

Session 5: Introduce and play YouTube clip of the human digestion system. Remind the children that this is what it looks like in our body. Class discussion. Compare real pictures to apron images – how are they different and how are they similar.

Session 6: Revise parts of the digestive system and their purpose. In groups of three, children to design a model of the digestive system using a range of collected recycled materials – different sized boxes, cardboard tubes, plastic bags, stockings and masking tape. Groups to explore materials and consider what might be best for each part of the digestive system. Draw the model.

Session 7: Children make their model. They then test it by passing a snaplock bag of peas through the model. Make a prediction of what the peas might look like when they have gone through the model.

Session 8: Again, trace around the body of each child onto butcher paper. With their new-found knowledge, each child is to draw what they think happens to their food on these life-size tracings.

Consider the following questions related to Case study 16.3:

1. What science education PCK can be seen in this case study? Identify and describe the content knowledge, educator confidence, context, educator's orientation to learning and teaching, and knowledge of students relevant to Kaye.

2. Reflect on how simply reading this case study could be adding to your science education PCK. What aspects of the story appealed to you? Why did these aspects appeal to you? How could you use them in your science learning and teaching?

3. How many different representations of the digestive system did Kaye use? Why did she use so many? How is this a reflection of Kaye's science education PCK?

REFLECTION

Strategies to enhance science education PCK

In the discussion above, key elements essential to the development of science education PCK were highlighted: the educator's content knowledge, their confidence, the learning context, educator's orientation to learning and teaching, and knowledge of children. In considering how each and all of these can be enhanced, it is important to realise that PCK develops over time, through experience (Loughran, Berry & Mulhall, 2006). However, each element can be examined to consider ways to improve it: content knowledge can be gained by explicit application to understanding and knowledge of science; confidence is improved through successful experiences, so success will come with greater content knowledge and improved pedagogy in science; the learning context, orientation to teaching and learning and knowledge of children can all be improved through strategic focus. Lastly, reflection on teaching, which examines all these elements as part of an educator's professional practice, will enable professional growth of PCK.

Professional development for science education learning has traditionally occurred through the medium of workshops and conferences that focus on particular elements of practice, activities and ideas, and skills and content knowledge. While this 'skills and knowledge' approach can be valuable and efficient in disseminating information and ideas, it may not be as effective in challenging and supporting more fundamental aspects of pedagogy and beliefs (Hoban, 1992). Long term professional learning that is sensitive to the needs of educators and their context, and supports the needs and concerns of the children, is necessary to support significant educator development (Campbell et al., 2007).

Conclusion

This chapter introduced professional learning, with a strong focus on the use of reflective practice as it assists educators in examining and reviewing their own teaching and their children's learning. A range of strategies to assist in reflective practice were presented. Science education PCK and its components were introduced highlighting the importance of knowing what to teach and how to teach in order to engage students in science. Reflective practice offers educators the opportunity to expand their own science understandings, while enabling the young children in their care to undertake meaningful science explorations.

16 References

Appleton, K. (2006). Science pedagogical content knowledge and elementary school teachers, in K. Appleton (ed.), *Elementary Science Teacher Education: International Perspectives on Contemporary Issues and Practice*, Mahwah, NJ: Lawrence Erlbaum, 31–54.

Bain, J. D., Ballantyne, R., Mills, C. & Lester, N. C. (2002). *Reflecting on Practice: Student Teachers' Perspectives*, Flaxton, Queensland: Post Pressed.

Campbell, C., Chittleborough, G., Hubber, P. & Tytler, R. (2007). Educating for the future: Technological advantage? Paper presented at the annual National Association of Research in Science Teaching Conference, New Orleans, US.

Campbell, C. & Jobling, W. (2010). A snapshot of science education in kindergarten settings, *International Research in Early Childhood Education*, 1(1), 3–21.

Cartmel, J., Macfarlane, K. & Casley, M. (2012). *Reflection as a Tool for Quality: Working with the National Quality Standard*, Canberra: Early Childhood Australia.

Department of Education, Employment and Workplace Relations (DEEWR). (2009). *Belonging, Being & Becoming: The Early Years Learning Framework for Australia*, Canberra: Commonwealth of Australia.

Duchesne, S. & McMaugh, A. (2016). *Educational psychology for learning and teaching* (5th edn), Melbourne: Cengage.

Hoban, G. (1992). Teaching and report writing in primary science: Case studies of an intervention program, *Research in Science Education*, 22, 194–203.

Loughran, J., Berry, A. & Mulhall, P. (eds) (2006). *Understanding and Developing Science Teachers' Pedagogical Content Knowledge*, Rotterdam: Sense Publishers.

Maloney, C. & Campbell-Evans, G. (2002). Using interactive journal writing as a strategy for professional growth, *Asia Pacific Journal of Teacher Education*, 30(1), 39–50.

Nolan, A. (2008). Encouraging the reflection process in undergraduate teachers using guided reflection, *Australian Journal of Early Childhood*, 33(1), 31–6.

Nolan, A. & Raban, B. (2015) *Theories Into Practice*, Melbourne: Teaching Solutions.

Richert, A. E. (1990). Teaching students to reflect: A consideration of programme structure, *Journal of Curriculum Studies*, 22(6), 509–27.

Ryan, M. & Ryan, M. (2015). A model for reflection in the pedagogic field of higher education, in M. E. Ryan (ed.), *Teaching Reflective Learning in Higher Education: A Systematic Approach Using Pedagogic Patterns*, Cham, Switzerland: Springer, 15–24.

Wenger, E. (1998). *Communities of Practice: Learning, Meaning and Identity*, Cambridge: Cambridge University Press.

Appendix 1

Activity plans

Chapter 3

Bush, bricks and bugs

A range of ideas are presented below for children to continue to explore experiences central to the three case studies, 1) A day in the bush, 2) Building with mud bricks and 3) Spiders.

1. A day in the bush

> Ensure rugs are available for making an indoor tent during free play.
>
> Find areas in the school grounds suitable for nature play and visit regularly.
>
> Walk mindfully through the nature play area using a range of senses. Stop, be silent, breathe deeply, feel the breeze on your face, look up in awe of the moving clouds, or shape of a leaf on a tree.
>
> Do observational drawing, sketch same object/place in different seasons, note changes, record pictorially in own journal.
>
> Take a book (e.g. *Leaf Litter: Exploring the Mysteries of a Hidden World* by Rachel Tonkin) and read to the children outside.
>
> Children find their own special place in the school ground (still all visible to the teacher). They spend time silently and by themselves in the fresh air in nature. They close their eyes: what can they hear, smell, touch? Imagine.

Learn the names of five plants that the children didn't know. Invite the groundsperson in to give a tour of significant plants in the school ground. Make a map (2D figure or 3D model) of the school grounds locating where the plants are. Keep adding as knowledge is broadened.

Redo the colour cards / alphabet search in potential nature play area of school – discuss the difference between this and what we found in 'A day in the bush'.

2. Building with mud bricks

Make your own bird's nest using natural material such as mud, feathers and sticks.

Make mud of different consistency, and make thin to thick mud balls.

Set up a mud pie kitchen using seed pods as cups.

Make mud hand prints on different surfaces, compare different size and shape hands. Play 'Whose hand is this?'

Create mud sculptures and leave them to be weathered by the elements.

Explore how mud has been used in the past, culturally, in building construction.

3. Spiders

Class newsletter with each child sharing something they have learnt about spiders. If possible show the change in their understanding of an aspect of spiders.

An end of term spider celebration – dress up as a spider showing and labelling correct anatomy. This could be done at school or at home.

Class cooking – make a spider – correct anatomy.

Make a wall (or electronic) display of all the different local spiders that have been identified at school and home, continue to add throughout the year.

Put unknown species onto a citizen science app such as Bowerbird.com and scientists will identify.

Invite other classes to share spider information.

Chapter 4
Challenging developing concepts

Through providing children with appropriate scaffolding and resources, an intentional educator can enhance children's conceptual development.

1. Provide children with a small number of items, one at a time, to test for 'floating' in a clear container of water. Try to include items they may have used in water play previously (such as a plastic lid or a small piece of wood) along with objects which they are unlikely to have used in water play (such as a small candle or a paper clip).
   a. Ask them to predict what will happen when they place the item in the water.
   b. Have them observe closely from above but also through the side of the clear container. Ask them what they notice about the item – Is it floating, sinking, on the top, on the bottom or somewhere in between?

2. Provide children with materials so that they can draw their observations with the educator annotating the diagram. Use the drawing to develop children's concepts about floating items – they are on or in (suspended) the water. They are not on the bottom.

3. A follow-up activity would be to provide children with the same set-up, but with items which challenge their understanding. For example, provide children with a ball of plasticine, which will sink when they test it. Ask them to alter the shape so that it floats. Given success in this activity, children learn that an item with a boat shape can float if it contains air.

4. Further activities can be used to develop concepts around the idea that it is the material an object is made of that influences whether it floats or sinks.

Chapter 5
Exploring an interactive approach

Exploring concepts of air – children had been asking the question 'Where does wind come from?' on a particularly windy day. The educator decided to set up some small experiences for children to explore some common ideas about air so that they could develop their own understanding of where wind came from.

1. Provide children with a small plastic freezer bag and ask them to collect air. Discuss with them where they found air. Use the children's own experiences and effective questioning to draw out the key idea 'the air is everywhere'.

2. Once they establish that air is everywhere, demonstrate the idea that air pushes on things. Children can stand in an open space (all facing the same way), holding a piece of paper (A4 size) to their chest. They commence running and once they have moved about two meters, they let go of the paper. It stays in place until they slow down. Ask the children why it stayed in place. They will begin to understand that air pushes on things as they move through air.

3. A simple activity is to drop a piece of paper and ask children why if falls slowly to the ground – what is affecting its fall? Repeat the activity, this time with two pieces of paper, but the second piece of paper screwed up. Ask children to predict what they think will happen when both are released at the same time. Most will answer that the scrunched up paper is heavier.

4. Introduce this as a discrepant event – have them double-check the two pieces of paper before you start a second demonstration to establish that the paper is identical in size, and repeat the drop. This time ask the children what else might be affecting its fall. Some will start to link the air pressure idea with the falling paper.

5. The final activity involves children in blowing a piece of string. Asking them questions, they come to the conclusion that they have created wind. Support the idea of air as wind by using an electric fan or a small concertina fan to create 'wind' in the stationary air.

6. At this point, as children have experienced that air is everywhere and can exert a pressure (it can push on things), they can bring together the ideas to understand that wind is moving air.

Chapter 7
Play pedagogy activities

1. Read the story *Mr Archimedes' Bath* (by Pamela Allen) to the children and discuss the various characters and their role in the story.

2. Set up a scientific role-play area which relates to the story. Provide resources for imaginary play related to the story. As children gather around the resources, scaffold their ideas.

3. Video and photograph the children's role play and upload it to the pre-school internet site, then:
   ▪ show the children the video and ask them to provide a drawing of the play
   ▪ use the drawings and the photographs of the role play to make a 'big book' for children to refer to and re-read.

Chapter 8
Exploring sound

A range of ideas are presented below for children to continue exploring sound.

Activity 1: Read *The Very Noisy House* (by Julie Rhodes) which describes five different noises in a house. As a new noise is introduced on each page have the children repeat that noise. Can the children remember the order of the noises and what caused them – clomp from the walking stick, woof from the dog, meow from the cat, whaaa from the baby, and squawk from the bird? Children role play the story with props for each of the different sounds.

Activity 2: Discuss different sounds that children might hear – people talking, birds singing, car moving. Take the children outside and sit quietly with eyes closed. Have a discussion on the sounds they hear. What do they think is making that sound?

Activity 3: Go on an environmental walk and listen for different sounds. Record the sounds onto a mobile device. Mad Map HD is an excellent app to do this. Twelve different sounds can be recorded. These sounds can then be played back as music.

Activity 4: Develop a sound garden for children to explore and create music with. This could include found items such as pots and pans, wooden and metal spoons, water bottles with rice or small marbles added, large water filter bottles, hub-caps and tapping sticks. These items, along with a triangle and xylophone, could be placed on benches or strung from branches of a tree.

Activity 5: Talk about quiet and loud. Ask the children what objects make quiet sounds and what objects make loud sounds? Challenge the children to be as quiet as possible (whispering) and then as loud as possible (shouting). Using the sound garden, ask the children to make sounds that are quiet and sounds that are loud?

Chapter 10
Science exploration with natural materials

Using a science exploration or discovery table, set the table up with a range of natural material from outside – leaves, twigs, gumnuts.

Activity 1: Using magnifying lenses, children observe material closely. Ask children to describe what they see on the table and where they think it comes from. They share their descriptions with each other.

Activity 2: Using pencils and paper, children draw one of the items and then in turn discuss this with the larger group. Have children describe how they drew the object and what details they were concentrating on.

Activity 3: Children's drawings form the basis of the construction of a diorama or artistic collection of natural objects, e.g. children construct trees from twigs and leaves, other surfaces using bark and grass, or arrange the natural material onto a sheet of paper and glue into place.

Activity 4: Take photographs and project one of them onto a screen so the whole class can see. As a class, describe the object in detail.

Activity 5: Create a book from the photographs and annotate it with children's comments.

Chapter 12
Activities based on Case study 12.2: bush kinder environments

Activity 1: Children view the components of the weather while outside. They sketch what they see.

Activity 2: Using a digital camera, children take photographs of their components of weather.

Activity 3: When back inside the normal kindergarten setting, children use the computer and iPad with educator assistance to looks up clouds, rain or their own weather 'component'. They compare the digital image to their own photos and drawings, reflecting on similarities, differences and key characteristics.

Activity 4: Children construct 'weather cards' which include downloaded pictures of weather components, e.g. different clouds. The educator laminates these for outside use.

Activity 5: Children take their cards outside for the next bush kinder and keep a watchful eye on the weather to see if they can recognise any of the components and match to their weather cards.

Chapter 13
Activities relating to the theme of the sea

The activities presented below are an expansion of some of the ideas presented in the mind map in Figure 13.1, relating to the theme of the sea.

Activity 1: Shells. What animals live in shells? Discuss the importance of shells as a 'home' for some animals. How are shell homes similar and different to the homes that people have? Present a range of shells of different sizes, shapes and colours. Describe and/or draw the shells in detail. Classify the shells in different ways. Count the shells. Provide small 'treasure' boxes for children to collect their favourite shells?

Activity 2: Fish market. Show YouTube clips of fish markets from around the world. Who buys their fish at fish markets? Set up a fish market learning centre. Have a range of fish in sealed plastic bags. These should be placed in a chilled container. On a table have butcher's paper, sticky labels, thick pen,

FIGURE A1.1   Seaweed and shell art

and paper bags. Also have aprons for the children to wear. Children select a fish from the chilled container, wrap it in the butcher's paper, place a sticky label on the paper, write a 'price' on the label, and then place the package into a paper bag. This can then be delivered to the educator or some other adult in class.

Activity 3: Seaweed art. Present a range of seaweed of different sizes, shapes and colours. Discuss what seaweed looks like, feels like and smells like. How long is some of the seaweed – is it longer than the children? Have four pieces of doweling (or sticks). Children use the doweling to create a square, rectangle or triangle frame and then select various pieces of seaweed (and shells) to create a picture within the frame. Children describe and photograph their seaweed art.

Activity 4: Flotsam and jetsam. Discuss what the term 'flotsam and jetsam' means, highlighting that it refers to marine debris. What is the difference between flotsam and jetsam? Flotsam (or floatsome) refers to debris in the water that has not been thrown overboard, while jetsam refers to debris that has been deliberately thrown overboard. Research where the names came from? Present a range of flotsam and jetsam that has been collected from the beach. Describe each object and predict where it may have come from. Sort and classify the objects. Link to sustainability and the importance of looking after the environment.

Chapter 14

Activities based around Case study 14.1: observing and drawing

Activity 1: Ask the children to take one of their pencils and to draw it. This will be a superficial drawing. Hold up a giant pencil and describe it in detail. As a class draw this pencil in detail while thinking aloud. Have children look back at their own pencil and draw it in detail. Compare first and second pencil drawing.

Activity 2: As a class, select one object in the classroom to draw. Take a photograph and project it onto a screen so the whole class can see. As a class, describe this object in detail. Then children each draw this object. Have children describe how they drew the object and what details they were concentrating on.

Activity 3: Children bring objects from home to draw in detail.

Activity 4: Drawing seedlings – see Case study 14.1.

Activity 5: Bring in another plant with different roots, leaves and possibly flowers. Go through the process of describing as a class the detail of the plant, identifying the roots, stem, leaves, and flowers (if any) and then have the children draw and label the plant.

Activity 6:   Bring in a different plant and get the children to draw individually (with no class discussion beforehand).

Activity 7:   Observe leaves up close with magnifying glass and light tables. Children draw these in detail.

Chapter 15
Movement

This lesson was adapted from Primary Connections 'Movers and shakers' and is an introductory lesson to focus children on movement. In science, movement is seen as the precursor knowledge to an understanding of forces. This lesson was designed to capture children's interest and find out what they know about how an object moves.

1. During a music session, introduce children to a game of statues. Children move to music but when the music stops, they have to freeze. When the music starts, they can start.

2. Talk to them about being still. What does this mean in the game? When have they had to be still before?

3. Introduce a new variation of the game where one child moves to the music and the other child observes the movement while remaining still. Play the game and swap the partners around so that they see both movements and practise being still.

4. Scaffold the children's observations by asking questions:
   - When the music stopped, did your partner move at all?
   - Did you see any part of their body move?
   - What sorts of movements did you see?

5. Ask the children to make different shapes with their bodies. Discuss the shapes that they made and what features of the shape the children used.

6. Introduce a class science journal and note in it what children thought of their game, their different shapes and ask them how they can find out more about things that move.

Appendix 2

Examples of simple science statements or concepts

Biological sciences

Animals

Some animals change from one form to another during their life cycle. For example, a caterpillar turns into a butterfly.

Each type of animal has its own life cycle.

An animal is alive even during stages at which it appears to be inactive, such as during hibernation or in a chrysalis.

Some animals, once they are born, have the same form for the remainder of the life cycle. Examples of this are chickens, cats, dogs and humans.

Animals include slugs, snails, worms, star fish, mussels, spiders, crabs, insects, fish, amphibians, reptiles, birds and mammals. Humans are animals.

Small animals perform a vast number of important functions in our ecosystem, such as pollination, and aerating and fertilising soil.

Small animals have a variety of external features that help them survive.

Small animals live in different places where their needs are met.

Many animals have skeletons.

Some skeletons are made up of bones.

The shape of a bone can be used to identify its likely position in the skeleton.

It is possible to gain information about how an animal may have moved by looking at the skeleton.

It is possible to gain information about the size and shape of an animal by looking at the skeleton.

The skeletons of a particular type of animal are very similar to each other.

It is possible to gain information about what the animal may have eaten by looking at the teeth in the skeleton.

By comparing the skeletons of other animals to the human skeleton it is possible to gain information about how the animals may have differed from, and been similar to, humans.

Birds have different ways of moving compared to other animals.

Birds eat a variety of foods.

The shape of a bird's beak is related to how it eats.

Each sort of bird has a distinct flight pattern.

Plant seeds are food for many birds.

Nectar from plant flowers is food for many birds.

Small animals are food for many birds.

The shape of a bird's feet is related to the way the bird lives; for example, webbed feet are found on water birds.

Most birds are active only in the daytime.

The times at which the majority of birds are most active are the hours after sunrise and the hours before sunset.

Some birds, such as owls, are more active at night than in the daytime.

A bird's habitat depends on the location of suitable food, nesting sites and safety.

Many birds have characteristic songs that can be used to identify them.

Birds communicate with one another by means of sound and/or body movements.

There are patterns in the way birds behave.

Plants

Many plants form seeds.

Seeds can be found in fruit, cones, pods or nuts.

Seeds absorb water.

Seeds need water to germinate.

Seeds need the right temperature to germinate.

Seeds need air to germinate.

Some Australian seeds need fire to germinate.

Seeds vary in their rate of germination.

Seeds develop from flowers.

Seeds form a significant part of the world's food supply.

Seeds are living; they are in a state of dormancy.

Humans (and other animals) consume different parts of plants, such as leaves, stems, flowers, fruits and roots.

All flowering plants have a similar life cycle.

Wood is the natural product of plant growth.

Natural forests supply us with some of our wood requirements.

Plantations provide us with wood not naturally found in Australia.

Trees provide us and other animals with homes.

Wood differs from metals and rock in that it was once part of a living entity.

Properties of living things

All living things have a life cycle.

The way living things are classified has changed over time. Animals and plants are the main 'kingdoms', but fungi, mosses and viruses have their own separate kingdoms.

All living things exhibit the following characteristics that define them as living, with the acronym MRS GREN being used to help us remember them:

- movement
- respiration
- sensory response
- growth
- reproduction
- excretion
- nutritional requirements.

Chemical sciences

Materials

Everyday materials can be physically changed in a variety of ways.

Different materials have different properties, such as colour, strength, texture, smell, hardness, flexibility and also cost, which determine their applications and likely use.

The properties and structure of materials are inter-related and determine their behaviour. Their uses are determined by their properties, some of which can be changed and enhanced by processing.

Natural materials are often selected for applications that exploit their properties and are also used because of their availability or cost of production.

Natural materials can be combined, mixed, heated or treated in a combination of ways to produce processed materials with changed or enhanced properties.

Matter

Matter consists of solids, liquids and gases.

A solid: retains a fixed volume and shape, is not easily compressed and does not flow easily.

A liquid: assumes the shape of the container it is in and retains a fixed volume, is not easily compressed and flows easily.

A gas: assumes the shape and volume of the container it is in, can be compressed and flows easily.

The input of heat energy can change the state of matter from solid to liquid, liquid to gas or solid to gas.

The removal or loss of heat energy can cause a change of state from gas to solid, gas to liquid or liquid to solid.

Melting involves a change from a solid to a liquid, caused by heating, such as ice to water.

Freezing is the opposite of melting: a change from a liquid to a solid, such as water to ice.

Substances tend to melt at certain temperatures.

For pure substances, such as ice, melting is reversible.

Some substances, when heated, are irreversibly changed (e.g. when bread is toasted it cannot be turned back to bread).

Melting is different to mixing and dissolving. Melting requires heat energy.

Mixing refers to the addition of various substances together where no new material is formed. A good example of a mixture is muesli.

Dissolving refers to the mixture of a solid (e.g. salt) to a liquid (e.g. water) to produce a solution (salty water).

Evaporation involves a change from the liquid to gas state, such as water to water vapour.

Condensation is the opposite of evaporation: a change from gas to a liquid, such as water vapour to water.

Water will evaporate at warmer temperatures, with water vapour entering the air.

Fog or water appearing on cold surfaces is due to condensation of water vapour from the air.

Substances can react together to form new substances that are quite different from their original properties.

A gas is a possible product of a chemical reaction.

Combustion is a chemical reaction.

A flame needs oxygen to keep burning, as the oxygen reacts with the burning substance.

Substances can be grouped (e.g. acid/base) according to their chemical properties.

Earth and space sciences

Earth and space

The Earth is in the shape of a ball.

'Down' refers to the centre of the Earth (in relation to gravity).

The Moon appears in the sky due to reflected light from the Sun.

Stars are still there during the daylight.

The Moon's gravity is much less than that on Earth.

The Earth rotates, which makes the Moon, Sun and stars appear to move.

The universe is extremely large.

Instruments such as telescopes and binoculars can be used to view objects in the universe.

There are many different types of objects in the universe.

The rotation of the Earth on its axis in relation to the position of the Sun gives us night or day.

The planets in the Solar system differ in size.

- The Solar system is a large place.
- Space travel is very difficult.

Rocks

The Earth is covered with rocks, soil, water and ice.

The Earth's crust has many specific formations, such as volcanoes and mountains.

Rock layers are located under rocks, soil, water and ice.

Natural rocks are made in many different ways.

Rocks slowly become smaller due to the action of rain, wind and ice.

Crumbled rocks form part of soil.

Rocks that we find at a particular place may have been made elsewhere.

Rocks can be made of one or more minerals.

Some rocks are harder than others.

Rocks can be a single colour or contain many colours.

Minerals can form crystals.

Crystals have straight edges and flat sides.

Rocks can vary in shape, texture and mass.

Some rocks act as magnets.

Some rocks are conductors of electricity.

Some rocks contain prints or filled parts of plants and animals.

Rocks that take a long time to form underground have large-sized minerals.

Rocks that form quickly underground have small-sized minerals.

Some rocks are good conductors of heat energy.

Some rocks, such as gold and diamonds, are highly valued by humans.

The varying hardness of rock is an important factor in its usage.

Humans' knowledge of rock association helps them to find oil and precious stones, such as gold, opals, and emeralds.

Rocks can be altered by humans to make materials for use in their everyday lives, for example, steel from iron ore.

Weather

Daily and seasonal changes in our environment affect daily life.

Observable changes occur in the sky and landscape.

Serious weather phenomena have impacts on communities.

Weather prediction is important for our life and communities.

Physical sciences

Force and movement (motion)

Forces can be thought of as 'pushes and pulls'.

Forces can make things move or stop or hold things up or squeeze things.

Friction is a common force that stops things moving or slows things down.

Gravity is a force that makes things fall.

Air and flight

Air is all around us.

Wind is moving air caused by changes or differences in air pressure.

Air occupies all space if allowed.

Air has weight.

Air exerts a pressure in all directions.

Air expands upon heating, causing a pressure increase.

Reduced pressure causes a force imbalance, which appears as 'sucking'.

The pressure of air is used in many applications (e.g. tyres and hoists).

A moving stream of air has reduced pressure.

Air exerts a resistive force on objects moving through it.

The shape of an object affects the nature of air flow around it.

Air consists of a mixture of gases, one of which (oxygen) is necessary for burning.

The force from air on a moving object depends on the surface area and the shape of the object.

Objects can be shaped to either minimise or maximise the force of air on them.

A flat object, such as a plane wing, a boomerang or a paper tube, can be supported by forces that arise due to differences in air flow across the top and bottom surfaces of the object.

For every action there is an equal and opposite reaction: a stream of air (or water) forced from a balloon or rocket will cause a force back on the balloon or rocket to propel it.

Hot air is less dense than cold air, and subsequently hot air rises.

Electrostatics and electricity

Circuitry can be used to make working models that use electricity.

Some materials can conduct electricity, while others cannot.

Friction can cause static electricity.

Objects can be made to attract or repel using static electricity.

Voltage is the energy supplied by a battery to each charge. It is a measure of the 'strength' of a battery.

Resistance refers to the blockage of the flow of current, and causes energy to be lost as heat.

Conductors allow electricity to flow.

Insulators prevent electricity from flowing.

A circuit is an unbroken flow of electricity around a path.

Energy/heat

Heat is a form of energy.

The Sun is the Earth's most important heat source.

Temperature is a measure of the hotness of an object.

Heat affects different living and non-living things in different ways.

Heat causes objects to change (e.g. change of state or change of colour).

Changes due to heat can be observed.

Heat travels in different ways – conduction, convection and radiation.

Sources of energy are:

- chemical energy
- electrical energy
- kinetic energy
- nuclear energy
- potential energy
- solar energy

- sound energy
- wind energy.

Floating and sinking

Objects float or sink depending on the materials they are made of.

Whether something floats depends on its density, which comprises both mass and volume. (Concepts relating to density are quite challenging for young children and should be taught in the later years of primary school.)

Objects float if they are light for their size and sink if they are heavy for their size.

An object can be light for its size if it contains air, such as a hollow ball.

Objects are more buoyant in salt water than fresh water.

Materials that are boat-shaped will float because they displace a large amount of water.

Water surfaces have a cohesive force, called surface tension, which acts like a 'skin' to the water.

Small, dense objects can 'float' on the surface of water without breaking it, or small insects can 'walk' on the water, due to this surface tension.

Water pressure increases with depth.

Light, sight and colour

Light travels in straight lines.

Some objects (e.g. a globe, the Sun, a flame) are sources of light; most things we see reflect light.

The Moon is not a source of light; rather it reflects the light of the Sun.

Ordinary surfaces reflect light in all directions.

Some surfaces reflect more light than others. Black surfaces reflect least light.

Light is bent going into or out of water or glass, and this can cause distortions in the shape or position of objects such as straws placed in the container.

Glass and water can break light rays into their constituent colours as they bend.

White light consists of the colours of the rainbow (red, orange, yellow, green, blue, indigo and violet).

Light is refracted or bent in water so objects such as a pencil appear to be broken in two.

Shadows require a light source and an object. Shadows are formed when light cannot pass through the object.

The size and shape of a shadow depend on the shape of the object that has blocked the light, the angle of the surface on which the shadow falls, the distance between the object and the light source, and the brightness of the light source.

The image in a mirror is inverted and symmetrical with the object.

Our image in a mirror is equally far behind the mirror as we are in front of it. Curved mirrors cause images to appear distorted.

Sight is a very important sense we use to interpret our world.

We see when light is reflected from objects into our eyes.

Having two eyes is necessary for judgement of depth.

Our brain puts together the stereo view we have of the world.

Our eyes and brain can be misled.

Colours can be mixed together in different ways to give different results.

The basic (or primary) colours of paints and pigments are different from the basic colours of light. Paints and pigments – red, blue and yellow (magenta, cyan and yellow in a printer). Light – red, blue and green.

Magnets

Magnets work by pushing ('repelling') and pulling ('attracting').

Magnets only work on objects made of iron, cobalt, nickel and steel.

Many toys contain magnets.

Some magnets exert more force than others.

Magnets have many different shapes and sizes.

Magnets are used in many ways; examples include metal catches, fridge magnets, magnetic films on swipe cards, loudspeakers, and the generation of electrical energy in power stations.

Magnets are strongest at their ends.

The ends of magnets may push or pull other ends of magnets.

Magnetic forces work through non-magnetic materials.

Magnetic force extends into the space surrounding the magnet.

The Earth has magnetic properties.

Sound

We hear sound with our ears.

Our sense of sound is very acute.

Sound can travel through solids (e.g. wood), liquids (e.g. water) and gases (e.g. air).

We use two ears to judge where sounds come from.

Sound bounces off surfaces.

Sound is caused by objects vibrating.

Objects have their own natural vibration pattern and can give a characteristic note when hit (or blown).

Large or long objects vibrate slowly, causing sounds of low pitch. Short or small objects vibrate quickly, causing sounds of high pitch.

Sounding boards amplify sound and are important in instruments.

Vibrating strings form the basis of stringed instruments.

Vibrating air is the basis of wind instruments.

Many materials can transmit sound; they include strings, metal and wood.

Time

Reaction times differ for each person. (Reaction time is the time taken to perform a task, such as catching a dropped object.)

Clocks can be made from many different devices, such as candles and shadow sticks.

Pendulums help us to keep time.

We can tell time by measuring many things.

We can tell the time from our perception of the movement of the Earth in relation to the Sun.

We view time as a duration.

Time is also a sequence of events.

These concepts were adapted from the following resources:

Bruton, P. & Thornton, L. (2010). *Science in the Early Years: Building Firm Foundations from Birth to Five*. London: Sage.

Howitt, C. & Blake, E. (eds) (2010). *Planting the Seeds of Science*. Perth: Australian Learning and Teaching Council.

Hubber, P. & Tytler, R. (2005). *Ideas for Teaching Science P–8*. Geelong, Victoria: Deakin University Press.

Kelly, L. & Jane, B. (2002). *Ideas for Teaching Primary Science*. Geelong, Victoria: Deakin University Press.

Victoria Curriculum and Assessment Authority (VCAA), AusVELS, 'Science', ausvels.vcaa.vic.edu.au/science/curriculum/f-10#level=1, accessed 20 July 2014.

Index